THE TITANIC EFFECT

T0163865

ENDORSEMENTS

"The gripping story told in this book masks the expert research and deep insights upon which it is based. Don't let the fun of reading this book fool you—it is must-reading, not just for entrepreneurs launching and growing their ventures but for anyone remotely interested in how our entrepreneurial economy functions."

David B. Audretsch
Distinguished Professor
Ameritech Chair of Economic Development,
Director, Institute for Development Strategies
Global Award for Entrepreneurship Honoree
School of Public and Environmental Affairs, Indiana University

"I love it! The whole concept of hidden debt is perfect and something very real that I've experienced but never defined before. I highly recommend this to both first-timers and seasoned entrepreneurs."

Chris Baggott
Founder, ExactTarget, Compendium, Tyner Pond Farm, and ClusterTruck

"The advice in this book is not just for tech entrepreneurs. As a restaurateur, I have had my share of successes and failures. Both came down to the right or wrong decisions I made regarding the people, the product, and/or the market I was targeting. Being aware in advance of the 'debtbergs' described in *The Titanic Effect* would have helped me save a lot of time and money."

Gary Brackett
Owner and CEO, Stacked Pickle; Super Bowl Champion, Indianapolis Colts

"The Startup Ladies were fortunate to have hosted a *Titanic Effect* workshop. The book is a life jacket for a first-time founder. It helps you understand, anticipate, and solve problems that are just below the surface of a startup."

Kristen Cooper
CEO and Founder, The Startup Ladies

"This aptly named book is an outstanding treatise on navigating uncertainty. It is essential reading for any physician who has a penchant for the entrepreneurial world. The authors' many years of experience as both innovators and educators uniquely qualify them as seasoned 'captains' who would be welcomed on any physician's entrepreneur journey to success."

Anthony C. Chang, MD, MBA, MPH, MS
Chief Intelligence and Innovation Officer
Medical Director, The Sharon Disney Lund Medical Intelligence and Innovation Institute (MI3)
Children's Hospital of Orange County

"*The Titanic Effect* is a no-nonsense and easy-to-understand 'field guide' to startups. For entrepreneurs, it offers critical, hard-earned insights that are typically only learned through failure. For early-stage investors, it gives wisdom and tools to effectively evaluate startups and determine your own investment strategy."

Barb Cutillo
Financial Consultant and Investor in Early-Stage Companies
Co-Founder/CFO/CAO, Stonegate Mortgage Corporation

"The nature of entrepreneurship is to venture into unfamiliar territory. As an investor, we often see entrepreneurs who teach themselves lessons the hard way, through trial and error. I would encourage all would-be entrepreneurs to absorb the several great lessons in this volume to anticipate common pitfalls and strategize corrective action to speed the iterative process of business-building."

Dan Gebremedhin MD, MBA
Principal, Flare Capital Partners

"The investment world often debates distinguishing factors between luck and skill. Both are necessary, but neither alone is sufficient for success. *The Titanic Effect* unpacks the skills and helps decipher luck, and is a must-read for entrepreneurs to navigate their journeys to target destinations."

Ting Gootee
Chief Investment Officer, Elevate Ventures

"I have read dozens of books on starting companies, but this is the first that accurately captures why startups fail and provides a tool for entrepreneurs and investors to measure and manage these sources of failure."

Michael Hatfield,
Co-Founder, Cerent, Calix, Cyan, and Carium

"As a retired surgeon, serial entrepreneur, life-science and healthcare investor and champion, as well as Co-Founder and Chairman of the Board of the Society of Physician Entrepreneurs, I am thrilled to see a book directed to improving the success of innovators, both in our sector and in general. This is a well-organized, thoughtfully written work, both from the perspective of the entrepreneur as well as the potential early-stage investor.

"I often counsel and mentor young entrepreneurs that they have three important assets to monitor and nurture as they grow their companies. They are Money, People, and Time, each of which seems to take on different prominence and priority depending on the various stages of the company's development. My suggestion is that they read *The Titanic Effect*, and in doing so they might save some money, associate with the right people, and recognize that time is truly their most precious commodity."

Jeffrey N. Hausfeld, M.D., M.B.A., F.A.C.S.
Chairman of the Board and CMO, BioFactura Inc.
President, Memory Care Communities LLC
Chairman and Founder, The Society of Physician Entrepreneurs

"One of the biggest blind spots for an entrepreneur in building a startup for the first time is 'you don't know what you don't know.' The things that keep me up at night are not usually the problems I am aware of or the decisions I know I need to execute. The sleeplessness is usually from the anxiety of 'What am I missing right now that is going to be a problem later?' *The Titanic Effect* goes a long way in giving answers to that very question and gives any reader immediately more wisdom.

"I have known Todd, Kim, and Michael for over ten years, and all three have played a part in advising me on how to navigate the choppy waters of entrepreneurship. I am excited to see all of their expertise consolidated and made available to founders everywhere."

Scott Hill
Executive Chairman and Co-Founder, PERQ

"Todd, Kim, and Michael are experts on the entrepreneurial journey. Together, they provide the perfect combination of experience, teaching ability, and research-backed best practices. *The Titanic Effect* simplifies a lot of complex concepts that affect startup success and gives founders tools to stay afloat when navigating the icebergs of venturing. Any leader willing to brave the waters of building a high-growth business should read this book."

Matt Hunckler
CEO and Founder, Powderkeg

"I am honored to have known Todd for almost two decades. Todd, Kim, and Michael have been pillars in Indiana, guiding entrepreneurs and promoting venture-building in the area. They have figured out a novel way to explain to entrepreneurs and investors how not to get into traps by creating massive debtbergs (akin to icebergs that doomed the *Titanic*) during the course of an entrepreneurial journey. [This book is] an interesting must-read for aspiring and established entrepreneurs and investors. I am sure a reader will spot such patterns in his/her entrepreneurial journey and proactively apply the learnings from this book."

Mukund Krishna
Founder and CEO, Suyati Group India

"They say hindsight is 20/20, and this is typically true. The terrible *Titanic* tragedy is a dark yet very real and valuable metaphor for the many events or 'debts' that lead to startup failure today. These events (as trivial as they may seem) often combine for a multiplicative effect that culminates in failure. The irony is that most of the debts we know of are obvious (e.g., the iceberg sticking out of the water). *The Titanic Effect* takes a much deeper dive into the more vague, yet critical 'hidden debts' that can cripple and sink any company, no matter how big or how small. This is an essential read for anyone in the 'entrepreneurial community' that interacts, advises, or just exists alongside these startups. The comparisons between the *Titanic* event and the startup world also make this book entertaining and historically educational. Highly recommended!"

Oscar Moralez
Managing Director, VisionTech Partners and VisionTech Angels

"There are many books on entrepreneurship but very few that capture the insights, understanding, and actionable ideas shared in *The Titanic Effect*. I've had the opportunity to partner with all three authors, and they bring a wealth of knowledge and experience to light in an entertaining and meaningful way for all entrepreneurs."

Dave Wortman
CEO, Diagnotes
Former CEO, Made2Manage

"In my years in business development and strategy in the US and China, I have had the opportunity to work with large corporations as well as new technology firms. Both startups and larger firms can learn a lot from the ideas in *The Titanic Effect* regarding the perils of innovating without attention to tradeoffs. I particularly appreciate the effort to include entrepreneurial stories of founders and startups outside of the United States, in addition to the excellent examples of US ventures."

Gilbert Wu
President, Greater China, Aventics

THE
TITANIC EFFECT

Successfully Navigating the Uncertainties that Sink Most Startups

TODD SAXTON   M. KIM SAXTON   MICHAEL CLORAN

NEW YORK

LONDON • NASHVILLE • MELBOURNE • VANCOUVER

The Titanic Effect

Successfully Navigating the Uncertainties that Sink Most Startups

Published in New York, New York, by Morgan James Publishing. Morgan James is a trademark of Morgan James, LLC. www.MorganJamesPublishing.com

ISBN 9781642792140 paperback
ISBN 9781642792157 eBook
Library of Congress Control Number: 2018908706

Cover & Interior Design by:
Christopher Kirk
GFSstudio.com
With contributions from Stewart Moon, Moon Design

Morgan James is a proud partner of Habitat for Humanity Peninsula and Greater Williamsburg. Partners in building since 2006.

Get involved today! Visit
MorganJamesPublishing.com/giving-back

DEDICATIONS

To my parents, George and Lois Saxton. They provided me with all of the tools, capabilities, and love and support to develop the passion, experience, and persistence I have as a teacher, researcher, and entrepreneur. They always valued being part of and contributing to a strong community. And thanks to Ruth Saxton and Suzanne Musselman, who became part of our extended family and support group and were very helpful to Kim and me throughout our partnership. --*T.S.*

To my parents, John and Sandra Fradd, who taught me the value of working both smart and hard, encouraged me to go for my dreams even when they weren't sure I had a great plan, and found me the little indulgences that spoke to my heart and let me know how much I am loved. A person can accomplish almost anything when they know someone has a safety net ready to catch them and stand them back up again. --*M.K.S.*

To my parents, Larry and Maureen, who are the most successful people I've ever met—living life to the fullest while raising my four awesome siblings and teaching us the value of love, honor, ethics, and a higher purpose. And to my wife Elyse, whose inner light shines on her "five" boys and inspires everyone around her to stand a little taller, live a little better, and do a little more for others. And to my many cofounders, friends, coworkers, mentors, and even competitors who helped lead me to the realization that, in its most honorable form, *Capitalism is Service*. --*M.E.C.*

TABLE of CONTENTS

FOREWORD

The authors' deep experience that derives from researching startups and assisting entrepreneurs has provided them with the great insights they share in this book. I have been fortunate to have worked with them on various entrepreneurial endeavors over the better part of two decades. Working with Todd and the Indiana Venture Center from 2001 to 2008 yielded ample evidence that he is able to translate academic knowledge, research, and experience to practical lessons for entrepreneurs. Adding Kim's background in marketing strategy and research and Michael Cloran's deep knowledge as a serial tech entrepreneur makes for quite the team. Collectively, they have a strong understanding of the challenges of startups.

The concept of a startup incurring "hidden debt" across the key areas of Human, Marketing, Technical, and Strategy "Oceans" is a quite valuable one. This important view is not one commonly identified in entrepreneurial literature. Given the limited resources available in a startup, this debt is inevitable. *The Titanic Effect* raises the consciousness about how this happens and how to mitigate the risks associated with it. The Iceberg Index translates the concepts into a valuable and actionable tool that founders and investors can leverage to identify these debts, which would otherwise be hidden, and successfully navigate around them.

Using the debt incurred in the *Titanic* project is a perfect means to illustrate the consequences of poorly incurred debt. It also provides the basis for an interesting and entertaining metaphor using icebergs, oceans, seas, and navigation. The icons are a nice added touch to visually guide the reader along the journey.

For entrepreneurs, this book provides wisdom that, if heeded, will help the founders increase their likelihood of success. For those curious about startups, it provides a deeper understanding into these fledgling organizations and the challenges they face. For everyone, the book provides an engaging telling of a well-known tragic event in a unique way.

xiv | **The Titanic Effect**

On behalf of current and would-be entrepreneurs and their supporters, I would like thank the Saxtons and Michael Cloran for this important contribution to entrepreneurship.

Michael Hatfield is a serial entrepreneur who has founded, built, and exited from several startups including Cerent, Calix, and Cyan. He is currently the Executive Chairman and Co-Founder of Carium, a healthcare-based software firm headquartered in Petaluma, California. Michael is an alumnus of Rose-Hulman Institute of Technology and IU's Kelley School of Business.

PREFACE and ACKNOWLEDGEMENTS

We have each spent more than twenty years working with hundreds, collectively thousands, of entrepreneurs, students, alumni, members of venture communities, and our own startups. As angel investors and venture community participants, we have also seen hundreds of startup pitches. Throughout this activity, we noticed some consistent patterns in how entrepreneurs' early decisions constrained them later, limiting their success—or causing them to sink. As you will see in Chapter 2, we set out to capture these learnings and share them with our students as well as new entrepreneurs and early-stage investors. What started out as a presentation and workshop became the seeds of this book. We would like to thank Oscar Moralez for suggesting we write this book, giving us access to many startups through VisionTech Partners, Indiana's largest angel network, and encouraging us throughout the process.

Writing a book these days is a bit like starting a company. We began with a product idea (knowledge) that we thought could help address a pain point in the market (startup failure). We hypothesized our initial customers were entrepreneurs and investors. Next, we had to develop that idea into an actual product (book, tools, and a workshop), figure out how to scale its production, and disseminate it efficiently. We incurred our own hidden debts along the way, but were fortunate enough to have help and support that rendered them bergy bits as opposed to sink-worthy iceberg islands.

We started with the same challenge we recommend entrepreneurs address early in their journey—finding product/market fit. We'd like to thank the partners at DeveloperTown and VisionTech Angels for letting us test our early framework and the *Titanic* metaphor with them and their stakeholders.

Next, The Innovation Showcase in Indianapolis gave us a platform for investor training with the framework. Our beta test came from Kristen Cooper and The Startup Ladies, who were the first entrepreneurs to learn about and use The Iceberg Index. Positive feedback from these entrepreneurs gave us proof of concept. We most commonly heard, "where were you three years ago?" Our apologies—but we are here now!

Distribution is key for any venture once product/market fit is established. You have to find a way to get your product to the market. Some of our team was familiar with academic publishers, but our target wasn't only students and professors. Instead, we needed to figure out how entrepreneurs and investors would find this book. We were surprised to find out how complex the book-publishing business is. We were especially intrigued to learn which publishers care more about the size of your following than your content. Our favorite comment was, "Call us back when you have an email list of 50,000 people." We were fortunate to discover our publisher, Morgan James Publishing, through an author and former student—thanks, Mike Bensi.

Now, we had the book equivalent of wireframes (an introductory chapter and book outline) and a publisher who believed in us. Next, we had to develop the product—that is, write the damn book. Enter founder debt (see Chapter 3). With three strong-minded and passionate "co-founders," we each had our own ideas about how to move from idea to manuscript. So, we moved into just writing it and getting market feedback to solve our own A/B/C test. Thanks to Mike Hatfield and Jenni Burton who were willing to share how "our baby was still a bit ugly but had potential." Their feedback led to a major shift in organizational structure and the use of examples.

We also want to thank others who shared instrumental feedback about which core concepts were difficult to interpret—former students Chris Hanahan and Suddan Shanmugasundaram, as well as friends and family members Greg Townsend, Brad Saxton, George Saxton, Lindsey Saxton, and Mackensey Saxton. Many others provided feedback on pieces of the puzzle.

As we discuss in Chapter 3, founders rarely have all of the knowledge and capabilities they need for success. In our case, we had a notable void in knowledge about a key component of our narrative: icebergs. Shout out to Professor Grant Bigg of The University of Sheffield for sharing his insights and providing a sanity check on our iceberg facts. His research team also kindly provided the iceberg pictures in Chapter 2.

At this point, we had a semblance of a product—the book's words. However, words alone do not make a powerful user experience. Thanks to Contributing Editor Amanda Cross for taking our initial writing and refining it to be easier to read as well as mechanically correct. This would have been quite a different reader experience without her help. More importantly, Amanda had the difficult task of creating a similar voice across three co-authors with very different writing styles.

Stewart Moon then helped bring our ideas to life with visuals and design features that make the content easier to remember and work through. Sophia LeFevre, Joe Cummings, and the crew at DeveloperTown provided helpful input on design and technical knowledge. Sandra Fradd shared her research from Titanic Belfast and her pictures of glaciers, which sparked other creative ideas that are included on the website. We also want to thank Kari Peglar for her research on the academic support for our ideas and Tanner Coulter for his research on the *Titanic* itself. And certainly the team at Morgan James deserves kudos for bringing all of these elements together in an excellent final product.

Every startup exists in an ecosystem with organizations as well as people. We want to acknowledge the firsthand experience we've gained from the Venture Club of Indiana (VCI), Powderkeg, the Indiana Venture Center including Steve Beck, Elevate Ventures, VisionTech Angels, the Society of Physician Entrepreneurs (SoPE), and The Startup Ladies. We are fortunate to be affiliated with a first-class business school that not only recognizes and rewards research but also supports efforts to bridge that research to the business community—thank you to IU's Kelley School of Business for time, support, and resources to accomplish this book. Kelley's support also led to our global exposure to entrepreneurship through the Max Planck Institute for Economics in Germany and the angel network in Brisbane, Australia.

We are also humbled by the entrepreneurs who have inspired us and allowed us to work beside them. They are too numerous to name, but we want to especially thank a few—Scott Hill and Andy Medley of PERQ, Joe Muldoon of FAST BioMedical, Chris Baggott of ExactTarget/Compendium and a portfolio of food/technology startups, Dave Wortman of Diagnotes, Frank Dale of Costello, and Bharath Bynagari of MavenSphere. We cannot end this list without acknowledging our own first major startup effort with Joe Milazzo, Jared Pentecost, and Bob Toller. Again, the collective insight of many others contributed greatly to our work—you know who you are.

Startups cannot exist without funding. We hope our book has relevance for early-stage investors and supporters of startups. We'd like to acknowledge other investors whom we learned from in addition to the angels already noted. Thanks to Dan Gebremedhin of Flare Capital Partners, Jonathan Root at U.S. Venture Partners, David Golden at Revolution Ventures, and Bill Whitaker of Golden Seeds for sharing the VC investor perspective on fundable startups and growing ventures.

Finally, thanks to all of the "entrepreneurs next door" for inspiring us with your passion, sharing your experiences, and demonstrating your persistence in pursuing your dreams. We hope this book becomes a helpful navigation tool on your journeys.

CHAPTER 1:

~~~~~~~~~~

INTRODUCTION

"And as the smart ship grew
In stature, grace, and hue,
In shadowy silent distance grew the Iceberg too."

–Thomas Hardy

"Start me up."

–Rolling Stones

It was a cool but clear day in April of 1912 when the *Titanic* set sail from Southampton, England, bound for the United States. Close to midnight four days later, the *Titanic* encountered the destructive mass of an iceberg and began its descent into the icy depths of the Atlantic. It was still far from the New York Harbor that the White Star Line and its passengers had envisioned as the ultimate destination when they launched. Over half of these passengers were lost, along with the majority of the crew.

The *Titanic* has become emblematic of epic failure. Its tale has inspired countless stories and movies portraying the disastrous implications of thinking you are "too big to fail." Despite all the story's retelling, though, most people still have never heard about the series of small decisions that culminated in this calamity.

The White Star Line was dealing with a lot of *uncertainty* in building and launching the *Titanic*. Could the company overcome a history of technical problems and tragedies with ships? How big was too big for an ocean liner? Could the shipyard build the *Titanic* to standard while building two other similarly sized ships nearly simultaneously? Could the staff necessary to crew an engineering marvel also serve as able-bodied seamen for other tasks? How would a product designed for the wealthy and famous first-class passengers also serve the needs of the high-volume, third-class passengers? What accommodations for luxury and aesthetics could the company

1

adopt without sacrificing safety? The owners and builders had to make many choices without full knowledge of the consequences of these decisions. Unfortunately, the consequences were fatal.

Navigating uncertainty is the essential task of the entrepreneur. What to build, how to build it, whom to partner with, whom to sell to, and how to fund growth are just a few of the many uncertainties entrepreneurs face. Each decision on these dimensions creates unintended consequences—ramifications most entrepreneurs and their supporters are not able to anticipate that have an impact on the *startup*'s viability. These unintended consequences create constraints, obligations, perceptions, and expectations that can limit success or even sink the emerging startup. We call these hidden consequences of navigating uncertainty *hidden debts*.

Indeed, like many failed *ventures*, the story of the *Titanic* is one of an accumulation of hidden debts that might as well have been little icebergs battering holes into the hull of the ship before she even got close to the big berg. Ultimately, failure came from cumulative effects of those little debt icebergs—or "debtbergs" —not the single incident of an unstoppable force meeting an immovable object.

For the *Titanic*, these hidden debts accumulated in all aspects of the project:
- the people who financed, built, and operated the ship
- the diverse needs of the customers who embarked upon that fateful journey
- the engineering challenges involved in designing and building this large and luxurious vessel

What Are Hidden Debts?

Most of us think of debt in financial terms—how much you owe the bank or other creditors for your mortgage, credit card, or car loan. For the entrepreneur, financial debt may be money the company borrows if she is able to get a bank loan. These debts are fairly easy to identify and assign a value. They certainly are important to manage, and if you can't pay them back, it can create trouble!

However, in the startup context, debt often takes on other, less tangible forms. Like an iceberg, the visible component of debt above the surface masks the much larger and more problematic non-financial debts that lurk beneath the surface. When navigating uncertainty, identifying the *tradeoffs* and assessing the results of key decisions are difficult. As such, we define *hidden debts* as the unanticipated consequences of navigating uncertainty. The uncertain nature of entrepreneurship means that founders might not be able to identify these debts easily or know how to avoid or repay them. Taking on these debts may be necessary and can buoy a startup—or sink it. Our hope is to help entrepreneurs and their supporters identify where these hidden debts might lie, and help them navigate successfully through the Oceans of debtbergs that await.

Where Do Hidden Debts Come From?

Even though most people haven't heard of them, hidden debts are not new; many have historical precedent. They have haunted entrepreneurs for centuries—and founders as auspicious as President Abraham Lincoln fell into traps of hidden debt with his failed grocery store venture (see Chapter 3).

The people involved with starting a company, from the founders to the investors and advisors to the first employees, are one source of hidden debt. The early team probably won't have everything it needs to launch the company properly, but it proceeds by incurring a hidden debt in skills and resources that it will need to make up later.

After human-related hidden debts, we talk about marketing and technical choices as areas where the startup must get by on less than it really needs. The latter area might not be unfamiliar to you: the notion of *technical debt* as the early choices or mistakes tech entrepreneurs make that end up limiting the scalability or growth potential of their ventures has been common parlance in the IT sector for some time. See Chapter 2 for our origin story about how the authors' discussions of technical debt led to our broader narrative regarding hidden debt.

With the popularity of the *Lean Startup* and rapid experimentation and iteration, entrepreneurs worldwide have embraced the *pivot*—the notion that, in the early stages, founders should experiment and redirect rapidly based on market feedback.[1] There is much to be said for getting customer reaction and market feedback before going all in on the direction of the company. However, each pivot also creates a series of hidden debt icebergs that a startup must navigate. These debtbergs can ultimately result in a Lean Startup joining the countless carcasses of venture concepts that, like the *Titanic*, riddle the floor of the economic ocean.

For the *Titanic*, hidden debts manifested in multiple ways. For example, you might not know these tidbits:

- White Star Line, the company that owned the *Titanic*, changed builders prior to building the *Titanic* and its sister ships at the insistence of a major investor.
- The *Titanic* did not meet design specifications in its key bulkheads so that it could accommodate a larger and more luxurious dining room for wealthy travelers.

---

1   Ries, Eric. *The Lean Startup: How Today's Entrepreneurs Use Continuous Innovation to Create Radically Successful Businesses.* New York: Crown Business, 2011.

- The rivets used in the exterior parts of the ship were of substandard materials.
- The crew was sadly lacking in able-bodied seamen who knew how to load lifeboats.

These elements and more set the stage for the *Titanic*'s sinking, which had ripple-through effects on maritime law and safety practices for decades. These systemic changes persist even today. In the startup world, we have seen similar ripple-through effects. For example, the JOBS (Jumpstart Our Business Startups) Act of 2012 helped small and new businesses overcome uncertainty in many ways, but also created new sources of uncertainty and hidden debts for some startups.

Foreshadowing

Fourteen years before the sinking of the *Titanic*, author Morgan Robertson penned the novella *Futility*. In this novel, a massive ship called *Titan*, largest of its kind, collided with an iceberg and sank in the month of April. While many lauded Robertson for his clairvoyance, he simply noted that increasing ship size and traffic in the iceberg-ridden shipping lanes made such an event increasingly likely. Still, the ship's name does make the coincidence downright eerie.[2]

FUTILITY
THE WRECK *of* THE TITAN

MORGAN ROBERTSON

Why Did We Write this Book?

You may have already noticed that this is not a feel-good book about being a rock star entrepreneur and finding the key to vast riches. If we wanted a tale of inspiration, full of promise, we likely would **not** have included "Titanic" in the title. We can tell you verbatim the reaction (by email) of one publisher:

> "*...a book on hidden hazards of entrepreneurial financing/funding and how to navigate them: genius! First reaction to a book with the Titanic as central metaphor (for an audience seeking success): are you crazy?*"

Nevertheless, we think the venture world is ready for a tell-all book on the challenges of starting a company without an informed approach to the hidden debts founders will undoubtedly accumulate. Taking on debt isn't necessarily bad—as long as you are aware of and manage it. We can learn from our own failures and those of others to better spot and avoid future disaster.

---

2   Heba Hasan, "Author 'Predicts' *Titanic* Sinking, 14 Years Earlier," *Time*, April 14, 2012, accessed August 20, 2017, http://newsfeed.time.com/2012/04/14/author-predicts-titanic-sinking-14-years-earlier.

Popular media is full of optimistic tales of the promised land of venturing and the rock star entrepreneur—the joys of pivoting and the nobility of camping in your parents' basement, bringing the garage startup to life. What are less celebrated are the long years of work, the hundreds of thousands of failed startups, the millions of hours of wasted effort, and the hundreds of millions of investors' dollars lost in failed enterprises. Then-Harvard Professor Noam Wasserman explored some of the reasons for these failures, which he describes as "founder's dilemmas."[3] He elaborates on different stages in startup development and the hard choices founders must make. Our work builds on this more problem-focused (and more realistic) depiction of the entrepreneurial journey.

We know that somewhere between 70% and 80% of ventures fail.[4] That does not even reflect the nascent ideas on the back of a napkin that never really get off the ground. Is this a cautionary tale? Absolutely. However, we seek to educate you, gentle reader, on the hazards of hidden debt so that you may successfully navigate the dangerous waters of launch and find the promised land of startup traction as part of your journey.

For Whom Did We Write this Book?

We had several types of readers in mind as we wrote this book: the entrepreneur, the investor and supporter of the entrepreneur, and the general reader.

For the early-stage entrepreneur,[5] our work raises important questions about venture formation and progress:

- Have you set up a *vesting schedule* for founders and others to earn *equity* over time?
- Are you timing your experiments in the market so you don't burn your best and most likely early customers?
- Is your technology platform inexpensive enough that you have not "bet the farm" without market feedback, but flexible and scalable enough to grow the venture without crashing and burning?

---

3   Wasserman, Noam. *The Founder's Dilemmas: Anticipating and Avoiding the Pitfalls That Can Sink a Startup.* Princeton, NJ: Princeton University Press, 2012.

4   There are many sources of data on venture failure. See Shane, Scott, *The Illusions of Entrepreneurship: The Costly Myths that Entrepreneurs, Investors, and Policy Makers Live By* (New Haven, CT: Yale University Press, 2008) for failure rates over a ten-year period. The following article summarizes venture failure rates and reasons for the failure: Patrick Henry "Why Some Startups Succeed (and Why Most Fail)," *Entrepreneur Magazine*, February 18, 2017, accessed August 20, 2017, https://www.entrepreneur.com/article/288769. The Kauffman Foundation (https://www.kauffman.org) is also a good resource for data on entrepreneurship activity and failure. Most sources converge on failure rates between 50 and 70% five years after startup launch, and over 70% after 10 years.

5   We define an early-stage entrepreneur as someone with an idea or searching for an idea who plans to launch, is in the process of launching, or has launched a venture but not yet secured financing above $1.5 million. In other words, the person might be in the "self-funded" through "seed stages" of financing, but typically not to the A-round.

- Do you have a *strategy* to navigate the human, technical, and marketing sources of debt as you move through cycles of financing?

This book should help you identify some of the pitfalls and problem areas that can sink your idea before or during its maiden voyage. We call out some specific suggestions for identifying and avoiding icebergs in Navigation Plan tips throughout the book. While these tips may be most relevant to the entrepreneur, they also serve to help the investor/advisor and venture supporter as well.

 Look for this icon to find Navigation Plan tips quickly.

For the *early-stage investor* and supporters of entrepreneurs, we offer guidance on how to assess the startups you might be considering for investment or assistance. Early-stage investing can be hazardous, with 70% or more of your investments likely to earn the big goose egg (in other words, zero return). However, investing can also be rewarding, both financially and in terms of helping a concept reach scalable reality. Many early-stage investors struggle with how to assess a startup's potential and identify any skeletons in the closet. Just as this book can help an entrepreneur self-assess hidden venture debts, it can help the early-stage investor identify red flags that can help separate the golden goose from the goose egg. We call out some of these red flags specifically as Lookout tips for the investor/advisor, as well as the founder, as a kind of early-warning system for possible iceberg damage.

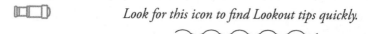 *Look for this icon to find Lookout tips quickly.*

For the *general reader*, even if you do not plan to start or invest in a company, you no doubt will run across those who do. We want our book to provide you an entertaining and informative way to follow—and perhaps even contribute to—discussions with the would-be founder when you hear the phrase "so I have this idea…" We also hope you enjoy the richer and deeper insights into the *Titanic* and her sinking, as well as some fun facts on icebergs and startup anecdotes.

How Does the Savvy Reader Navigate this Work?

We have tried to design the book in a user-friendly way to ease the journey. Here are some ideas on how to get started:

- If you are on board for the whole journey, read on and enjoy. You will
  learn about the *Titanic*, startups, and many failed and successful ventures.

- If you are less interested in history, the *Titanic*, and icebergs—but are enthused to learn about startup hidden debt—skim Chapter 2 on the history of the *Titanic* and icebergs and move to the core content Chapters 3-7.
- If you want to use our framework, the Iceberg Index, to begin to measure the hidden debt of your own venture or that of an investment, you might begin with Chapter 8. You can also see our website (http://www.titaniceffect.com) for more tips and a tool to set up and manage your Index as you work through the chapters.
- If you need a primer on the terminology, flip to our glossary for some definitions and examples that might help you quickly understand and digest unfamiliar terms. Glossary terms appear in italics throughout the book.

We hope this book is more than a one-time read—we'll know we've succeeded when we hear about the dog-eared, highlighted, and often-consulted copy a founder keeps on the edge of her desk as she navigates the entrepreneurial journey.

What Will You Find in this Book?

When you turn the page following this introduction, you will find a chapter sharing our own origin story for the book and providing a history of the White Star Line and the *Titanic* for context. We also detail how icebergs are born, how they travel and change, and the types and sizes of icebergs waiting in the ocean. We wrap up the chapter by outlining our Iceberg Index, which guides you through identifying, assessing, and managing the various types of hidden debt. In this chapter, we will show you how hidden debts are like icebergs and talk about the fact that much of what can sink your ship is below the surface.

We continue the metaphor by identifying the four different sources, or "Oceans," of hidden debt in our four core chapters (3, 4, 5, and 7):

- Human Ocean, which includes the co-founders, investors, and advisors; early employees; and other people-related sources of debtbergs
- Marketing Ocean, which includes segmentation, *positioning*, and implementation debtbergs due to customer and market-related choices
- Technical Ocean, which includes validation, design, and development debtbergs that result from early product and technology choices
- Strategy Ocean, which includes the integrative challenges across the other Oceans that create debtbergs

We briefly digress before talking about the Strategy Ocean to lay out some of the more important points in the definition of strategy and how they relate to uncertainty for startups.

Each of these Oceans of debt reflects decisions founders face in launching their startups. Within the chapter about each Ocean, we detail major categories of hidden debts (Seas) and then identify specific hidden debts (debtbergs of various sizes) that can sink ventures. In this framework, you can think of the venture as a ship attempting to navigate the perils of iceberg-laden Seas in various Oceans of activity.

Each core chapter includes similar components:

- We identify some of the non-financial hidden debts that the White Star Line and *Titanic* acquired in the early stages of their journey within that Ocean.

Look for this icon next to stories of the Titanic.

- We discuss the sources of hidden debt for ventures in that Ocean.

These icons point out discussions of hidden debts.

- We include examples of both failed and successful ventures that high-light these debtbergs.
- Both within and at the end of the chapter, we offer some tips for how entrepreneurs and investors can navigate the sources of uncertainty that can sink their startup.

Find help navigating hidden debt next to this icon.

Identify red flags that suggest trouble next to this icon.

The Lookout and Navigation Plan tips that we offer map directly to the Iceberg Index tool that we detail in Chapter 8. Also watch out for glossary terms in italics.

Origin Stories

We rely on a number of examples to illustrate our concepts. A few of these, including Clif Bar, Airbnb, Instacart, Chesapeake Bay Candle, and TRX, appear at multiple points in the book to explore how different debtbergs affected these companies across Oceans. As familiar brands that span different types of products and markets, these companies demonstrate how even ultimately successful startups can encounter damaging icebergs along the way. Other ventures to which we refer in the examples never sailed far enough to become widely recognized brands, succumbing to the hidden debt they accumulated early in their journeys.

To enable those examples, let us introduce the founders of these interesting and ultimately successful ventures who encountered various forms of hidden debt but survived.[6]

Clif Bar/Gary Erickson

Today, Clif Bar is a household name in energy bars. Founder Gary Erickson worked helping manage a bicycle seat company and raced bikes, but had the entrepreneurial bug to start a company from his early school years. Erickson's entrepreneurial appetite intersected with his mom's culinary skills for his first foray into founding a company. He launched Kali's Sweets & Savories, named after his grandmother. Kali's business was making Greek calzones distributed through delis in San Francisco. The venture was not significant enough to make ends meet, and Erickson kept his day job. Then, one day in 1990 on a 175-mile ride, Erickson had his epiphany when he tried to choke down his sixth power bar—the world needed a tasty but healthy energy bar for outdoor enthusiasts and active athletes. The seeds of Clif Bar were sown.

Instacart/Apoorva Mehta

Instacart was not founder Apoorva Mehta's first startup. In fact, the *LA Times* reports that Mehta had twenty failed ideas before hitting it big with the grocery-delivery company.[7] With his first major effort, a social network for attorneys, Mehta raised a million dollars, but the venture promptly cratered due to human debt. His IT background and supply chain experience at Amazon had given him the enthusiasm for innovation that he would need to succeed, but not the knowledge he would need about lawyer networks. Fortunately, his love of entrepreneurship, logistics, and technology eventually intersected with his loathing for the grocery-store experience to lead to the idea of Instacart, founded in 2012.

Airbnb/Joe Gebbia

Joe Gebbia started Airbnb to address a very specific need: his rent had increased 25% and paying the bills was becoming increasingly challenging. He and his roommate were pursuing multiple venture ideas in San Francisco circa 2007, but Airbnb started out of desperation. Their need to supplement income for rent intersected with a specific event: a design conference in San Francisco that had sold out all the hotel rooms in the area far in advance. Gebbia and his roommate had extra space and some

---

6 A special thanks to the Guy Raz podcast series *How I Built This from NPR*, https://www.npr.org/podcasts/510313/how-i-built-this as one source of much of the material for these stories.

7 Tracey Lien, "Apoorva Mehta had 20 failed start-ups before Instacart," *Los Angeles Times*, January 27, 2017, accessed August 20, 2017, http://www.latimes.com/business/technology/la-fi-himi-apoorva-mehta-20170105-story.html.

airbeds they we willing to share with conference attendees. Gebbia's education at the Rhode Island School of Design made him comfortable with the target market. Gebbia also had personal experience letting a stranger crash at his place when he was leaving Providence—through a series of circumstances, he hosted a stranger new to the area overnight, and found it initially discomforting but ultimately rewarding. Stars aligned and AirBed and Breakfast (Airbnb) emerged.

Chesapeake Bay Candle/Mei Xu

Mei Xu, founder of Chesapeake Bay Candle Company, was born and raised in China, where she trained as a diplomat. Xu joined a select group in a special training program to enhance China's commercial relationships with other countries. Her first post was far from glamorous, logging inventory in a factory far from her husband. The couple was able to immigrate to the United States, however, and Xu's training in import/export, combined with Chinese fluency, provided a solid base for her work in New York with a medical equipment exporter. She spent extra hours—many extra hours—touring the floors of Bloomingdale's to window shop, close to her employer. However, her husband was in Washington, D.C., and the job was far from stimulating. Xu determined to leave her job in 1994 and start something new that leveraged her cross-cultural training and awareness, her import/export background, and her fashion sense cultivated by hours in an uptown high-end department store. After experimenting with various products, candles became her focus. Chesapeake Bay Candle Company evolved from this journey.

TRX/Randy Hetrick

On an antipiracy mission in Southeast Asia in 1997, TRX System founder Randy Hetrick was a Navy Seal looking for a way to exercise in the limited confines of his small military quarters. Exercise equipment and resort gyms are typically not plentiful under these circumstances. Fortuitously, Hetrick had accidentally packed an old Jiu-Jitsu belt and had access to parachute webbing. Necessity was the mother of invention. After bit of sewing and a lot of experimentation, Hetrick invented the TRX System, or the Total Resistance eXercise System. It was a modest start and eventual success took a lot of sewing, business training, and the tenacity one would expect of a Navy Seal. TRX officially launched nearly eight years later in 2005, creating a substantial business and helping many fit athletes.

Your Nautical Mileage May Vary

While we hope our work has relevance to many types of entrepreneurs, investors, and startup contexts, there are certainly exceptions to some of the navigation plans we create.

Life science ventures, for example, face a very different trajectory in terms of fundraising and regulatory approval process than, say, software ventures. Those differences render our balanced approach to navigating technical, marketing, and human debt inappropriate. A medical device company may invest tens of millions of dollars in development and regulatory approval (navigating the Technical Ocean) before it even encounters some of the icebergs we talk about in the Marketing and Human Oceans. For a biotech firm developing a new drug, that number could be over $1 billion. Alternative energy and other highly regulated industries are in the same boat, so to speak. These kinds of cases may need to stretch some of our guidelines to identify and manage icebergs in the Human, Marketing, Technical, and Strategic Oceans.

There are also icebergs that fall outside of our model. Legal sources of hidden debt, for example, can be equally important for a founder to navigate. When and how to protect intellectual property, what legal and tax structure to employ upon launch, what aspects should remain proprietary as part of the "secret sauce," and how and when to employ trademarks and copyrights are all important questions. We encourage founders to consult their accountant, attorney, or local Small Business Development Center or Chamber of Commerce for guidance in these areas.

Weighing Anchor

As Steve Case notes in his book, *The Third Wave*,[8] the next generation of entrepreneurial opportunity will require stakeholders to put more thought into the development and execution of strategy. Getting the app you created in your dorm room to go viral is less and less likely. The new generation of founders must overcome sophisticated competition, leverage partnerships, and tackle unprecedented uncertainty to navigate the dangerous startup seas.

For the Captains Courageous who start companies, fund them, or support the venture community, read on! It's time to weigh anchor and get underway.

---

8   Case, Steve. *The Third Wave: An Entrepreneur's Vision of the Future.* New York: Simon & Schuster, 2016.

CHAPTER 2:

WHY THE *TITANIC* and ICEBERGS?

"There is only one Iceberg that has gripped the imagination of the world, one Iceberg that has humbled the arrogance of men who believed in technology, one Iceberg that tells us of the wonders and dangers of the North Atlantic Ocean. That Iceberg sank the Titanic.*"*

–Richard Brown

"You're as cold as ice."

–Foreigner

Our own origin story helps answer the questions that this chapter poses: What the heck does the *Titanic* have to do with *startups*? Furthermore, how do icebergs figure into the picture?

It goes back a few years to a presentation two of the authors of this book, the Saxtons, attended on technical debt. The third author, Michael Cloran, was presenting. Cloran and his partners launched DeveloperTown, a design- and development-consulting firm and shared workspace for startups, to help startups and larger firms better understand and manage technical debt. He was presenting on the perils of technical debt, and how DeveloperTown used tools and tactics to avoid its damaging impact.

Technical debt is not a new term, nor is it ours. It refers to the early choices startups make about software and technology development, which can limit future scalability or growth potential (see more in Chapter 5). In both his public speaking engagements and his work through DeveloperTown, Cloran frequently advised entrepreneurs and innovators on how to avoid or manage technical debt.

For the Saxtons, Professors of Marketing and Strategy/Entrepreneurship, the discussion of technical debt provided a framework to identify other categories of such debts. They saw similar struggles related to early customer communication and validation, market targeting, and brand choices. Startups can use early marketing choices to test messaging and value proposition—but those same choices can leave the market with an outdated understanding of what the company is all about when it inevitably *pivots*. Similarly, the people involved in a startup (co-founders, investors and advisors, and the first employees) can be an asset—or a giant anchor that weighs the startup down.

Based on these observations, the Saxtons approached Cloran about a joint presentation that would shed light on many of the choices that could incur different kinds of *hidden debts*, not just technical debts. Our logic chain went as follows:

1. Entrepreneurs must navigate *uncertainty* in launching their *ventures*.
2. Navigating uncertainty requires choices that have unintended consequences because founders can't possibly anticipate everything.
3. The unintended consequences manifest as hidden debts in different parts of the startup, including human, marketing, and technical arenas.
4. These hidden debts can subsequently limit the potential of or even sink a startup.
5. Entrepreneurs and *early-stage investors* would benefit from being able to spot, measure, and manage these sources of hidden debts.

Our mission became to help entrepreneurs and their supporters identify and manage these hidden debts, which are a natural byproduct of navigating uncertainty. With the vision of hidden debt as a driver, icebergs immediately leapt to mind, as so much of an iceberg's mass is out of sight, below the water. When starting from icebergs and the damage they cause, who does not think about the *Titanic*?

The title of our first presentation thus became *The Titanic Effect: How Hidden Debt Can Sink Your Venture*. It is a provocative title, but we wanted to make sure the *Titanic* was more than a compelling label. That's where the research began. Our findings not only reinforced our instincts that the *Titanic* was a good comparison, they also provided startling insight into its sinking and led us in completely new directions in using the story as a metaphor for startup failure.

The parallels started with the processes for designing, building, and operating the ship. Choices in these arenas both enabled the disaster and increased casualties. Connecting the *Titanic* to technical debt was easy. The history of the White Star Line, the company that built the *Titanic*, and its leadership, investors, and crew offered fodder for comparison to hidden human debt for startups. The overly diverse customer base and mixed value proposition made a great comparison to marketing debt for startups.

Our first presentation at Indiana's Innovation Showcase, in July of 2015, seemed to be well received. Over the next two years, the ideas evolved and we gave the presentation multiple times to entrepreneurs and early-stage investors. Soon we realized, as any good entrepreneur does, that scaling our ideas and sharing them with a larger base of entrepreneurs, investors, and supporters of startups would require a new mechanism of communication. The book idea was born.

But was a book enough? We were concerned that a book would be too abstract to be actionable for entrepreneurs and investors. We needed to develop and offer a companion tool that would help the reader translate the ideas into something concrete. Enter the Iceberg Index.

The Iceberg Index is our attempt to implement the concepts from this book and allow interested readers to improve their startup's chances of success. There is more on the Iceberg Index itself later in this chapter, and the tool is the focus of Chapter 8.

Now that you see how meaningful they have been to us in our own story, some prefatory information on the history of White Star Line and the *Titanic* seems to be an appropriate launching point for our journey. You will also learn about icebergs, the gold rush in Australia, what is important about the 48th parallel, what sounds icebergs make when melting, and other bits of potpourri. We hope you find the additional color interesting and entertaining, even if some of the factoids stray slightly off-track from our principle narrative.

If you have no interest in the White Star Line, the *Titanic* Iceberg, or icebergs in general, you can skim the first part of this chapter, but make sure to look for bold terms and their definitions. These definitions are important for fully understanding the iceberg metaphor we use throughout the book. Also, read the Iceberg Index section carefully. That will be helpful later for understanding how to measure hidden debt for a startup.

On the other hand, if you find nautical history and the majestic and deadly wonders known as icebergs as fascinating as we do, read on!

History of the White Star Line and the *Titanic*

Let's start by looking at the history of the White Star Line. This company came to be a leading force in moving people to promised lands from the mid-1800s to the early 1900s. Founded in 1845 in Liverpool, England, the White Star Line originally provided passage on clipper ships to the gold rush of the late 1840s...in Australia (see callout box). The booming economy and search for treasure "down under" had created quite the demand for passage to Oz, and White Star was happy to fulfill it.

Australia's Gold Rush

Yes, there was a gold rush in Australia. The Australian gold rush began in earnest in 1851, when Edward Hargraves drew on his experiences in California to discover gold in a location in Australia. He subsequently named that location Ophir, in homage to the resource-rich biblical town of King Solomon's time. The Australian states of New South Wales and Victoria became hugely popular destinations for would-be gold miners, and many did strike gold. Australia came to generate over one-third of the world's gold in the 1850s, and Victoria alone grew from a population of 77,000 to over 540,000 in two years during the boom. By comparison, the '49ers that went to California during the two peak years of its gold rush numbered only about 170,000.

These and other gold rushes of the 1800s had global ripple-through economic effects:

- Many countries that used a silver or bimetallic standard for their currencies changed to the gold standard as the annual production of gold tripled compared to the previous 250 years.
- Governments had to redefine property rights to deal with the miners "staking a claim."
- Huge influxes of immigrants changed the ethnic make-up of the countries.
- Technologies for gold extraction enjoyed a huge boom and led to advances in extraction of other metals and minerals.

White Star's first loss occurred in 1854 when its clipper ship, RMS *Tayleur*, ran aground on the island of Lambay, Ireland, on its maiden voyage to Australia.[9] The iron in the ship's hull apparently confounded both the compass and the crew, who believed they were sailing south through the Irish Sea. Meanwhile, they were actually headed straight west toward Ireland.

The ship sank due to a combination of navigational and sailing errors. It did not help that the crew comprised less than 50% seaman, and ten of the crewmembers did not speak English. Over half of the 652 passengers died. Technology and human error combined to cut short a journey that had hardly begun and that became known as the "First *Titanic*."[10]

Despite this early setback, the White Star Line organization grew and remained profitable for its first twenty or so years, focusing mainly on transporting passengers to Australia. In 1867, however, the Royal Bank of Liverpool, which had funded White Star's strong growth, failed. This left White Star lacking capital and in dire finan-

---

9   Bourke, Edward J. *Bound for Australia: The Loss of the Emigrant Ship* Tayleur *at Lambay on the Coast of Ireland.* Dublin: Edward J. Bourke, 2003.
10   Starkey, H. F. *Iron Clipper* "Tayleur": *The White Star Line's "First* Titanic." Merseyside: Avid Publications, 1999.

cial straits. Following the company's bankruptcy, Thomas Ismay acquired White Star Line's assets in 1868. Ismay was a man with a family history with boats and sailing and a passion for iron ships. He decided to expand the focus on steamships and serve the increasingly popular route to the United States. Another promised land beckoned.

White Star's first ship under the new ownership was the RMS *Oceanic*, built in 1870. The *Oceanic* became one of White Star's stalwart transports in the late 1800s thanks to a number of innovations that improved ship performance and passenger comfort. Despite a brief interruption to address overheated bearings on its maiden voyage, the *Oceanic* was a success.

RMS: What is a Royal Mail Ship?

RMS stands for Royal Mail Ship. Initiated in 1840, the classification designated a level of quality and on-time performance for passenger ships. Ships that met the standards delivered mail as well as passengers, but also incurred heavy penalties for lateness. Initially, the Admiralty and Royal Navy undertook mail operations themselves. In 1850, private companies operating passenger ships took over for the Royal Navy. Both White Star and its competitor, Cunard, carried the RMS stamp of approval.

Today, air transport delivers most mail. Only four ships retain the RMS designation.

In 1873, however, White Star suffered another catastrophic loss. The RMS *Atlantic* was the second ship built for White Star's new owner. With eighteen successful voyages under her belt, the *Atlantic* set out for New York on March 20 of 1873. Because the *Atlantic* needed coal, it added Halifax, Nova Scotia to its itinerary. In part due to stormy weather—but also because of a series of crew errors, including not having the appropriate lookouts, being twelve miles off course, and not seeing a lighthouse—the ship ran aground. Over half the crew and passengers were lost due to improper loading of lifeboats and the treacherous conditions of the rocky shore. For a second time, conditions and poor decision-making led to fatalities and significant loss for White Star Line.

Ismay was not to be deterred. Again rebounding, from the 1880s to the turn of the century, the White Star organization thrived, providing transport to America and differentiating itself based on its speed. The RMS *Teutonic*, for example, was one of several White Star ships that won the Blue Riband award in 1889 for fastest passage across the Atlantic.

During this period, Ismay engaged with investor Gustav Christian Schwabe. In exchange for funding White Star's growth, Schwabe mandated a change in shipbuilders. He wanted White Star to use a company called Harland and Wolff. It was no coincidence that Schwabe's nephew, Gustav Wolff, co-founded Harland and Wolff. The *Titanic* was one of the ships from the new builders.

White Star and its primary competitor, Cunard, engaged in their own "space race" of the 19th century to have the fastest ships. However, improvements in speed became harder and harder to maintain, particularly with larger boats. The race cost money, but transport rates were falling due to increasing competition. This combination landed White Star in financial straits once again around the turn of the century. J. P. Morgan's newly formed International Mercantile Marine Co. purchased White Star Line in 1902.

J.P. Morgan—The Man, The Company

John Pierpont "J.P." Morgan was born in 1837 and lived until 1913, the year after the *Titanic* sank. He had scheduled passage on the *Titanic* on her maiden voyage, but fortunately for him, last-minute conflicts prevented his trip. He had quite the resume, with involvement in the formation of General Electric, AT&T, International Harvester, and U.S. Steel Corporation.

He was also instrumental in heading off a banking crisis the year the *Titanic* was conceived. During the Panic of 1907, widespread concerns about New York banks led to mass selling of stocks. However, Morgan worked with legislators and other bankers to both provide subsidies to failing firms and purchase stocks and assets.

The firm survives today as JPMorgan Chase after a merger with Chase Bank in 1996. It is one of the largest banks in the United States. Many of you might recall the banking crisis and Great Recession that began in 2007, exactly 100 years after the Panic of 1907. In this reincarnation, JPMorgan Chase again bailed out banks like Bear Stearns and Washington Mutual through acquisition in 2008. However, unlike the savior status their actions earned them in 1907, this time the government perceived their actions as predatory and destabilizing, resulting in a $13 billion fine by the Department of Justice in 2013.

Two thoughts to take away from this: first, history does repeat itself, and second, you should consider shorting bank stocks in 2107!

In 1907, Thomas Ismay's son, J. Bruce Ismay, was Chairman of White Star. He met with Lord William Pirrie, Director of both White Star and Harland and Wolff, to concoct a new *strategy* for White Star over drinks and dinner: SIZE. If winning with speed would be too costly, perhaps a change to size and luxury would be more sustainable. This met the approval of new owner Morgan. The *Titanic* and its sister ships, the RMS *Olympic* and HMHS *Britannic*, reflected this change in focus from speed to size. It was a pivot of disastrous proportions.

As you can see, the *Titanic* and White Star Line faced a number of organizational and personnel changes, challenges, and issues. Transitions in ownership, demands of investors, new shipbuilders, and crew capabilities all preceded the creation of the *Titanic*. All played a role in the designing, building, and operating of the doomed *Titanic*.

On Icebergs

When we began planning this book, the iceberg that sank the *Titanic* was a side note, a backdrop to our story. As we learned more about not only the *Titanic*'s sinking but also icebergs themselves, we became intrigued.

Icebergs are complex and varied structures that may take centuries to form and as little as weeks to disappear. They are deceptively small to look at, though even the part you can see might be bigger than you can really comprehend. Icebergs are such a slow and massive presence that people, to their peril, can stop noticing them in the great scenery of the ocean—and forget their power. These poetic similarities to the forces that sink startups inspired us to expand the role of icebergs to become a fundamental part of our ideas for measuring and managing hidden debt.

Icebergs begin as part of much larger ice masses, such as ice shelves or glaciers. Once icebergs are "birthed" by breaking off this larger mass, a process also known as "calving," their time is limited. They follow the tides and currents of the oceans, gradually melting away until they became part of them. This process may take weeks or months, depending on the size of the iceberg and the water temperature.[11]

Icebergs Writ Large and Small

Over 80% of the icebergs in the Atlantic originate in the massive ice cap of Greenland. A half million years ago, Greenland was indeed a green land, but centuries of falling snow and frigid temperatures turned it into an inhospitable place and a prolific iceberg factory. The iceberg season in the Atlantic runs from about February 1 to July 31.

Not surprisingly, the other primary home for icebergs is near Antarctica, at the other end of the planet. The word "iceberg" derives from northern European languages and their words for ice mountains (likely the Dutch word "ijsberg").

---

11   Thanks to Professor Grant Bigg, The University of Sheffield, for reviewing this chapter for accuracy and relevance.

The Massive Iceberg of 2017

Sometime between July 10 and July 12 of 2017, one of the largest icebergs ever recorded broke off the Larsen Ice Shelf in Antarctica. Scientists and avid iceberg watchers had been following its likely calving for months. This behemoth initially weighed in at a trillion tons and was almost 6,000 square kilometers. For perspective, this is roughly the size of the state of Delaware or the nation of Luxembourg.

Icebergs come in many shapes and sizes. The two basic categories of shapes are:

- *Tabular*. Tabular icebergs have steep sides and a flat top.
- *Non-tabular*. Non-tabular icebergs include more interesting and exotic profiles, such as domes, pinnacles, and wedges.[12]

A tabular iceberg credit: *Edward Hanna, University of Lincoln*

A wedged iceberg credit: *Julie Jones, University of Sheffield*

---

12 See the National Ocean Service's website at http://oceanservice.noaa.gov/facts/iceberg.html for more information and examples of these icebergs.

A tabular iceberg credit: *Darrell A. Swift, University of Sheffield*

A domed iceberg credit: *Edward Hanna*

You probably think of icebergs as massive, but they come in a variety of sizes. Though they eventually become small enough to put in your vodka tonic, according to the National Snow & Ice Data Center, they must be at least five meters, or about sixteen feet, to achieve the lofty title of "iceberg."[13] Smaller subcategories of icebergs have colorful names such as "**growlers**" (small car or truck size) and "**bergy bits**" (storage-unit or train-car size). The largest iceberg masses are dubbed "**iceberg islands**." The tallest iceberg recorded peaked at over 550 feet, taller than a 55-story building.[14]

---

13   See the National Snow & Ice Data Center's website at https://nsidc.org/cryosphere/quickfacts/icebergs. html for "Quick Facts on Icebergs."

14   "Iceberg Facts," *Canadian Geographic*, March 1 2016, accessed August 20, 2017, https://www.canadiangeographic.ca/article/iceberg-facts.

A bergy bit credit: Sandra Fradd

We use several different sizes of icebergs in our Iceberg Index, which we discuss later in this chapter. See the table on the next page for a size comparison chart.

Given the relative density of ice versus seawater, Archimedes' Principle suggests that, at inception, about 90% of the iceberg mass hides underwater. As the iceberg moves into warmer waters, the submerged portion melts faster than the exposed part so that the iceberg may "roll" when it becomes top-heavy. This is an awesome sight, but keep your distance!

SOLAS and Maritime Safety

In 1914, following the *Titanic* disaster, the International Convention for the Safety of Life at Sea (SOLAS) formed to establish international guidelines for lifeboats, emergency equipment, safety procedures, and radio communication. Though these guidelines were not completely implemented for years due to delays caused by World War I, they have saved many lives over the last century plus.[15]

We think of icebergs as silent and majestic denizens of the ocean, but apparently, icebergs make a variety of noises.[16] When trapped gasses escape as icebergs melt, they make a crackling or fizzing sound known affectionately as "bergy seltzer." German scientists have also discovered that water from melting ice running through icebergs can make a high-pitched tune that, with slight modification, is audible to the human

---

15 International Maritime Organization, "International Convention for the Safety of Life at Sea (SOLAS)," 1974, accessed August 20, 2017, http://www.imo.org/en/About/Conventions/ListOfConventions/Pages/International-Convention-for-the-Safety-of-Life-at-Sea-(SOLAS),-1974.aspx.

16 "Iceberg Facts," *Canadian Geographic*, March 1 2016, accessed August 20, 2017, https://www.canadiangeographic.ca/article/iceberg-facts.

Sea Ice Forms Useful Size References

Brash: less than 2 m (6 ft.) across

Growler: less than 5 m (16 ft.)
Pancake: 30 cm – 3 m (1 – 10 ft.)

Bergy Bit: 5 – 15 m (16 – 50 ft.)
Ice Cake: 3 – 20 m (6 – 65 ft.) across

Small Berg: 15 – 60 m (50 – 200 ft.)
Small Floe: 20 – 100 m (65 – 328 ft.)

Medium Berg: 61 – 122 m (201 – 400 ft.)
Large Berg: 123 – 213 m (401 – 670 ft.)

Medium Floe: 100 – 500 m (328 – 1,640 ft.)
Very Large Berg: Greater than 213 m (670 ft.)
Big Floe: 500 m – 2 km (1/3 – 1 mile)

Relative iceberg size chart

ear—not unlike the sounds created by volcanic tremors and akin to an orchestra warming up.[17] The calving that is part of the birthing process is both chaotic and loud as well, producing roaring and crashing sounds worthy of the best Hollywood action features. While majestic, at least in some stages, icebergs are anything but silent!

The *Titanic* Iceberg

Many theories have surfaced through the years as to the age, origin, and path of the iceberg that sank the *Titanic*, often called the "*Titanic* Iceberg." Nearly all agree that it originated in Greenland and followed a path in ocean currents to where it met the *Titanic*. It is described as being between 200 and 400 feet long on that date, which was significantly smaller than what its original size probably would have been: as much as a mile long. Notions of how long that journey took and the original size of the iceberg vary quite considerably.

Initial reports of the iceberg came from eyewitness accounts from survivors of the *Titanic* and passengers on other ships in the general area. A number of vessels, including the *Birma* and the *Mesaba,* were in the vicinity, and some had, in fact, sent telegraphs warning of the iceberg danger earlier in the day. It was the RMS *Carpathia*, however, sailing from New York to Austria/Hungary, that ended up arriving to aid the survivors. This ship, owned by the rival company Cunard Line, rescued over 700 passengers and crew from the frigid waters and lifeboats. Sadly, due to miscommunication, the closest ship did not response to distress calls until the next day. The *Californian,* reportedly closest to the *Titanic* after impact, did not respond until the following morning, apparently due to a request from the *Titanic* to cease communication.

Picture taken from the *Carpathia* of a possible *Titanic* Iceberg

---

17   Christopher Mason, "Singing Icebergs," March 1, 2006, accessed August 20, 2017, https://www.canadian-geographic.ca/article/singing-icebergs.

A book devoted to the *Titanic* Iceberg, *Voyage of the Iceberg* by Richard Brown, was published in 1983. Brown writes that the primary suspect calved off the Greenland ice cap at Jakobshavn Icefjord eighteen months or more prior to the *Titanic* disaster in April 1912. He describes it as being 100 yards long and a million tons at the time of impact, with 100 feet above water and 500 feet below. Brown's narrative is poetic in composition and paints a beautiful picture of the majestic berg and her journey from Baffin Bay to the Grand Banks of Newfoundland. Truly, the sublime storytelling belies the deadly nature of the subject matter.

Titanic Facts website,[18] a treasure trove of information about many aspects of the *Titanic*, contains facts about the *Titanic* Iceberg that most experts consider true, such as the following:

- It was birthed in 1909 and took two-to-three years to reach the point of impact.
- Survivors estimated the iceberg to be 50-to-100 feet tall.
- Only about thirty seconds passed between the crew observing the iceberg and the *Titanic* colliding with it.
- It was traveling a leisurely eight miles per day around the time of impact.
- The early snow pack forming the glacier would have been fallen about 15,000 years earlier.

The 48ᵗʰ Parallel

It is south of the 48th parallel north that icebergs begin to enter the shipping lanes and cause issues for ships navigating the Atlantic. The parallel runs 48 degrees north of the equatorial plane and cuts across North America, the Atlantic, and the Pacific, as well as Europe and Asia. The band is popular enough to have spawned both a beer called Latitude 48 IPA (Boston Beer Company) as well as a brewery in Fishers, Indiana.

Within the last few years, research by Professor Grant Bigg of The University of Sheffield and team offers some confirmation and some different findings regarding the life of the *Titanic* Iceberg. Bigg literally wrote the book on icebergs with *Icebergs: Their Science and Links to Global Change*, published in 2016.

The British newspaper the *Daily Mirror* reported that Bigg's research with colleagues, as documented in the book, suggests that the *Titanic* Iceberg started to form

---

18   Dave Fowler, "*Titanic* Facts: The Life & Loss of the RMS *Titanic* in Numbers," *The History in Numbers*, accessed August 20, 2017, https://titanicfacts.net/.

from snow that fell over 100,000 years earlier,[19] much earlier than previous estimates. His team has extensive data on ocean currents through the years, which allows for more insight into the likely path and length of the voyage.

The team also conducted research on weather patterns suggesting that an unusually warm and wet spell four years earlier led to conditions favoring calving. This relatively short period of time, by global standards, should not lead us to think the *Titanic* was an early victim of global warming! This research offered an alternative to previous theories suggesting sunspots and tidal surges were the cause for increased iceberg activity in the shipping lanes of 1912.[20]

The International Ice Patrol

Formed in 1913, the year after the sinking of the *Titanic*, the International Ice Patrol's mission is to "monitor the iceberg danger in the North Atlantic Ocean and provide relevant iceberg warning products to the maritime community." The Patrol primarily uses airplanes for visual and sensor scanning of dangerous areas during the ice season from February to July. No ships that have received alerts of iceberg dangers from the International Ice Patrol (and listened) have been lost in its over-100 years of existence.[21]

Did the captain of the *Titanic* know that icebergs had been spotted in the area? Likely yes: the ship had received eight iceberg warnings by telegraph during the two days prior to the collision. However, telegraph technology was new to shipping, and the ship probably didn't have a process to communicate the frequency and strength of the warnings to the key decision makers. This provides a good lesson for entrepreneurs: Information is not enough! You need a mechanism not only to get good, current information, but also to communicate that information to the right people and a way to act on it.

The Iceberg Index

Part of our goal is to help entrepreneurs and early-stage investors not just identify, but also measure and manage the hidden debts startups accumulate. With that goal in

19   Adam Aspinall, "Iceberg that sunk the *Titanic* was 100,000 years old and originally weighed 75 million tonnes," *Mirror*, March 6, 2016, accessed August 20, 2017, http://www.mirror.co.uk/news/uk-news/iceberg-sunk-titanic-100000-years-7506651.

20   Paul Rodgers, "Where Did The *Titanic*'s Iceberg Come From?" *Forbes*, April 10, 2014 accessed August 20, 2017, https://www.forbes.com/sites/paulrodgers/2014/04/10/revealed-the-origin-of-the-titanics-iceberg/#6440274cb5b0.

21   Lt. Stephanie Young, "Top 10 facts about the International Ice Patrol," *Coast Guard Compass*, March 7, 2012, accessed August 20, 2017, http://coastguard.dodlive.mil/2012/03/top-10-facts-about-the-international-ice-patrol.

mind, we created the Iceberg Index. This tool guides you through finding and quantifying these debts.

In our metaphor, the startup is the ship. The founders and crew are navigating this ship through a variety of Oceans and Seas representing the different dimensions of the venture—people (Human Ocean), markets (Marketing Ocean), and product ideas (Technical Ocean). The "debtbergs" are manifestations of specific hidden debts that populate these Seas and can damage or sink a startup. It is neither a perfect nor a literal metaphor! However, we believe it captures the dangers of sailing the startup seas, and that the *Titanic* is an interesting and colorful story to serve as a backbone for this metaphor. The theme also reflects the uncertainty that founders must navigate as part of starting their company.

The largest body of water the startup must navigate is an **Ocean**. Each Ocean contains a set of **Seas**, or categories within the Ocean (oceanographers, please bear with us putting metaphorical Seas inside of Oceans). Each Sea contains iceberg drifts, or related collections of icebergs, with specific sources of debt being icebergs of various sizes.

We develop four Oceans of hidden debts (all separate chapters), each with several Seas as noted below:

- *The Human Ocean.* This chapter explores how people related to the startup can create hidden debts. The Seas include Founders, Investors/Advisors, and Employees.
- *The Marketing Ocean.* This chapter explores how relationships with customers and competitors can create hidden debts. The Seas include Segmentation, Positioning, and Tactics.
- *The Technical Ocean.* This chapter explores how the technology base for the product, service, or software can create hidden debts. The Seas include Validation, Design, and Development.
- *The Strategy Ocean.* This chapter explores how the overall direction of the venture and interrelationships between the three oceans can create hidden debts. The seas include Integration, Measurement, and Accountability.

After detailed descriptions of these dimensions and their components, Chapter 8 provides more information on how to use the Iceberg Index to your advantage. See our website[22] for more on tools that can help you calculate and track your startup's iceberg index score over time.

---

22   See the website for this book at http://www.titaniceffect.com.

Several icebergs have been accused of being the culprit that sank the *Titanic* because they were seen in the neighborhood and fit the general description—a sad case of glacial profiling. We likely will never know with certainty which iceberg was indeed involved. In a case worthy of a Sherlock Holmes' mystery, the evidence quite literally melted away within a few weeks. Science and history can offer only conjecture, not certainty. However, the incident will forever be memorialized as a key event in nautical lore, a trigger for lifesaving safety improvements—and now, the inspiration for a tool that allows entrepreneurs and investors to monitor the effects of hidden debts on their emergent ventures as they navigate uncertainty.

The most likely *Titanic* Iceberg Picture credit: *Wikimedia Commons*

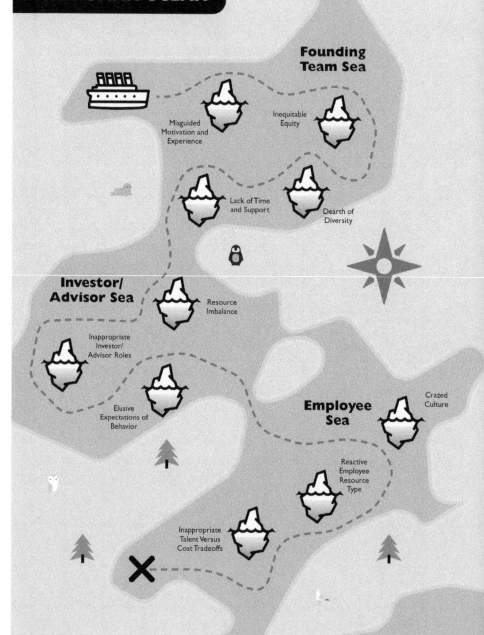

THE HUMAN OCEAN

Founding
Team Sea

Misguided
Motivation and
Experience

Inequitable
Equity

Lack of Time
and Support

Dearth of
Diversity

Investor/
Advisor Sea

Resource
Imbalance

Inappropriate
Investor/
Advisor Roles

Elusive
Expectations of
Behavior

Employee
Sea

Crazed
Culture

Reactive
Employee
Resource
Type

Inappropriate
Talent Versus
Cost Tradeoffs

CHAPTER 3:

THE HUMAN OCEAN

"Life is a shipwreck, but we must not forget to sing in the lifeboats."
–Voltaire, paraphrased by Peter Gay

"We all need somebody to lean on."
–Bill Withers

The first category of *hidden debt* we will explore is human. With any good story, one must understand the central characters as well as the supporting cast to appreciate the plot. The founder is not the only person involved in the *startup* journey. The presence—or absence—of co-founders, support team members (like advisors and investors), and the first hired hands of a startup all contribute to its trajectory. These make up the crew, who can help launch and sail the promising startup to success. They may also be the founder's only companions if the lifeboat needs bailing out—and if the founder chooses well, the ones willing to sing while they do it!

You learned a bit about the history of the White Star Line and the *Titanic* in Chapter 2, including the history of the organization and some of its key and colorful players. In this chapter, we delve further into the three Seas of icebergs in the Human Ocean for startups and reveal a little more on the *Titanic* people issues as well. Human behavior is unpredictable, so navigating *uncertainty* would be incomplete without a rich discussion of the debtbergs people can create for even the most promising startup. The Seas in the Human Ocean include:

- **The Founding Team Sea**—Have the right leadership team on the bridge
- **The Investor/Advisor Sea**—Find the right funders/supporters
- **The Employee Sea**—Hire the right crew

The Founding Team Sea

White Star Line had an interesting and changing set of leaders who ran the company. Each signaled a different strategy and focus for the company and brought a different set of relationships.

Founders John Pilkington and Henry Wilson started the company in 1845 in Liverpool, England offering passage to Australia. Leadership and ownership transferred to Thomas Ismay in 1868 following the financial troubles of the 1860s. The move to steamships and serving the UK-to-US market were major strategic departures from the past. The RMS Oceanic was the first ship built during this period, and it marked a directional change toward a Titanic*-like ship.*

Upon the passing of Thomas and with White Star facing further financial distress, eldest son J. Bruce Ismay took over the leadership of the company. He brought in new investor/owner J.P. Morgan and shifted the core value proposition from speed to size and luxury—all pivotal events preceding the building of the Titanic.

Obviously, startups don't exist without founders. Where would Apple be without Steve Jobs? Amazon without Jeff Bezos? Uber without Travis Kalanick? Snapchat without Evan Spiegel? However, these business icons all had colleagues who helped them launch their businesses. Take a look at the zany bunch in Figure 1: Do you recognize Bill Gates in the lower left corner? Even then, he put himself in the middle of a team that was essential to getting Microsoft off the ground.

Figure 1: Founding team, Microsoft

The composition of the founding team and how it shares ownership, responsibility, and accountability are key success factors for a startup, and potential sources of devastating human debt. As we discussed in the introductory material, each Sea contains iceberg drifts, which hold related debtbergs. The four iceberg drifts of the Founding Team Sea we focus on are:

- Misguided Motivation and Experience
- Inequitable Equity
- Dearth of Diversity
- Lack of Time and Support

Misguided Motivation and Experience

Starting a venture is hard work and requires a combination of passion, experience, and persistence (we affectionately call this the *PEP model*). Launching a startup without appreciating the core of what it provides its customers is shaky ground to start from, but it does happen. Some entrepreneurs may be motivated by the lure of being their own boss, making a million bucks, or being the next entrepreneurial rock star—but have little passion about the actual product. Successful venturing starts with the right motivation.

One example comes from Chris Baggott, cofounder of ExactTarget (now Salesforce Marketing Cloud). Baggott is a serial entrepreneur in the tech space as well as an innovator in local food growing, marketing, and delivery (for example, ClusterTruck). Baggott's first "startup" was a dry-cleaning business he purchased. He saw the opportunity to apply marketing tools that were just emerging in the 1990s, such as email marketing, to revolutionize how dry cleaners communicated with clients and managed their client relationships. The potential of the technology intrigued Baggott, but as he is fond of saying, "I neglected to appreciate that at some point you have to press the customer's pants." He loved the technology, but not the core business itself.

While the dry-cleaning venture failed, the lessons Baggott learned on the technology side of the business became the core value proposition of ExactTarget. This startup went on to go public, and eventually Salesforce.com acquired it for $2.5 billion. That's a lot of pressed pants! Successful entrepreneurs must discover what they are passionate about and match that to the core value proposition of the startup.

Apoorva Mehta's company Instacart demonstrates the importance of deep experience and the insight it yields. For Mehta, his attempt to build a social network for lawyers scratched his entrepreneurial itch to start something, and that project did overlap with some of his interests and capabilities. However, the startup concept did not match Mehta's experience or give him meaning. "After going through all these failures, releasing feature after feature, I realized it wasn't that I couldn't find a product that worked—I just didn't care about the product," Mehta said. "When I went home, I wouldn't think about it because I didn't care about lawyers. I didn't think of what lawyers did day-to-day."[23]

Like Baggott, Mehta did not connect in a meaningful way with the core product of his first startup. Then, Baggott came upon helping companies connect with customers and manage customer relationships with ExactTarget, and Mehta discovered a vehicle to get groceries without the pain of hitting the store aisles via InstaCart. That's when they fulfilled a deep need with which they were intimately acquainted and the PEP pieces came together.

On the other hand, deep passion and commitment for the core of the business incurs its own type of debt. When Gary Erickson had an opportunity to cash out of his position in Clif Bar, he was too attached to the business to let it go (it has to be hard to sell your company that you named after your dad). Reddit founders Steve Huffman and Alexis Ohanian walked away after a nice sale to Condé Nast, but returned to the company out of a sense of obligation to the platform and the stakeholders when the company struggled. Launching something you really care about improves the odds of success and avoids motivation icebergs, but can create new and different icebergs of hidden debt.

> **Lookout:** *Beware the founder who has no passion for the problem the business solves—but also the founder who is so committed they appear unwilling to consider negative feedback. Good founders are passionate and persistent, but coachable.*

Inequitable Equity

The next place where founders begin to incur debt is the division of *equity*, or ownership of the firm. Whether two, three, four, or more founders, people tend to start by dividing equity equally across all who are part of the initial discussions about an idea—those at the table when the team puts ink to napkin. It just feels right to share equally, and it is great fun at first. However, how many team projects have you worked on where all members equally carry their weight over time? Opportunity costs and energy simply vary across team members over time, and really only one or two members are likely to have the time and capacity to champion the effort through all stages.

---

23   Tracey Lien, "Apoorva Mehta had 20 failed startups before Instacart," *Los Angeles Times*, January 27, 2017, accessed August 20, 2017, http://www.latimes.com/business/technology/la-fi-himi-apoorva-mehta-20170105-story.html.

We call this the "Curse of Thirdsies" (for ventures with three founders). Consider Bob, April, and Gerry, who have a great idea for the next app to revolutionize weight loss and exercise. They meet a few times over coffee or beers and hash out the beginnings of a business concept. They all agree to share equally in the rewards when they go public or get acquired. Woo-hoo, everyone wins! "We all own 33.33% of the next Facebook!"

Then, reality sets in. After three months, Gerry has a promotion at work and needs to travel a lot with a new position. His wife starts to raise concerns about his status as absentee husband and father of their young family. Bob and April are understanding and forge on…after all, Gerry's wife Sara is so nice, also a working professional, and was April's roommate in college. Besides, Gerry will make it right eventually! However, as time goes on, it gets harder and harder to reengage with Gerry. He has his equity, and the venture isn't really going in the direction he envisioned in the first place, so he avoids his partners. The more time passes, the more difficult the conversation about changing the equity distribution gets.

Whether because of intentional shirking or life simply getting in the way, co-founders usually end up with one free rider who has an equal share of the equity but does not pull his weight. This debtberg can weigh on founders and create challenges for funding down the road when inactive founders are on the *cap table*, but not contributing to the startup progress.

Splitting equity 50/50 between just two founders also has associated decision-making problems if the two founders share control of decisions equally. Moving forward requires both partners to agree completely on critical strategic initiatives, which may not always be the case.

Erickson of Clif Bar faced a huge decision in the year 2000. A large acquirer wanted to buy the company following a wave of similar transactions in the snack bar category, such as the acquisitions of Balance Bar and PowerBar.[24] The offer on the table was $120 million, which was quite a nice premium for a company with $40 million in sales.

Circle back to Clif Bar origins. Remember from Chapter 1 that Erickson's first company was Kali's Sweets & Savories, a Greek pastry company. Erickson had brought in Lisa Thomas to help run Kali's. When he started Clif Bar, he started it within Kali's and never legally separated the companies from each other. Instead, he ran Clif Bar while Thomas continued with Kali's. As a result, Thomas owned half of both businesses.[25]

Not surprisingly, Thomas was enthused about the $120 million offer and committed to cashing out. Erickson, however, was less enthusiastic. He was concerned

24   Melanie Warner, "Clif Bar's Solo Climb," *CNN Money*, December 1, 2004, accessed August 20, 2017, http://money.cnn.com/magazines/business2/business2_archive/2004/12/01/8192527/index.htm.

25   Nadine Heintz, Bo Burlingham, and Ryan McCarthy, "Starting Up in a Down Economy," *Inc.com*, May 1, 2008, accessed August 20, 2017, https://www.inc.com/magazine/20080501/starting-up-in-a-down-economy.html.

about what becoming a small product in a large company would do to the brand, the product, the employees, and the company. He got cold feet and decided to pull out in the final hours before closing.

Unfortunately, in this case, the 50/50 ownership status from early Kali's/Clif days carried a $60 million debtberg. With a 50% interest in the company, Thomas was just as entitled to sell the company as Erickson. When he prevented the $120 million deal, Thomas wanted the money she would have gotten. It took Clif Bar and Erickson nine years and many payments to melt this iceberg island down to a bergy bit. That's a lot of Clif Bars!

Making sure founders earn equity over time as they demonstrate commitment and contribution and the venture meets milestones limits the negative effects of founder debt. We further discuss *vesting* and additional strategies for overcoming this debt at the end of the chapter.

 Navigation Plan: *Never split equity 50/50. Have a clear majority owner and decision-maker if there are two founders, or require majority agreement for major decisions if there are more founders. The startup's operating agreement can state the specifics.*

 Navigation Plan: *Vesting, or allocating equity over time, is a great vehicle to balance contribution and progress with incentive for founders and early employees.*

Dearth of Diversity

Every good founding team needs some combination of technical skill, financial understanding, marketing savvy, and sales hutzpah. One angel investor we know calls this the 3 Hs—every venture needs a Hacker (technologist), a Hustler (salesperson), and a Hipster (visionary with great hair who tells the story). This is hard to embody in one individual.

In Gimlet's Startup podcast, investor Micah Rosenbloom of the Founder Collective says, "I would much rather bet on two people or three people than a single founder...I think startups are a team sport...the probability of success goes up."[26]

---

26   Alex Blumberg, interview by Robert Smith and David Kestenbaum, "Planet Money Episode 569: How to Divide an Imaginary Pie," NPR, September 17, 2014, accessed August 20, 2017, http://www.npr.org/templates/transcript/transcript.php?storyId=349034928.

Healthy discussions about innovation and disruption require opposing viewpoints and diverse perspectives to be successful. However, founding teams often comprise people who share history, interests, and work experience. Too much overlapping perspective can result in significant blind spots for the startup. Worse, it can lead to *groupthink*, where the members begin to see a shared view of the world that may or may not resemble reality.

A strong venture team has not just coverage of key functional areas, but also ideally some startup experience, access to funding sources, and complementary networks for identifying customers and employees. The blind spots created by a lack of diversity create significant debtbergs in the form of a limited perspective on reality and appreciation for possibilities.

 Navigation Plan: *Be sure to incorporate diversity, including demographics such as gender and race as well as functional experience, early in the life of the startup. This can be through the founding team, the early hires, or advisors who counsel your firm.*

There are many ways to broaden and diversify capabilities:

- Randy Hetrick of TRX had plenty of passion for his product and persistence helpful to a founder navigating the iceberg-laden Oceans. However, he had little business training, so he went to Stanford to get his MBA. He relentlessly used TRX as fodder for group projects and class discussions to bring out diverse perspectives.
- When Joe Gebbia and co-founder Brian Chesky of Airbnb hit on a model they thought could grow, they realized they needed more than design talent. They recruited a CTO in Nathan Blecharczyk, a former roommate.
- Mei Xu turned to friends and family as far away as China to help broaden resources as Chesapeake Bay Candle began to expand.

Founders can add diversity of capabilities over time and through multiple vehicles. This approach balances the financial burden of adding more talent against the human debtbergs stemming from a dearth of diversity.

Lack of Time and Support

Starting a venture is hard and requires constant attention. It is virtually impossible to make significant headway if starting a company is extracurricular—done after the founder's day job, in the evenings and weekends.

President Lincoln and Human Debt

Problems with founder diversity, commitment to the product, and talent are not new issues. For one example, let's go way back, even before White Star Line was conceived, to a period in Abraham Lincoln's life before he was President. In 1832, Lincoln and his partner William Berry purchased a general store in New Salem, Illinois. Through a series of events, they also acquired the assets of the other two stores in the small town, making them a virtual monopoly.

The appeal to Lincoln was that a store was a place to build community, share jokes and stories, and discuss politics. Lincoln did all of these—but was not very good at selling items from the store, and his honesty often got in the way of closing a deal. He particularly liked to dissuade customers from purchasing "sinful" (but high margin) products like tobacco and alcohol. His partner Berry did little to help, being

more interested in whiskey and gossip than running the business. The store folded in less than a year, leaving Lincoln with debt, but many lessons learned about engaging in political discourse, which served him well.

This is especially true as the business grows and begins seeking outside funding. Investors will rarely put money into a startup with a part-time CEO. Yet, resources are scarce and most early-stage ventures cannot support a full-time salary—let alone three for Bob, April, and Gerry. Taking time and energy from the day job, family, or other relationships takes a toll on both the founder and the founder's friends and loved ones. Being the first among the founding team to leave the day job and work full-time on the venture should also have an associated increase in equity.

While often ignored, relationship debt and the obligations a founder builds while launching a company are not insignificant. Having no salary may create financial debt, which is relatively easy to measure. However, founders should not ignore the difficult-to-measure, non-financial debts they incur to current employers, partners, and others as they deal with the stress, energy, and peaks-and-valleys of early-stage venturing. These debts can result in poor work performance and strained or severed relationships with loved ones.

Social news and media aggregation site Reddit co-founders, Huffman and Oha-nian, had their struggles at several points in their entrepreneurial journey balancing venture needs, personal challenges, and friendship. Huffman and Ohanian met at the University of Virginia. Their relationship started with unfulfilled expectations—Alexis was to live in the room across from Huffman in their dorm. Seeing the name Alexis, Huffman thought it was cool that he would have a female hall mate—until he actually met Alexis, a male student! However, the two became friends and co-conspirators. Coming up on graduation a few years later, the two friends embarked upon their entrepreneurial dream journey together.

The first concept was a food ordering system for gas stations to reduce wait times. They named it My Mobile Menu, or MMM for short. The system would allow patrons to communicate their food order from the pump while filling up. The idea for Reddit came later, at the urging of Paul Graham, founder of Y Combinator (a well-regarded accelerator in Silicon Valley). Graham liked the two as a team, but not MMM as an idea—so he encouraged them to turn their talents to a new concept. During their fif-teen-year journey, challenges to Huffman and Ohanian's relationship and involvement in Reddit came in extreme forms:

- a girlfriend's accident resulting in a coma
- a mother's cancer
- a period of detachment following the sale of Reddit to Condé Nast

Despite these challenges, Huffman and Ohanian worked together to build Reddit as the "front page of the Internet." They persisted through periods of strife and stress on both sides to keep moving forward. Like a marriage, good founder partnerships must survive not just venture but personal obligations and distractions as well. We all need somebody to lean on.

As you have toured the Founding Team Sea, you have seen how the founder cate-gory of human debt can include:

- experience and motivation
- how equity is shared
- diversity of talent and experience
- time and support to devote to the venture

Matching passion for the problem the startup solves to the venture value prop-osition, careful building of a diverse founding team, vesting of equity over time, and stage-appropriate founder investment of energy can help mitigate these possible human debtbergs. PEP is essential. At the end of the chapter, we offer some more detailed suggestions for how to manage and mitigate these hidden debts.

The Investor/Advisor Sea[27]

With each generation of leadership came a new set of financial sup-porters and advisors for White Star. The initial banking relationship with the Bank of Liverpool, central to White Star's success through the mid-1860s, dissolved with the bank's collapse in 1868. The bank failure sank White Star's source of funds. This triggered the need for new investors. Enter Christian Schwabe. Schwabe brought in new builders Harland and Wolff. Another round of financial distress in the early 1900s led to the entrance of owner, investor, and confidante J.P. Morgan, coinciding with the Bigger is Better strategy and the building of the Titanic. *It is impossible to disentangle White Star's history from the investors who influenced (or coerced!) the company's leaders at key inflection points leading to the* Titanic.

As any startup grows, bringing in investors may become important to continue fueling that growth. Initially, such funds might come from *friends and family* members. Both may be able to invest some modest amount, perhaps up to $50,000 to $100,000, without significant paperwork and regulatory constraints. Angel investors or groups, and possibly even *venture capital*, can fuel growth beyond that.

Along the way, the founders may engage with a variety of formal or informal advisors and advocates as well, who may help the team to overcome obstacles, connect with customers and funding sources, and provide other invaluable guidance and feedback. However, investors and advisors are not a one-way street for dollars and advice. They can also be a drain, a source of major hidden debts that can constrain future growth, flexibility, and action. With both advisors and investors, founders need to be aware of the following debtbergs in the Investor/Advisor Sea:

- Resource Imbalance
- Inappropriate Investor/Advisor Roles
- Elusive Expectations of Behavior

Resource Imbalance

Founders must manage the input of many versus the power of few. Crowd-funding, for example, seems like a great way to raise money from hundreds of friends, neighbors, and supporters without having to go, hat in hand, to a small number of major investors. However, when you are up at 2:00 AM answering the twentieth email from investor number 245, you might feel otherwise! Plus, having large numbers of small investors on your cap table might create regulatory barriers and discourage investors in later rounds. Such investors might also be able to provide little help beyond the small check, and not have expertise in launching and growing

---

27   While investors and advisors can play very different roles, the debt involved is similar. We will discuss them both at the same time.

a startup. Crowd investing and funding from the masses has some benefits, but can create debtbergs as well.

What is Crowdfunding?

While popular and rapidly evolving, *crowdfunding* is a term that is often misunderstood and misused today. First, there are several types of crowdfunding. All focus on connecting the customer or supporter directly to the organization, as opposed to working through an intermediary like United Way, a bank, investment group, or the stock market.

Platforms like Kiva and DonorsChoose.org provide a mechanism for small loans or donations to causes of the donor's choice. Equity and products typically are not involved.

Kickstarter, Indiegogo, and others connect startups with customers and enthusiasts who can preorder products or receive gifts or swag such as t-shirts, access to unique information, or signed memorabilia. (As some readers might recall, we experimented with a Kickstarter as part of writing this book). These are rewards-based and don't involve equity.

The JOBS (Jumpstart Our Business Startups) Act of 2012 also allowed for the third category: people who aren't *accredited investors* putting money into startups for equity. Though implementation varies by state, this allows "regular folks" to invest in startups for a small piece of ownership through platforms like Localstake. New technology, social preferences,[28] and regulatory change have all enabled much of crowdfunding's potential—potentially democratizing early-stage investment, but also creating possible debtbergs. Will crowdfunding revolutionize early-stage investing and launch waves of startups, or sink as naïve investors lose money when paired with naïve entrepreneurs? The jury is still out.

On the other end of the spectrum, landing "Danny Deeppockets" for a $200,000 check feels great and allows you to start hiring first employees. However, after the third time in a week that Danny drops over for dinner to tell you whom you should hire and what product tweak he wants you to make, you may feel less enthusiastic—as Ismay might have felt when he had to shift shipbuilders to Harland and Wolff.[29] Balancing the value added and power of one or a small number of large investors versus a large number of small investors is tricky—each path builds a different kind of investor debt. Hunting for minnows versus whales takes different weapons, and each approach has its own downside.

---

28   For more on these trends, check out Steven Johnson's *Future Perfect: The Case for Progress in a Networked Age*. New York: Penguin Group, 2012.

29   This is not a comment on Harland and Wolff's capabilities—it was a well-regarded shipbuilder. However, changing suppliers of a major component of your strategy is never easy or comfortable, especially when dictated by an investor.

Inappropriate Investor/Advisor Roles

Another important consideration with investors and advisors is the role they play. These roles might involve their capabilities—what they are good at, like marketing, finance, or technology; their experience, based on what they have done and know about growing and launching a startup or the industry; and/or their network, as in who they know and can get access to. All of these roles can be helpful to a startup. However, "investment" in these relationships is a two-way street and can add debt in the form of wasted time and effort.

It is important to use advisors and investors to add diversity and expand networks. Diversity from investors and advisors can efficiently offset the debtberg of a dearth of diversity among the founders described previously. However, while local advisors whom founders already know are easy to find, those advisors may not expand the founders' capabilities or network.

 Navigation Plan: *Look for a diverse mix of advisors who add functional expertise, industry knowledge, startup experience, and relationships with new customers and/or investors. Building an advisory board, even an informal one, of people exactly like you brings little new or different in terms of experience or relationships and builds hidden debt. These kinds of advisory groups create obligations that outweigh the value they bring.*

On the investor side, similar issues to those for advisors can set up a startup for success or failure. Many founders see investors, at best, as arm's-length sources of funds and, at worst, as adversaries to battle at every turn. Both approaches create debtbergs in the form of missed opportunity and unnecessary angst. Certainly, some investors can be sources of funds only, but at least a few should add value in other ways. Good investors are not adversaries but partners and allies in growing the startup.

 Navigation Plan: *Particularly early, you should seek at least some investors who bring more than money to the table. Startups need a lot of help, guidance, and connections. Seek some investors who have experience investing in and guiding the companies they support, and others who have industry experience and connections.*

Chris Sacca, renowned serial *early-stage investor*, worked relentlessly to help Twitter raise money, get visibility, and succeed—it was his first big investment, and he was determined to have it pay off. However, Sacca also acknowledges founders may find him overly aggressive in his interference. The *Fortune* cover featuring "Venture

Cowboy" Sacca (April 2015) says it all with his quote: "When I invest, I am in your face." Passive investors have a time and place, but advocates dedicated to a startup's success can be worth more than their weight in checks. Entrepreneurs must be strategic and selective in what they want from their investors. Ultimately, investors have a vested interest in any company they invest in to be successful. That's a lot of vests!

 Navigation Plan: *Ask potential investors questions early in the relationship regarding their willingness to leverage their experience and network.*

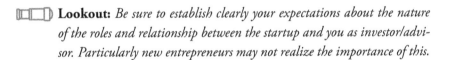

 Lookout: *Be sure to establish clearly your expectations about the nature of the roles and relationship between the startup and you as investor/advisor. Particularly new entrepreneurs may not realize the importance of this.*

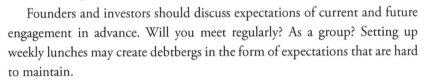

Elusive Expectations of Behavior

Founders and investors should discuss expectations of current and future engagement in advance. Will you meet regularly? As a group? Setting up weekly lunches may create debtbergs in the form of expectations that are hard to maintain.

Similarly, meeting as a group when you really only need select advice on a particular topic may over-involve one advisor and waste the time of the others. For investors and advisors, it should be clear whether their input on strategic matters is expected generally on a regular (monthly or quarterly) basis, in specific circumstances, only when there is a crisis, or not at all. Time and money are the entrepreneur's most valued resources. A general guideline would be quarterly board or advisor meetings with select engagement individually as otherwise needed. However, it is also a good idea to communicate monthly or even every two weeks during key phases of experimentation or fundraising for input via email or other communication form.

 Navigation Plan: *Prepare monthly or quarterly email updates for distribution to advisors/investors with important updates and needs. Don't be afraid to ask for help in critical areas and acknowledge problems.*

Lookout: *Encourage portfolio companies to provide regular monthly or quarterly updates including not just numbers but insight into customer trajectory, product changes, and venture needs.*

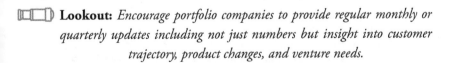

For future engagement expectations, if a startup is successful, it will likely need additional funding rounds and capital. In fact, the more successful a startup is and the faster it grows, the more likely it is to need money to fuel that growth—and sooner than most would think. Startups often need to hire sales and marketing help, invest in product improvements, and bring on employees for service and support in advance of when revenue comes in the door. Those hires burn cash and require funding. Will existing investors step up for additional funding rounds? Are they connected to new sources of funds, particularly institutional sources, that can help fund future growth? Tying a venture to a set of shallow-pocketed investors with no broader investor network can be a large and limiting source of debt when trying to scale the company.

Other types of strategic partners can fall into similar expectation icebergs as well. Clif Bar, for example had a handshake deal with two distributors in the growth stage. They did not clearly establish expectations, and, in Erickson's eyes, the distributors failed to perform. He terminated the deal, and the distributors sued and tried to wrest control of the whole business away from him. While Erickson eventually won and avoided sinking, the period was stressful and consumed time and energy that he should have used on growing the business. To make matters worse, this iceberg came with a $2 million cost to settle with the distributors, a significant iceberg to overcome for a young, growing startup. This relationship debtberg overlaps with *technical debt* (Chapter 5) in designing and developing distribution systems to get your product to the customer.

The venture Alikolo provides another interesting example of some of the collective challenges of founder and investor debtbergs.[30] Alikolo was an e-commerce platform serving Indonesia, founded in Medan, North Sumatra in 2014. Danny Taniwan, a software engineer trained at the Technical University of Berlin, was the company founder. Upon graduating, Taniwan returned to Medan and moved from jobs in insurance to car modification. He had an entrepreneurial itch and motivation to do something big, but neither insurance nor automotive businesses scratched it. There was no PEP!

Seeking to exercise his software skills, Taniwan read up on the hugely successful Chinese firm Alibaba, the ecommerce equivalent of Amazon in Asia. He was determined to build a similar company in Indonesia. He was able to interest two investor acquaintances in his idea.

Taniwan lacked entrepreneurial experience and did not seek out co-founders. Further, the two investors had experience in commodity businesses like timber, but also lacked technical and startup experience. To their credit, they were able to rent an office, start a company, and launch a working product—but the venture demonstrated little traction after launch.

---

30 Nadine Freischlad, "This guy's story of failing in Indonesia is refreshingly honest. Now he's getting up and starting again," *TechInAsia*, June 19, 2015, accessed June 23, 2018, https://www.techinasia.com/danny-taniwan-alikolo-startup-failure-indonesia.

By the time Taniwan began to increase his set of advisors, network in the venture community, and land on a strategy, Alikolo was out of money. Taniwan was able to interest venture capitalists in his revised vision, but the venture capitalists' *due diligence* revealed that the early angel investors owned the majority of the company. These early investors were unwilling to take a less significant stake or be flexible with terms with a new investor. Unwilling to fund the startup further, the investors shut down Alikolo.

As Taniwan reflects on his experience, he notes, "Now I know I did everything wrong. I shouldn't have tried to start a company alone, without co-founders. I should have done my research. I should have started small and *bootstrapped*. And I never should have let the investors become majority shareholders." Undeterred but better prepared, Taniwan has moved onto his next venture, AFFORIA, an online premium private shopping experience, with enthusiasm—but also with a co-founder and a much better understanding of the debtbergs of founder and investor debt.

In summary, relationship expectations with advisors and investors create debts that can mount to serious time sinks and constantly changing venture direction or a lack of resources and help when a founder needs them. Both groups can be an entrepreneur's biggest allies and advocates, and can help overcome deficits in the founding team. However, they can also be a drag on time and energy if these debts go unmanaged.

The Employee Sea

Strategy and financial capital were not the only challenges facing the White Star Line and Titanic. *Building such large ships required incredible numbers of workers—over 14,000, in fact. This exhausted local skilled talent for wood and metalwork, such as riveters. Further, some of the crew challenges that accompanied the losses of White Star's* Tayleur *and* Atlantic *persisted or even accelerated with the new strategy and the launch of the new line. As an "engineering marvel" and due to the luxurious treatment high-end passengers expected, the great majority of the nearly 900 crewmembers were mechanics/engineers and staff responsible for preparing and serving food. White Star recruited most of the crew only weeks before the maiden voyage, and none of the crewmembers were permanent. Only about sixty-five, or less than 8% of the crew, were trained, able-bodied seamen who understood emergency procedures—for example, how to load lifeboats. This imbalance contributed to the catastrophic losses in lives the* Titanic *suffered in 1912.*

How rewarding to hire that first employee! If all goes well, the first employee will continue to contribute to the company as it "grows up" and share in some of the rewards. However, the growing startup has a complex set of needs, and staffing the scaling organization can be a big source of hidden debt. Let's not forget that payroll is both a real financial debt and a hidden emotional one. Some founders find they have sleepless nights after launch, growth, and securing outside capital, as they sweat cash flow to be able to pay employees their monthly salaries.

Understanding and managing employee debt is an important consideration early in the life of a startup. The categories or iceberg drifts of employee debt we will elaborate on are:

- Inappropriate Talent Versus Cost Tradeoffs
- Crazed Culture
- Reactive Employee Resource Type

When to Hire the First Employee

Being too early to hire your first full-time employee creates debtbergs, but so does being too late. There are no hard and fast rules as to when to hire the first full-time employee, but here are some guidelines as to when to pull the trigger:

- *When the startup can afford it.* If there is cash to last six months or more, the startup is in a position to offer stability for at least that much time—but should communicate the risks to recruits.
- *When the needs of the business dictate it.* Once a startup has paying customers, it likely needs a dedicated resource to service them.
- *When there is a job to do.* When the startup has demand in one functional area that needs forty-to-sixty hours a week or more from a dedicated individual, it needs an employee.
- *When the opportunity costs on founders becomes too high.* Founders can carry the load only so far. When getting necessary work done precludes spending time on strategy and fundraising, it is time to hire the first employee.

Inappropriate Talent Versus Cost Tradeoffs

One of the first human resource challenges is the level of talent versus cost of the early hires. Human debt can come in the form of one prima donna, for example, the high-cost whale-hunter sales guy who had one prior success with a startup, but has no transferable skills to bring to the new venture. Equally problematic are the enthusiastic, bright—and cheap—fresh-out-of-college hires who exude energy, much of which might be misdirected. The founding team must balance getting people with experience in key areas with not breaking the bank on overpriced talent.

Interns are a great example. They may be inexpensive, and, appropriately trained and focused, they can be a great help to the cash-strapped startup. However, they **do** need training and focused help and direction from founders. If interns interact with customers, then these "helpers" will be the face of the startup—for better and for worse. Such exposure can create credibility debt with customers and others from which it is hard to recover.

Equally detrimental can be the high-end IT developer, marketing guru, or killer sales hire. Expertise in these areas can cost ventures upwards of $150,000-$200,000 a year in salary alone, plus incentives/commission and equity. If their expertise is deep but narrow, they may have little flexibility to adapt as the business inevitably changes direction. Moreover, the ego that goes along with past success can be a challenge to manage. Such employee debt can be, at best, distracting, and, at worst, devastating.

Lookout: *Be wary of founders or critical hires with one big success behind them (and no failures). They may be overpriced and have limited ability to function in a new context.*

Staffing at all levels is complex. Consider the *Titanic*. While the crew suffered from a lack of trained, able-bodied seamen, Captain Edward J. Smith was widely regarded as the most experienced (and best-paid) captain on the seas. He had a spotless record of forty years without a wreck. In fact, some suggested that Smith's lack of failure made him a little complacent and more willing to push for speed, despite the iceberg warnings, than he should have been. A strong CEO cannot make up for diversity and depth of talent that is lacking across the venture, and an unblemished record with no failures does not guarantee success.

Crazed Culture

Startups can be incredibly fun and stimulating places to work. Done right, they can attract the best and brightest and develop a culture of innovation and shared community that returns dividends for years. However, the Foosball or board game breaks, free pizza dinners, and spontaneous karaoke can also get out of control and be dysfunctional if things turn south. Setting expectations of a personal lunch with the founding team on an employee's birthday can be fantastic for employee number ten…but hard to maintain for employee number 100. Similarly, banging the gong for a new sale can be motivating in the emerging stage of a startup. Having that gong ring twenty times a day during growth, though, can be deafening—and the silence when in a twenty-day lull disquieting and dispiriting.

Sometimes investors push for limits on corporate cultures when those cultures appear to be building icebergs of hidden debt. Weichaishi, an Asian startup based in Shanghai, faced pushback from investors in the venture capital tightening of 2016. Weichaishi provides an online crowdsourcing platform to corporate clients. After scoring over $3 million in investment in 2014, the company took employees to Thailand, housing them in a five-star hotel and treating them to elephant rides. That sort of precedent is hard to maintain, let alone improve upon in future years! Following the pushback and increased investor vigilance, two years later even snacks and beverages for employees were rare at Weichaishi. Pei Qiao, founder, noted in his *Wall Street Journal* interview[31]: "We are becoming more practical and looking for tangible results."

Employees must recognize that the perks that accompany success are earned and not automatic. As the company grows, founders will have to work even harder at maintaining a unique and consistent culture. Patterns and expectations become culture in a way that is important to monitor and be intentional about, for better and for worse.

Reactive Employee Resource Type

Another balancing act that can be a source of human debt is the appropriate mix of part-time, full-time, and outsourced resources. Ventures simply cannot staff full-time employees for all tasks. It is too expensive, and there is too much uncertainty about which roles and capabilities are necessary in the long term. It is easy to be reactive to venture needs and hire at-will, but proactive planning can avoid wasted resources.

Contracting with the marketing expert for one or two days a week of help with social media or public relations can be a boon at one stage, but a burden at others. Sourcing work from India for some web app development and coding can be cost effective and help in a time crunch, but a waste of time and money and a big source of customer and technical debt in other circumstances. Having Cousin Vinny manage the books on the weekends might be a sound choice. However, individuals who are not full-time employees may never share the same bond and commitment to the blossoming enterprise.

A mix of types of employees and outsourced relationships can provide balanced and efficient capabilities for the growing firm. Each type of human resource creates some type of debt, and each needs appropriate management.

---

31   Juro Osawa, Newley Purnell, and Sean McLain, "Asian Startups Hit by Venture Capital Slowdown," *The Wall Street Journal*, May 12, 2016, accessed June 23, 2018, https://www.wsj.com/articles/asian-startups-hit-by-venture-capital-slowdown-1462986692.

Navigation Plan: *Never forget that outsourced human resources are not living and breathing for your venture. Over time, you need to own the key parts of the business, including product design, customer relationships, and financial performance.*

Consider Chesapeake Bay Candle, which provides a helpful example of dodging various employee debtbergs over time. As the company began to scale, Xu struggled to find adequate-quality raw materials for her scented creations. United States' sources demanded too large an order or were not up to the task. It would have been too costly at the time to build a plant in the United States, and the company did not have employees skilled in this kind of manufacturing.

However, Xu's sister and brother-in-law in China were willing to quit their jobs and pitch in. Xu's family connections got her through early growth, and supply ramped up. Not much later, to meet the demand of new account, Target, Chesapeake Bay Candle required a facility for inventory. Pressed for time, they found one that had capacity and was available, but had no lights. Low on power—both in the form of electricity and labor—Xu and friends manually unloaded crate after crate of candles by the light of car headlights. Entrepreneurs must be prepared to go the extra mile and roll up their sleeves to overcome resource imbalances!

Eventually, Chesapeake Bay Candle outgrew the China facility and moved to new manufacturing and storage several times, ultimately landing some production in the United States. Of course, Xu's family still had a plant in China, and the hidden family debt that accompanied her sister's career transition. To overcome the debtberg owed to her family members for leaving their former careers, Xu converted the original plant into a sourcing, testing, and design center, and it has continued to morph over time to fulfill other entrepreneurial ideas. This kept them employed and contributing to her ventures.

 Navigation Plan: *Family and friends can often fill resource gaps, but do not underestimate the long-term relational debts that can accrue.*

The Role of Individuals

As we discussed the iceberg drifts in the Human Ocean, we talked about people in general—"roles" and "human resources." Generalizing about "people" is fine, but each "person" is a unique character who contributes something wholly distinctive to the startup's story.

When Xu had difficulty reaching the buyer at Target for her product category, she did what many assertive and entrepreneurial founders would do—she went over the buyer's head to the higher-level buyer. She received a concise message from her initial contact essentially communicating that she had burned a bridge by going to the boss, and spent eighteen months in limbo with no positive progress until a new buyer moved into the position.

Hetrick saw a huge leap in demand, particularly from professional sports teams, when New Orleans quarterback Drew Brees' use of the TRX System contributed to a faster-than-expected, even miraculous, recovery from a labrum tear and shoulder surgery.

Airbnb had former President Obama to thank for two major inflection points in the company's history. The first was the 2008 Democratic National Convention in Denver, where Airbnb saw its first significant usage linking conventiongoers to places to crash for the big event. The second was in subsequent months when Gebbia and Chesky had tapped out their credit cards and faced possible termination of the startup. They created limited-edition boxes of Obama O's and Cap'n McCain's cereal to raise some extra funds and pay off their credit card debt (see callout box). While not a personal acquaintance, Obama helped Airbnb bail out from hidden and financial debts on two occasions.

Cereal Entrepreneurs

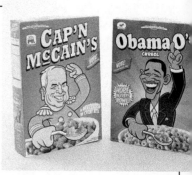

In 2008, Airbnb was in the early stages of conceptualization and had not proven its business model. This made it hard to raise money from investors. Instead, the founders found a creative way to raise money with a side gig through an Internet business playing on the election. The product was boxes of cereal labeled Obama O's and Cap'n McCain's, sold for $40. Even though it was unrelated to the core startup business of Airbnb, it provided enough cash to keep the startup running.[32]

In all three of these examples, single individuals played a significant role in the progress, or lack thereof, of one of our exemplar startups.

 Navigation Plan: *Don't discount the importance of an individual in navigating human debt. Every relationship, whether with a buyer, an investor, a customer, or even an unknown celebrity, can be a source of great power and advocacy, or an iceberg of insurmountable debt.*

---

32   Michael Carney, "Brian Chesky: I lived on Cap'n McCain's and Obama O's got AirBnB out of debt," *Pando*, January 10, 2013, accessed June 23, 2018, https://pando.com/2013/01/10/brian-chesky-i-lived-on-capn-mccains-and-obama-os-got-airbnb-out-of-debt/.

As the venture grows, the primary sources of human debt tend to shift from the founders to the investors/advisors to the employees. Initially, getting the right diverse founding team and appropriate equity structure in place is paramount. Then, getting the right mix of advisors and investors for sustained help becomes key. At this point, hiring employees and managing the company's culture through growth becomes the most important. It is incredibly rewarding to build a company with co-founders, bring in outside sources of ideas and funding through advisors and investors, and create jobs and establish a positive culture for an organization. Nevertheless, each stage, relationship, and type of contributor brings some common and some unique challenges and opportunities.

Navigating Human Debt

How does a founder begin to address some of these concerns? Thoughtful engagement with co-founders, advisors, investors, early employees, vendors, partners, and even customers can help mitigate and manage, if not eliminate, human debt. Here are three tips for doing so effectively.[33] They include doing due diligence, allocating equity slowly and vesting over time, and bootstrapping with stage-appropriate resources.

Do Your Due Diligence: Know the History

Just as the White Star Line had a questionable track record as reflected by the *Tayleur* and the *Atlantic*, most organizations and individuals have histories that suggest patterns of behavior—both good and bad. Just because a potential investor, employee, co-founder, or board member seems like a good person, don't just trust your instincts; dig deep into the candidate's history.

Similarly, some companies have a strong history of partnering with early-stage ventures for mutual benefit, while others have a track record of appropriating technologies and profits for themselves. Don't finalize an agreement until you are comfortable with the history of your partner. Google searches, checking out LinkedIn profiles, and contacting past partners and employees provides some good initial information. Before finalizing a significant relationship or investment, consider hiring a firm who does background checks.

For example, one telecommunications startup based in the Midwest had a nice *pitch* and early traction. It was raising $500,000 in growth capital. An angel group was interested in contributing over half of the $500,000 the startup was looking for. However, due diligence revealed that it was not the first time the same founders had raised money for a similar plan under a different name. In fact, the founders

---

33   For more depth on related themes, we encourage you to check out Noam Wasserman's *The Founder's Dilemmas: Anticipating and Avoiding the Pitfalls That Can Sink a Startup*. Princeton, NJ: Princeton University Press, 2012. Many of the dilemmas he explores relate to the Human Ocean.

had raised money twice before in two different Midwestern cities and subsequently filed for bankruptcy. At best, this suggested a history of not being able to convert investor dollars into returns. At worst, a cynic might suggest, it suggests a scheme with limited credibility. The angel group passed on the deal, and warned other similar groups locally of the history. Needless to say, the founders moved on to other pastures.

Lookout: *Do a background check on all founders before making an investment. Talk to other investors as part of the due diligence process as well.*

Please recognize that past failure is not *per se* a reason to forego an investment. As noted, Mehta of Instacart had more than twenty failures before translating these learnings to success; previous failure shaped Erickson of Clif Bar, Gebbia and Chesky of Airbnb, Baggott of ExactTarget, the Reddit founders, and many others. Many highly successful entrepreneurs have failures in their past. However, founders should be up-front about their history. What they learned from past mistakes can help them avoid similar mistakes in the future.

Founders who Failed First

Some of the most illustrious names failed in business before they struck it big:

- Evan Williams, Twitter, failed with podcasting platform Odeo.
- Chris Baggott, ExactTarget, failed with a dry-cleaning business.
- Sir James Dyson spent fifteen years and failed with over 5,000 prototypes before landing on his signature bagless vacuum cleaner.
- Reid Hoffman, LinkedIn, failed with dating and networking platform SocialNet.
- Kathryn Minshew, The Muse, lost almost everything with PYP Media due to founder and investor debt.
- Milton Hershey (chocolate) failed with three candy companies before succeeding.
- Arianna Huffington, Huffington Post, had her book rejected by thirty-six publishers.
- Abe Lincoln, President, failed at his grocery store.
- Vera Wang, designer, "failed" to make the US Olympic Figure Skating Team.[34]

---

34   Note that all of the authors of this book also failed to make the US Olympic Figure Skating Team.

Navigation Plan: *Be up-front with potential advisors/investors about past failures, but focus on what you learned and how you will avoid similar icebergs in your current startup.*

Due diligence goes in both directions for founders. Before spending time with a potential angel or venture capital firm, founders should check out its portfolio and talk to companies who have been accepted as well as rejected for investment. Good investors provide solid counsel to entrepreneurs, even when they do not invest. Spend time with those who have a track record of investing at your stage AND in your market if at all possible. Treat potential, as well as existing, portfolio companies as partners and colleagues. Most early-stage investors are not *"vulture capitalists"*—don't spend time with the few who are!

Allocate Equity Slowly and Vest Over Time

Alex Blumberg of Planet Money and This American Life (NPR) has a great segment in the Gimlet *StartUp* podcast on his search for a partner and the awkward equity discussions that ensued.[35]

Aptly named "How to divide an imaginary pie," one podcast covers how Blumberg and eventual Gimlet Media co-founder Matt Lieber came to agreement on equity distribution. Blumberg had already begun the journey of launching his new thing, prospected with investors, and had the idea for the podcast company originally dubbed "The American Podcast Company." However, he had no financial background or business training—just a huge advantage in understanding content generation and production of very worthwhile edutainment. Enter Lieber, the consultant at the Boston Consulting Group (BCG) with an MBA from MIT's Sloan School of Management. Lieber helped Blumberg shore up financial statements and put the concept in the form of a preliminary business plan.

Then came the discussion of how to split the equity, which at the time was 100% owned by Blumberg. Based on his discussions with his wife, other entrepreneurs, and colleagues, Blumberg thought a reasonable starting point would be 10% for Lieber—but he admitted he had no idea and was extremely uncomfortable with the whole conversation. It was his idea, he had done the hard work getting momentum, and equity is scarce—his wife said he should view giving it up like giving up his fingers.

Lieber, meanwhile, felt that his business acumen was critical to the venture, and wanted to be viewed as an equal partner, not a consultant. His starting point was a 55/45 split in favor of Blumberg to reflect the idea value. After much discussion,

---

35   Alex Blumberg, "Gimlet 3: How to Divide an Imaginary Pie," *Gimlet Media*, September 14, 2017, accessed June 23, 2018, https://gimletmedia.com/episode/3-how-to-divide-an-imaginary-pie.

angst, sleeplessness, and reflection, they settled on 60% for Blumberg, and 40% for Lieber.[36]

This is not an unusual situation. Founders agonize over how to share equity under conditions of great uncertainty. It is a highly emotional and potentially conflictual topic, even though the pie is, indeed, imaginary. Fortunately, we have some tips to help navigate these icebergs in the Founding Team Sea.

First, founders should allocate equity and earn it as the value of the startup grows. Many entrepreneurs team up and allocate 100% of the equity upon founding. Big mistake! This is like dividing the entire pie before you know what kind of pie you are making, who else will be joining you for dinner, who will be making the pie, and whether there is ice cream to go with it. OK, maybe the metaphor breaks down at ice cream. The point is this: if the venture is only 5% of the way towards becoming a real thing, you shouldn't assign 100% of the value.

In Blumberg and Lieber's case, maybe the relative value was fine—but with 100% of the pie allocated, the focus became the wrong things—who gives up what, potential relative contribution, and the contractual terms for an exchange. Of course, ego plays a role as well. We would have suggested in this scenario a 30% position for Blumberg and 20% for Lieber. An arrangement like this would reflect the incomplete status of the project they are undertaking, reward Blumberg for the idea, and give Lieber his same relative percentage as co-founder. Moreover, it would recognize that at least half of the upside value was still on the table. The founders (or others) can earn that 50% as it develops over time.

Next, Blumberg and Lieber could have focused on the shared expectations of future behavior and commitment, how to reward contribution over time, and the "rules of engagement." This kind of focus keeps the conversation on goals and possibilities and limits the risk that the founders will take the discussion personally. A *term sheet* can be helpful in laying out these expectations and understanding the "buckets" or categories of behavior for all sides. At a minimum, this should include:

- *Time frame.* How long the agreement is in effect and the duration of different expectations
- *Commitment of hours.* Approximate number of days per week each person is committing
- *Expected contribution.* What each person is tackling, relative areas of focus
- *Expected reward.* What equity or compensation is associated with those contributions

---

36   Listen to the whole *StartUp* by Gimlet Media podcast—it is definitely worth it! You can find it at https://gimletmedia.com/startup.

- *Metrics and milestones.* What are the milestones you expect to achieve and how does this affect any of the other categories

This does not have to be a legally binding agreement, at least initially, but it sets up a lot of healthy discussions about venture goals, metrics, and accountability. We discuss this concept more in the Strategy Ocean Chapter.

In short: Don't start by allocating 100% of the equity. At a minimum, set aside 20-30% in an option pool to allocate to future members of the leadership team and early employees. When that pool is already in existence, it is easier to use it to attract new blood—as opposed to each founder having to "give up" a slice of pie to late arrivals. At the more realistic end of the equity continuum, allocate equity only as the venture reaches specific milestones. At the idea stage, maybe that is 5-10% of the journey—and that is the amount of equity rewarded as well. A plan on a napkin is very far from an investible entity.

Lookout: *Be wary of startups that over-allocate equity early in the life of the business.*

Vesting is also a great tool to stage equity ownership by allocating a specified amount of stock or equity for a specific individual, but having them earn that equity over time. In other words, do not award equity immediately. Instead, award equity as the venture **and** individual hit key milestones. When the "Curse of Thirdsies" strikes, there is far less downside or chance of defection when the founder must earn equity over three years with specific milestones. If co-founders do not carry their weight equally, the pre-existing discussion and aforementioned term sheet documents the expectations of what effort and time period are associated with earning one's full share. Vesting may occur over months or years, but often for significant stakes may take three-to-five years to vest completely.

For example, in the Gimlet scenario, Lieber could have gotten his 40% if he and Blumberg chose to allocate all equity—but 10% could have been distributed upon signing the agreement and the remaining 30% earned over the next three years at 10% a year. What if BCG had raised Lieber's salary and given him a promotion to keep him? What if, after six months of painful venture struggle, Lieber decided to quit, go back to his former day job, or become a UFC cage fighter? Blumberg would have found himself with a deadbeat co-founder who owned almost half the company but offered no help. Conversely, Blumberg should have been on a vesting plan as well—even idea originators should have to earn their full stake over time.

Even after founding, future additions to the leadership team should follow the same practice. A company we'll call Startup Alpha was in growth mode and needed a lead salesperson to grow geographically beyond the venture's home market. Investors and founders agreed that it was time to bring in a "real" Chief Revenue Officer (CRO). They identified one, and he requested equity of 10% to offset a salary that was not as generous as he was making in his current position. In fairness, he was taking both a risk and a pay cut to leave his current job.

However, the venture was also navigating uncertainty as to whether the market and company were ready for a new sales approach and whether he was the right fit for the job. For those reasons, the new CRO came in with 2% equity immediately, and an additional 2% per year with certain sales and funding milestones. After eleven months, it became clear that the fit was indeed not right for either side. Though he had landed some high potential new accounts and created a playbook for future sales efforts, the approach to market necessitated a different skillset than his experiences had provided him. He departed amicably with 2% ownership and some upside to reflect his contribution, but far less than the 10% he would have earned over time with commensurate contribution.

Bootstrap and Target Stage-Appropriate Human Capital and Resources

Starting a company is a constant juggling act of balancing time, money, and resources. The human components we have discussed—founders, investors, advisors, and employees—are critical sources of value and progress but also sources of considerable hidden debt. So how else does the savvy entrepreneur balance these factors?

Another tool is to bootstrap whenever possible. What the heck is that? It has nothing to do with molasses. Bootstrapping is using resources creatively and paying as little as possible for them. Don't give up cash OR equity unless and until you have to. There are individuals or outside firms who provide accounting and finance, marketing, technical support, and other services for a combination of shared revenue, equity, and cash.

Ask other entrepreneurs at your stage for recommendations on local people who provide these services. A part-time outsourced CFO and CMO (Chief Financial Officer and Chief Marketing Officer) can add great depth and experience to the team without a full-time commitment and commensurate cash drain. Local colleges and universities can also be helpful in providing business or technically trained students to help with market research, competitive analysis, financial modeling, and other functional tasks—look for programs with a history of active engagement with the venture community. Students benefit from real-world experience and potential future employment or a reference, as well as course credit. You get some focused activity, labor, and a chance to get to know a possible future employee.

The second component here is to make sure the human resources are appropriate for the stage of the startup. A pre-revenue startup still developing its *MVP* (*minimum viable product*) does not need three full-time C-level founder employees and a board of directors—this would be too much hidden debt in terms of time and energy for the stage. Similarly, a venture raising growth funding of $1.5 million should not be operating with part-time leadership.

Planning Human Resources by Stage

When planning, the developmental stage of the startup matters. We discuss planning as it relates to four stages in that development journey:

- *Pre-Revenue.* Before the startup is actually selling anything and is early in concept development. This is sometimes called the ideation phase.
- *MVP (Minimum Viable Product).* The startup is honing in on a concept and has something to share with customers.
- *Launch and Early Growth.* The startup is selling something and moving from one to a number of paying customers.
- *Scalable Product and Business Model.* The startup is moving to a growing venture in terms of products, customers, and employees.

Again, every venture is unique—these are just general guidelines to help position stage-appropriate roles without building too much human debt.

Pre-Revenue: Developing Ideas	MVP: First Customers	Launch and Early Growth: Growing Customer Base	Scalable Product and Business Model: Exponential Growth
• No full-time founder, no employees. • Approach informal advisors. • Self-fund, up to $50,000.	• First full-time founder, no employees. • Start to build advisory board. • Fund through self, friends-and-family, $25,000 to $100,000.	• Solidify founding team. • Hire early employees. • Formalize advisory board. • Fund through angel investors, $200,000 to $1 million.	• Set founding team. • Grow employee base. • Establish advisory board and/or board of directors. • Fund through angel group and/or venture capital, $1 to $3 million or more.

Critical human activities by startup stage

In the early stages of the venture, during ideation and prior to revenue, a startup might have no full-time employees. Founders work part-time on validating the venture concept and developing an MVP. Typically, founders would self-fund a venture at this stage, with minimal investment required—maybe up to $50,000. Even now, it is a good idea to have an informal set of advisors who are individuals with diverse backgrounds, are a good fit with the founders' values, and help by providing feedback.

It might take fifty meetings to find five such people, but the investment is worthwhile! Over time, narrow this group to a trusted and responsive few: having too many advisors at this stage accumulates debt. Compensation for advisors at this stage might include buying them coffee or lunch, but likely not cash or equity yet—but keep this as an option as you move forward.

 Navigation Plan: *Avoid over-allocating equity to founders (or others) and use vesting during this phase. Minimize outside investors until you have a proven concept.*

As the venture grows and the MVP is in the hands of some (hopefully paying) customers, it is now time for somebody to take this on full time. The venture is unlikely to go anywhere without a champion. So at least one member of the founding team needs to go full-time, or a CEO identified and brought in. Investment needs grow, which may lead to money from friends and family, or perhaps one or two individual angels with a personal interest in helping. Bootstrapping is essential at this stage to get everything done with minimal cash drain or equity loss. You are really just settling in on the venture business model and scalability.

 Navigation Plan: *Again, in terms of human debt, avoid over-allocating equity and instead use vesting at this stage. Be wary of early investor terms that limit future flexibility. You are building a base for growth—no need yet for a deep set of employees, advisors, or investors. It is not too early, however, to solidify the founding team, with a few gaps filled by outsourced services.*

All being well, the venture will grow in revenue and potential—but also in need for human resources. It is likely time to start formalizing an advisory board, which may include giving up a small percent of equity. The membership commitment for the advisory board should not be more than one year, with an "opt-in" to continue. Don't keep advisors on indefinitely with only an option to opt-out. That creates potentially awkward transitions. You will start rounding out the founding management team, but keep salary low and use external resources wherever feasible. As you move to outside funding, look to investors who bring more than cash and have access to deeper pockets.

 Navigation Plan: *Be careful of mounting debts in cash flow, expectations of investors, and making long-term commitments to employees. You still may not have a handle on the type of workforce you will need, so adaptability in your early employees is helpful. They are also navigating uncertainty with you.*

Hopefully you will have the opportunity to reach the level of more significant funding through angel groups, and perhaps even *A-round funding* with venture capital (VC) investors (The A round is typically when Venture Capital and larger funds for growth are involved, and larger dollars of $3-5 million plus). Significant investment in product development and support, marketing, and sales may follow. You likely now have a board of directors as well as one or more advisory boards who might represent specific capabilities—for example, a life science startup might have a medical advisory board.

 Navigation Plan: *You may exceed the supply of local workforce talent in this phase—be sure you are building a flexible base of employees who can adapt to changing job demands as the venture grows. You are likely to move to a smaller option pool for employees, but small pieces of equity can still be motivating. At this stage, your board should be able to help guide you through some of the additional human debts you might incur. The board can also teach you how to limit overly aggressive terms from later investors.*

Like the White Star Line, ventures cannot go anywhere without people. Whether founders, investors, advisors, employees, or others, the relationships and expectations formed by all participants can help or hinder the high-potential startup. These participants can provide necessary resources to launch, grow, and be part of the advocacy necessary to get traction. However, they can drain resources including equity, mandate strategic and structural changes, and limit flexibility, creating significant debtbergs. White Star started by delivering passengers to the promised lands of Australia and later the United States. Founders must manage human debt so that it does not sink the venture in the middle of its maiden voyage and keep passengers and crew from the promised land of a successful venture.

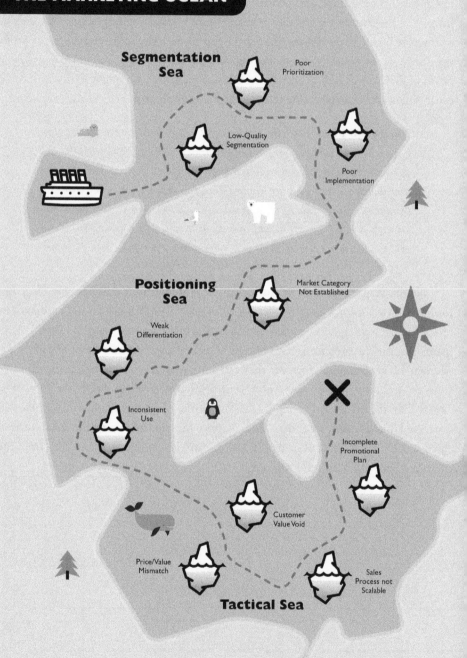

THE MARKETING OCEAN

Segmentation Sea

Poor Prioritization

Low-Quality Segmentation

Poor Implementation

Positioning Sea

Market Category Not Established

Weak Differentiation

Inconsistent Use

Incomplete Promotional Plan

Customer Value Void

Price/Value Mismatch

Sales Process not Scalable

Tactical Sea

CHAPTER 4:

~~~~

THE MARKETING OCEAN

"In a crowded marketplace, fitting in is a failure... not standing out is the same as being invisible."
–Seth Godin

"Just trying to keep my customers satisfied."
–Simon & Garfunkel

*O*nce constructed, the Titanic *was the largest ship ever built. How does a company pay for operating the largest ship? It starts by carrying a large number of passengers. In fact, the* Titanic *could carry more than 3,300 people, including about 900 in the crew. That meant it needed to convince 2,400 people to be paying passengers.*

For each voyage, White Star needed to do several things:

- *Find enough passengers that it could convince to pay for the privilege of crossing the Atlantic Ocean*
- *Communicate the unique value of sailing on the* Titanic *to a large audience on at least two continents—Europe (for the trip to America) and North America (for the return trip)*
- *Deliver on its promised value so that those passengers would become advocates and encourage others to pay for the privilege next time*

The first priority was to get enough passengers on that maiden voyage, but White Star wanted a repeatable process that could continue to generate sales over time.

Like many startups, White Star began by segmenting its market based on the amount the customer was willing to pay. Next, White Star needed to identify its positioning—the value it offered over other ways to cross the Atlantic—to each of those segments. Finally, it needed to implement and deliver what it promised to its customers, the passengers.

From a marketing perspective, the Titanic *took on considerable hidden debt. It had three different target markets it tried to serve at the same time. This created a lot of redundancy and many opportunities to make mistakes:*

- *Designing and delivering different features and benefits to each segment, within the same ship*
- *Advertising to those targets differently because the ship served different needs for each*
- *Communicating to the different target segments on multiple continents*

Then, to make matters worse, White Star Line wanted the market to know Titanic *for three different concepts—"largest," "finest," and "unsinkable." Trying to embody all three of these concepts simultaneously introduced design constraints that compromised the ship itself.*

That's a lot of hidden debt to mitigate.

As we'll see throughout this chapter, White Star, like many startups, took on marketing debt in each of these decisions. However, before we jump into the details of the *Titanic*, let's discuss the kinds of marketing decisions that lead to hidden debts for startups. These decisions, or lack of them, create debtbergs that cluster in Seas in the Marketing Ocean:

- **The Segmentation Sea**—Pick the right passengers
- **The Positioning Sea**—Make sure they are on the right ship
- **The Tactical Sea**—Make sure they find out about and can pay for the passage

The Segmentation Sea

Step one of Titanic *marketing was to figure out a way to motivate 2,400 people to buy passage to the Americas. The best way to do that was to break passengers into classes. That's what cruise ships do even today.*

At the high end, in first class, the best parlor suites cost as much as £870 at the time (about $4,000 in today's US dollars) and as little as £30 (about $150 now) for a one-way ticket. White Star designed first class to outshine all other first classes in terms of luxury, with the first-ever heated saltwater swimming pool, squash courts, a gymnasium, Turkish baths, a barbershop, kennels, a dining room that served the finest ten-course meals, and a Parisian café with French waiters.

There was also a second class (£12 to £13) and a third class (£3 to £8). What truly divided these three classes was wealth and social position, not simply the ticket price. This approach created three different target segments for White Star's marketing efforts. White Star aimed its first-class passage at the upper class, primarily businessmen, politicians, and socialites. Many of these multi-millionaires joined the Titanic *to be part of its his-*

toric maiden voyage. Expecting the lap of luxury, they traveled with entourages that might include a maid, a nurse for the children, a valet, and their dogs. They dressed up for dinner and viewed it as an experience to savor.

Next were the middle-class travelers in second class, including professors, authors, and prominent clergymen. Second-class accommodations were as luxurious as the typical first-class accommodations on other ships. Appointments included elevators, wood-paneled walls, linoleum floors, a promenade deck, and a smoking room for the gentlemen. These travelers were looking for a way to cross the Atlantic as part of their work life.

Finally, third class was for emigrants, primarily from Great Britain and Ireland but also from Scandinavia, Central and Eastern Europe, the Middle East, and even Hong Kong. Here too, White Star deviated from tradition by offering individual rooms and a dining service in third class, where other ships used dormitory-style sleeping areas and required passengers to bring their own food. These passengers were in search of prosperity in America and escaping their current circumstances—for as little as $15 in today's US dollars!

Here are pictures of the three classes of berths from National Museums Northern Ireland's Titanica *exhibit:*

A first-class cabin on the *Titanic*, highlighting its expansive space, ornate detailing, and well-appointed furnishings

A second-class berth on the *Titanic*, which is still spacious, but with far fewer luxuries

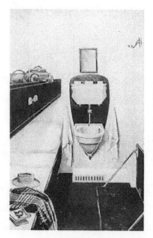

Berths in third class were quite small, with no additional accoutrements. They could hold a family of six.

While having different classes of rooms isn't atypical for a cruise ship, offering completely different amenities and services by class is very difficult to pull off operationally. As a result, each class had its own stewards and was physically independent. For example, grilles and retractable wrought-iron gates surrounded the third-class section. Stewards could open the gates, but mostly the gates remained closed. This separated the masses from the moguls, but also created hidden debt in the form of safety challenges.

Considering the complexity, it's not surprising that the Titanic *was not very successful in attracting customers. Only about one-half of the tickets for the maiden voyage sold, comprising about 40% of first- and second-class capacity, plus 70% of third class. While the exact counts of passengers vary by source, approximately 25% of the passengers were in first class, with 21% and 54% in second and third class, respectively.*

A serious challenge for startups is that investors evaluate them on the size of their addressable market—bigger is better—and yet startups cannot effectively target an entire market because of their resource constraints. Limited resources mean that startups need to focus on a single market segment at first. It's hard for a startup to choose a market segment that is big enough to generate a profit, but isn't so big or diffused that the startup can't afford to promote the product to it.

An example of a startup that struggled with segmentation is Bellabeat. Urška Sršen and Sandro Mur founded Bellabeat to help women monitor their own health. "All women" is an attractively large market of around eighty-six million people. However, a startup cannot tackle a segment as large and diverse as "all women." Instead, Bellabeat focused on pregnant women in the United States with a monitor that would let them hear their babies' heartbeats. This reduced the market to approximately four million women—the number of new births in the United States each year.

Even four million is still a big market, and it is highly diverse. Finding each of the pregnant women in the United States, especially each willing to pay $129 to listen to her baby's heartbeat, is tough. Bellabeat reportedly sold only 35,000 units of this first product, a *share* of less than 1% of the target market segment. (By comparison, Baby Einstein books sell about 250,000 units per year.) Later, Bellabeat shifted to defining its target segments by needs and psychographics (which we discuss later in this chapter) instead of demographics and enjoyed more success.

While targeting an entire market (in marketing parlance, this is called *mass marketing*) is not a great approach for a startup, appropriately segmenting and effectively targeting those segments in a stepwise process takes considerable effort. As we look to best practices and the choices that startups need to make, we'll review three iceberg drifts in the Segmentation Sea:

- Low-Quality Segmentation
- Poor Prioritization
- Poor Implementation

Low-Quality Segmentation

Segmenting customers takes careful consideration and effort. It starts with recognizing that product segments are NOT customer segments (for an example of product segments, see the callout box). The basic idea behind customer segmentation is that you can categorize potential customers into "buckets" where customers within the buckets are mostly similar and each bucket of customers is mostly different from each other—homogeneous within but heterogeneous across. Imagine that you have an endless line of potential customers in front of you—how many buckets are there? How do you separate each customer into the right bucket?

Customer Versus Product Segmentation

The term "market segmentation" often describes categories of products. For example, you can divide the snack food market into major and minor product groups:

- salty snacks
  - potato chips
  - tortilla chips
- chocolate candy
- yogurt
- non-chocolate candy
- natural cheese

- cookies
- crackers
- snack/granola bars
- pastry/donuts
- snack nuts

In this book, we use the term "segments" and "segmentation" to refer to categories of customers rather than products.

Historically, firms segmented customers based on demographics (for example, age, race, and income) because media sold advertising based on demographics. Over time, marketing practitioners have learned that demographics alone do not adequately represent the underlying differences in potential customers that matter in order to market to them effectively. Marketers want to connect with the hearts and minds of their segments. Demographics are not enough to reflect differences in customers' hearts and minds—for example, women may snack more than men, but they both prefer the same snack products in the same order (for example, both prefer chocolate most[37]), so the demographic of gender doesn't give the marketer useful information in targeting the segment.

Instead, a strong segmentation approach reflects segment differences leveraging two or more of the *bases of segmentation*:

- demographic
- behavioral, including both actual purchase behavior and "benefits sought" or needs
- psychographic
- geographic

The specific bases of segmentation vary slightly depending on whether customers are consumers (B2C, short for business-to-consumer, refers to companies that target individual consumers directly) or other businesses (B2B, short for business-to-business). Figure 4, on the next page, highlights variables that startups might use for each base of segmentation, depending on whether the startup is B2C or B2B:

For the sake of simplicity, we'll focus on how these ideas apply to B2C companies. We'll use snack foods as an example of how these bases of segmentation[38] work.

Elements related to **behavior**, the behavioral base of segmentation, include *what* customers buy, *how much* they buy, *how often* they buy, *when* they buy, and *how loyal*

---

37   Nielsen, "Snack Attack: What Consumers are Reaching for Around the World," September 2014, accessed July 28, 2017, http://www.nielsen.com/content/dam/nielsenglobal/kr/docs/global-report/2014/Nielsen%20Global%20Snacking%20Report%20September%202014.pdf.

38   See for example, Michael Lodato, "Market Definition is a multidimensional process," *BPTrends*, June 2006, accessed July 28, 2017, http://www.bptrends.com/publicationfiles/06-06-ART-MarketDefinition-Lodato.pdf.

Base	B2C	B2B
Demographic	Income, Age, Gender, Marital Status, etc.	Type, Size, Industry, Position, etc.
Behavioral	Volume, Usage, Frequency, Benefits Sought, Loyalty, etc.	Volume, Usage, Application, Benefits Sought, Buyer Requirements, Product Specifications, Loyalty, etc.
Psychographic	Interests, Attitudes, Personality, Lifestyle, etc.	Purchasing Approach, Operating Variables, Personal Characteristics of Buyers, etc.
Geographic	Location	Location

Figure 4: Variables for each base of segmentation

they are to a certain brand. For snack foods, you might segment your market into behavior groups like:

- heavy vs. light snackers
- daily vs. occasional snackers
- brand loyal vs. switchers

Another way of looking at the behavioral base of segmentation is by **needs** (also called "benefits sought"). This approach recognizes that people buy brands or products[39] because they have an unmet need they want to address by spending money. Buying snack foods meets several sets of needs. One study identified the needs that consumers address with snack food as a combination of functional and emotional. You can categorize these as "a small meal" (critical need = satiety) versus "better for you" (critical need = healthy energy for a workout) vs. "indulgent" (critical need = make yourself feel better).[40]

Frito-Lay found a segmentation approach that assigned functional needs to product benefits, such as the following examples:

- People in the Chewers segment like keeping their jaws moving with gum and prefer a snack that takes some work to get through.
- Crunchers are satisfied when their snacks deliver a crisp crunch, like celery and chips do.
- Smooshers don't want to chew and prefer snacks like yogurt that spread out in their mouths.

---

39   Note that, for readability, the term "product" indicates both products and services.
40   Jeff Gelski, "Three occasions define snacking segment," *BakingBusiness.com*, March 21, 2014, accessed July 28, 2017, http://www.bakingbusiness.com/articles/news_home/Trends/2014/03/Three_occasions_define_snackin.aspx.

- Suckers like a snack that slowly dissolves in their mouths.[41]

Functional needs are a good way to start. However, best practice is to understand more than just what customers want functionally. You also need to know how these functional needs help people fulfill their emotional needs and personal values.[42]

Defining a target segment based on what the people in the segment need is much more helpful than the product segmentation! Startup success Airbnb started by focusing on professional conferences. The founders recognized that conference attendees want to be close to the conference hotel, but may still feel like staying at a place that is homey—even more so if the convention hotel is not an option. They started renting their own apartment to attendees of an overbooked local conference. They launched their software platform at the National Democratic Convention in 2008. Over time, the product-based "conferencegoer" segment shifted to a needs-based "home-away-from-home" segment, which was a much larger opportunity.

The psychographics segmentation base describes segments based on the interests, activities, and attitudes of the people in them. There are several well-known psychographics segmentation approaches developed by research firms. One of these is the Values and Lifestyle (VALS) segmentation approach. The research firm SRI International developed VALS in 1978 based on the work of sociologist David Riesman and psychologist Abraham Maslow.

VALS includes eight different segments, like Experiencers, Makers, and Innovators.[43] Experiencers, for example, like to be the first in on a new trend, are very fashionable and sociable, and respond to visual stimulation. If you were introducing a new snack that had unique ingredients and was visually alluring, you'd want to recruit Experiencers as your early adopters so they could try it and share with their networks. Innovators, on the other hand, like science, R&D, and new technologies. Innovators make decisions based on facts rather than advertising. For Innovators, an appealing snack might focus on the best ingredients and overall health benefits.

These psychographic profiles tell you more about how to appeal to the people in your segments than knowing what product attributes and benefits they seek. Using psychographics as a segmentation base gives you the power to understand deeply who your customers are, what they want to accomplish in life, and how they like marketers to talk to them. This information is powerful for broad *promotions*, but it doesn't

41 Anne Marie Chaker, "Why Food Companies Are Fascinated by the Way We Eat," *The Wall Street Journal*, August 13, 2013, accessed July 28, 2017, https://www.wsj.com/articles/why-food-companies-are-fascinated-by-the-way-we-eat-1376434311.

42 Wansink, Brian, "New Techniques to Generate Key Marketing Insights," *Marketing Research*, Summer 2000, 28-36.

43 See, for example, Strategic Business Insights, "US Frameworks and VALS Types," accessed July 28, 2017, http://www.strategicbusinessinsights.com/vals/ustypes.shtml.

explain what motivates them in your product category—only behavioral, including needs-based, segmentation does that.

> ### Geodemographic Segmentation
>
> A few firms offer geodemographic segmentation that combines ZIP code with other socioeconomic variables. A company called Esri offers a geodemographic segmentation called Tapestry,[44] and another company, Nielsen Claritas,[45] offers one called PRIZM. This data is relatively inexpensive to buy. While a geodemographic approach brings more richness to a demographic base of segmentation, it is more superficial than a needs-based or psychographic segmentation.

While startups typically have limited market research budget (to be fair, maybe no market research budget), established brands typically conduct their own customer segmentation studies so that they have a proprietary view of the market's needs. These proprietary studies, while a best practice, are expensive, take months to complete, and generally require using a third-party market research firm. As a result, few startups have this level of detail about the market, even though it would be very helpful. However, startups can often find research articles that have used primary research to describe segments. Notice the studies we found online for snack foods. Repurposing other people's work is a good place to start. Over time, if funding and a need for clarity emerge, startups can consider conducting their own customer segmentation studies.

 Navigation Plan: *Don't try to target an entire market. Break customers into segments based on behavioral and psychographic variables. If there aren't funds for proprietary market research, scan the Internet and research databases for close equivalents.*

The more bases of segmentation you use, generally speaking, the better the customer segmentation scheme. More bases offer a deeper understanding of the customers. Of course, there is always a *tradeoff* among a complete, robust segmentation, the cost of market research, and the difficulty of undertaking this kind of research. As a rule of thumb, customers in many markets seem to cluster in about four different customer segments. Two customer segments are probably too few. Alternately, acting on six or more segments is probably too difficult for a startup.

---

44   See, for example, Esri, "Tapestery Segmentation," accessed July 28, 2017, http://www.esri.com/landing-pages/tapestry.

45   Learn more about Nielsen's Claritas Segmentation at https://segmentationsolutions.nielsen.com/mybestsegments/Default.jsp?ID=100&menuOption=learnmore.

"Low-quality segmentation" can mean not segmenting effectively or it might mean having a weak understanding of those segments. This understanding should include the segment's needs for this product, such as in the following examples:

- functional (e.g. crunchy)
- emotional (e.g. guilty pleasure because delicious foods are often bad for you)
- social (e.g. others also appreciate this)

In essence, a startup needs to figure out what job each segment is hiring the product to do. Harvard Business School professor Clay Christensen, who is known for his ideas on innovation, has also delved into the idea of the "Job to be Done" by a product.[46] The essence of the Job to be Done is that, when people pay money for something, they are hiring the product to do a job. Figure out what that job is and you understand the customer's most important need.

In addition, this understanding should include what chronic points of pain each customer segment regularly experiences in the product category with existing competitive offerings, as well as what would create value for each segment. A *segment profile* or *persona* (discussed later in this chapter) helps everyone in the startup consider this customer segment in their decision-making.

 Navigation Plan: *Segmenting customers is only a preliminary step. Once you have a good segmentation scheme, you have to get to know each of these segments in depth.*

Revisiting the Bellabeat example, trying to target all pregnant women was a low-quality, or at least incomplete, segmentation approach. There is a lot more variability among women and their needs than a demographic variable like "being pregnant." When Bellabeat changed to a more needs-based and psychographic segmentation, it could better describe its target segment as "women who want to track their health through all of the stages of their lives." Healthcare research with patients suggests that this is roughly 20% to 30% of all women.

To meet the needs of this target segment, Bellabeat developed multiple products for the different stages of life—an unborn-baby monitor, a health tracker that looks like jewelry and doesn't need charging, a smart water bottle, and a wellness coach app. Marketers call this "market specialization"—offering multiple products to one

---

46   See Clayton M. Christensen, Taddy Hall, Karen Dillon, and David S. Duncan, "Know Your Customers' 'Jobs to Be Done'," *Harvard Business Review,* September 2016, accessed July 28, 2017, https://hbr.org/2016/09/know-your-customers-jobs-to-be-done, and Christensen, Clay and Michael E. Raynor, *The Innovator's Solution: Creating and Sustaining Successful Growth,* Cambridge, MA: Harvard Business Review Press, 2003. See also Christensen, Clayton M., Taddy Hall, Karen Dillon, and David S. Duncan, *Competing Against Luck,* New York: Harper Business, 2016.

segment. So far, Bellabeat has survived the iceberg of low-quality segmentation and is now navigating the Segmentation Sea with a stronger plan.

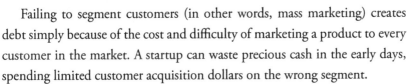 **Lookout:** *When founders say, "every customer could benefit from our product," they do not understand the importance of segmenting. They will most likely be unfocused and struggle to gain traction.*

Poor Prioritization

Failing to segment customers (in other words, mass marketing) creates debt simply because of the cost and difficulty of marketing a product to every customer in the market. A startup can waste precious cash in the early days, spending limited customer acquisition dollars on the wrong segment.

A key metric in marketing is *conversion rate*—the higher the conversion rate, the more effective the marketing effort. Consider if 100 potential customers visited a website. If 1% of them convert, that would be one customer. If 10% convert, the business would have ten customers. Conversion rates tend to be under 10% for any single marketing effort.

Having too many segments to pursue at once also creates debt. The purpose of segmenting customers is to be more efficient: spending less money while being more effective with a better conversion rate. Therefore, focusing more narrowly so you can convert at a higher rate is usually better than targeting broadly and converting at a lower rate. The goal of targeting a customer segment is to maximize penetration in that segment. Effective definition of a target market segment should result in 80% or more of the target segment buying the product after a series of marketing efforts. On the one hand, this sounds like a nearly impossible goal. On the other hand, planning to achieve this level of penetration can be powerfully motivating.

Reaching that goal means realistically identifying a segment that is small enough that you can understand how to win over a high percentage of its customers. TRX estimates that it has penetrated 95% of professional sports teams with its training offering. In part, that happened by luck—Drew Brees picked up the product while recovering from a shoulder injury and helped get the New Orleans Saints to adopt it. However, professional sports teams also picked up TRX because founder Randy Hetrick made more than 300 sales presentations over a two-year period to secure this target segment. He made that extraordinary investment to maximize penetration in a segment that could help influence others.

How is 80% Penetration Possible?

Some people see "80% penetration" and think "80% market share." Remember, the goal is to target a narrowly defined segment and know that segment so well that 80% or more of the customers in it raise their hands to be customers. Here's an example of a new pharmaceutical launch. There were three segments in the market. Less than half of the entire market, 45%, adopted the new brand. However, the launch was a success because the new brand converted 85% of its target segment:

Segment	Segment's % of Customers	Brand's % of Segment	Brand Adopters as % of Market
Expert Experimenters: They are disease experts who follow latest developments and like to try new products to see if they improve patient care. This was the most important segment to the pharmaceutical company.	20%	85%	17%
Show Me It Works: They see a large volume of patients and like new products but want the experts to validate them first.	30%	60%	18%
Tried & True Is Best: They are used to practicing medicine a specific way and worry that new products might not be safe enough for broad use.	50%	20%	10%
			Total = 45% of market share

The more segments a startup targets at once, the less likely the startup is to achieve that kind of penetration. Remember that the *Titanic* did best with the market segments that purchased passage in third class, but it struggled to fill capacity in its two other product segments—first and second class.

Big consumer products companies, like Procter & Gamble (P&G), target multiple segments through different brands. Startups, on the other hand, probably need to focus more narrowly at the start. The implementation challenges of targeting multiple segments require more resources in terms of people, time, and funding. For example, P&G has five laundry detergent products, each aimed at a different needs-based segment:

- Tide is for families and other people who need to fight stains.
- Cheer is for people who want to clean without fading colors.
- Gain is for people who feel clean clothes should smell good.
- Era is for those who want to get clothes clean at a more affordable price.
- Method is for those who want to clean in an environmentally friendly way.

Therefore, targeting multiple segments means different product offerings, prices, and messages. Most startups don't have those resources. Instead, when they say they are targeting multiple segments, they try to approach more than one segment with the same product offering, prices, and messages. Not only is this approach not a best practice, but also it is usually ineffective. Ideally, startups would focus on one well-defined segment where they can chart a path to adoption by a majority, or even 80%, of the segment.

> **Navigation Plan:** *Startups also need to plan to prioritize segments over time. When prioritizing segments, there is an inherent tension between segment size/profitability and interest in the product. The ideal situation is when the biggest/most profitable segment is the one most interested in your product—this is the low-hanging fruit. Unfortunately, that seems to happen very rarely.*

Startups should focus first on a segment that is the most interested in their product, even if that segment is small. It's much easier to convert a segment that already knows it has a problem, that is actively searching for a solution, and for whom a product already exists to fit its needs. Choosing a segment that is large but less interested incurs a debt in promotional costs because creating demand uses precious promotional dollars that could, instead, be converting the better segment.

In B2B segmentation, the classic challenge is whether to target larger organizations that might have a longer purchase path and a more complex buying process or smaller organizations, where users are more likely to be the buyer. Again, interest in and need for the product should be the determining factor. If bigger organizations get a bigger benefit, they are worth targeting, even if it takes longer and is harder. Whichever segment the startup chooses, it should choose just one, and really figure out how to maximize penetration. If each segment truly is different, targeting more than one segment means being less effective in each.

That said, a startup also needs a plan to how to expand over time. The startup needs a plan for which segments come next after penetrating the first segment. Investors want to see a large market opportunity. Targeting gives a foothold, but a startup should have a plan to expand over time.

> **Navigation Plan:** *As an aside, startups should consider that the ideas and information they use internally in marketing planning might not be the same information they share with investors. Investors want to see big markets with a path to long-term success. Marketing plans need to focus more narrowly and tactically on incremental successes that build over time. The investor pitch deck may appropriately focus on large opportunity and long-term success. For internal planning, though, the focus should be on winning the next five customers in the target segment!*

🔦 **Lookout**: *A startup should be able to explain its ongoing targeting plan. This plan should start with a narrow focus but expand over time. A strong plan shows how the startup will grow and that they have a strong understanding of the market. Simply knowing the first target segment and having no plan beyond that is not enough.*

Michalis Gkontas started Cookisto[47] in Athens, Greece with the idea to connect people who cook their dinner with people who don't like to cook. The non-cooks could buy homemade evening meals from the cooks who made more than they needed for themselves. Through an app, non-cooks could find out what cooks were making, and then arrange to buy the extras. Cookisto launched across the whole city at once. It got seed funding and used that money to recruit a whole bunch of new users.

Unfortunately, driving across town to pick up someone's extras was too inconvenient—people could just stop by a restaurant nearby for takeout. Despite Cookisto's promotional efforts, new users didn't convert to consistent users because it had targeted too broadly.

Next, Cookisto narrowed its focus to only people within an apartment complex—segmenting customers by location. Now, the food was nearby and convenient. That meant, though, that Cookisto had to build up volume apartment complex by apartment complex. This segmentation was too narrow.

Cookisto ended up folding due to initially low-quality segmentation, and then poor prioritization. To overcome the operational challenge of how to get food to hungry people and refocus, it relaunched as a made-to-order food delivery service called Forky. Now, Athens office workers can order the specific lunch they want and have it delivered to them within fifteen minutes by bicycle. Since its foundation in 2014, Forky appears to be going strong. It's clearly narrowed its focus—office workers at lunch in a large city. Time will tell if this approach will be more successful.

An Indiana food technology startup, ClusterTruck, had a similar idea to Forky about getting ready-made food to people ready to eat a meal. It deploys a similar made-to-order approach. However, it has segmented by geography. ClusterTruck started in a large metro area with a central downtown for day sales and a college campus for night sales. As ClusterTruck is expanding, it is concentrating on small footprints in mid-market downtowns and big college towns—like Bloomington, IN and Columbus, OH. There's lots of upward potential now that ClusterTruck has identified a great

---

47   Michalis Gkontas, "We're F*cked, It's Over. Or Is It?" *The Mission*, September 5, 2016, accessed July 28, 2017, https://medium.com/the-mission/were-f-cked-it-s-over-or-is-it-5abe1432471d.

target segment. ClusterTruck is still a burgeoning startup. Over time, we'll also find out if this approach was a good one.

Poor Implementation

Having a good segmentation scheme and prioritizing segments appropriately is a *strategy*. Startups also need tactics—a plan to use the segmentation on an ongoing basis.

In order to do that effectively, a startup needs a detailed persona for each segment. A buyer's persona[48] is a semi-fictional representation of the ideal customer based on market research and real data about the segment. Then, based on that persona and an in-depth understanding of each segment, the startup should create a plan to vary product, price, and promotion for each segment.

Navigation Plan: *B2B startups should give their sales representatives good discovery questions to evaluate in which segment a potential customer belongs. B2C startups should be able to develop a creener that includes a list of three-to-five questions that identify the consumer's segment. This kind of screener works well as part of an online registration form.*

Depending on the segment persona, promotion includes either the key messages and where those messages are placed for each segment, or media outlets the segment tends to see, such as magazines, TV, radio, Internet, and, today, social media.

This is one area where White Star did a good job of implementing its segmentation scheme. Advertisements and public relations aimed at first-class passengers stressed luxurious accommodations and appeared in the United States, mostly in magazines but also in newspapers. For third-class passengers, White Star placed newspaper classified in Europe, including England, to offer the promise of prosperity. This plan was good because it included a customized message and media channel for each segment. In retrospect, we can question whether the promotion plan was strong enough, given how much capacity went unfilled. It could have been a reach problem—these media didn't reach enough of the target audiences. On the other hand, it could have been a message problem, in that they key message wasn't motivating enough for each segment. Whatever the cause, the effect was that the conversion rate was low, showing how difficult it is to target more than one segment at a time.

---

48   See HubSpot and others for more information on crafting a buyer's persona—Paula Vaughan, "How to Create Detailed Buyer Personas for Your Business," *HubSpot Blog*, accessed July 28, 2017, https://blog. hubspot.com/blog/tabid/6307/bid/33491/everything-marketers-need-to-research-create-detailed-buyer-personas-template.aspx.

The mistake that many companies, including startups, make is trying to target two different segments with the same offerings and messages. In order to try to accommodate the needs of two different groups, the startup compromises on something that is only moderately attractive to both, rather than super attractive to the more important segment. Diluting the message in this way results in conversion for each segment being much lower than the target of 80%. Thus, the company incurs a debt just by trying to simplify implementation.

Academic researchers[49] have shown that segmented messages work because targets feel like they have been targeted: they see their needs expressed in the messages aimed at them. When they don't see their needs, they don't respond as well. Therefore, a startup should carefully hone each message to each target segment.

Hampus Jakobsson notes[50] how his Swedish B2B sales intelligence startup Brisk struggled to get segmentation right. Instead of mass marketing or identifying segments, Brisk customized its products for each customer, sometimes even multiple different users in the same firm. Marketers call this approach *one-to-one marketing*.

The goal of Brisk's product was to make the sales process more predictable. His team started with a base platform and customized an application on top for each customer. One customer organization, for example, had different customizations for the sales representatives versus the sales manager. They accomplished a flexible product, but no replicable story of a segment of customers with the same needs and goals. They did not have a use case that would appeal to more than one customer at a time. Moreover, supporting every individual customer took resources that Brisk might have used to secure new customers. In Brisk's case, poor implementation due to lack of focus created debt that swamped the *venture*.

Startups face a tradeoff—with too-narrow targeting, overall sales volume potential is too low. With too broad targeting, implementation is too difficult. Startups need to understand underlying customer segments so they can prioritize among them with a plan to expand over time. Then, they need to be able to differentiate their offerings to segments based on the product itself, the product's price, and how the company plans to promote the product. Each step away from this ideal creates debts in terms of reduced conversion and incremental costs.

---

49   See Alpert, Frank and M. Kim Saxton, "Can Multiple New-Product Messages Attract Different Consumer Segments? Gaming Advertisements' Interaction with Targets Affects Brand Attitudes and Purchase Intentions," *Journal of Advertising Research*, 55:3 (2015), 307.

50   Hampus Jakobsson, "How my failed startup failed due to being flexible, not focused," *Medium*, June 5, 2016, accessed July 28, 2017, https://hajak.se/how-my-failed-startup-failed-due-to-being-flexible-not-focused-227430ab1464.

The Positioning Sea

With three different target segments, product design and service delivery was a challenge for White Star on the Titanic. *So, too was advertising a challenge. Interestingly, Americans dominated first class. On the other hand, second and third class primarily appealed to the British and Irish. For first class, the main message focused on the luxurious offerings. For third class, the main message was access to the Americas. In order to accomplish this difference in geography, White Star had to distribute marketing messages on two continents. Moreover, with an ongoing schedule of trips, advertising was in full force prior to the maiden voyage. Consider how operationally difficult that must have been in 1912. In fact, to simplify this challenge, many ads for the* Titanic *included both the* Olympic *and the* Titanic. *After all, White Star needed to generate a constant stream of passengers for both of these large ships. Here are a couple example advertisements covering the two ships:*

Not only were there different messages for different segments, the content of the messages addressed the different needs of the segments. The primary and largest ads for the Titanic *noted its size—"45,000 tons, The Largest Steamers in the World." Newspaper ads suggested that the Titanic was the "Latest, Largest and Finest Steamer Afloat." Ads that were more specific showed the amenities in each class with first-class ads noting the swimming pool, Turkish baths, and other indulgent appointments.*

Luxury soap brand Vinolia Otto even co-branded ads with the Titanic, *noting that the Titanic had selected Vinolia for its first-class passengers. While most of us would not recognize the brand Vinolia (owned by Lever Brothers, known today as Unilever), in 1912 it was a well-known name.*

Unlike first-class passengers, third-class passengers didn't care about luxury. Brochures aimed at third-class passengers highlighted the prospects for prosperity in America. This means that the Titanic *actually attempted to fulfill different needs for these different segments—wining and dining first class as they returned home, and offering third-class passengers a way to change their long-term prospects through passage to the promised land.*

In addition to the challenge of meeting different needs for different segments, the Titanic *also burdened itself with complex and inconsistent messaging. The White Star Line positioned the* Titanic *based on its size and luxury. The biggest fear that customers have about the largest ship is "can it even stay afloat?" While none of the* Titanic's *ads themselves said the ship was unsinkable, it is the single biggest message that stuck in the market.*

How did the public get an idea about the Titanic *being unsinkable if it never appeared in any ads? The answer is that White Star offered other direct and indirect messaging beyond ads. First, White Star's brochures proclaimed, "as far as possible, these vessels are designed to be unsinkable." This idea caught on like wildfire via word-of-mouth. Eventually everyone, including employees of White Star, believed the* Titanic *was unsinkable. Even as the* Titanic *set sail, a VP of White Star in New York said, "We believe that the boat is unsinkable."*

The Titanic *wanted people to know it as the "largest" and "finest," but it also needed customers to believe "unsinkable." That's three different ideas to own simultaneously. Note that both the* Titanic *and the* Olympic *were the largest ships.* Titanic's *difference versus* Olympic *was in being the finest and latest. That kind of complex positioning is both hard to communicate and difficult to deliver on.*

Marketers have been preaching about the need to position a product appropriately since Jack Trout and Al Ries first published their book on this topic in 1981.[51] The basic idea behind positioning is straightforward—the human brain likes to sort and categorize information. Therefore, a company needs to make it easy for customers to understand to what category its product belongs. Marketers call that category the product's *frame of reference.* A frame of reference recognizes that customers are the ones who evaluate a product offering. Therefore, a startup needs to understand how customers will categorize the offering. Only by understanding customers' frame of reference will a startup understand who its real competitors are.

Knowing the frame of reference and competition helps a startup articulate why customers should buy theirs over competitors'—the product's point of differentiation (POD). Every product needs a strong and compelling POD. There are plenty of examples of big brands that have found an effective POD:

- FedEx = delivered in twenty-four hours
- Domino's = pizza in thirty minutes

---

51   *Advertising Age* recognizes this book as the most-read marketing book of all time. Trout, Jack and Al Ries, *Positioning: The Battle for Your Mind.* New York: McGraw-Hill, 1981, 2000.

- Nike = excellence
- Starbucks = relaxation
- Coke = always refreshing
- *Titanic* = unsinkable

In practice, this is more difficult than it sounds. Startups especially seem to struggle to position their products appropriately. More specifically, startups incur debt in the Positioning Sea from three different sources:

- Market Category Not Established
- Weak Differentiation
- Inconsistent Use

Market Category Not Established

Many founders get started thinking that nothing exists to compare with what their company is doing. If not that the idea is unique, founders might think that their solution is so novel that it's going to disrupt the industry.

If we go back to the idea that the human brain likes to sort and categorize information, though, we see that a product that's really that new and unique would actually face some big problems. Let's revisit snack foods. Most people generally know what a snack food is: a food item that is smaller than a meal and eaten between meals. Most people can also ascribe basic attributes to snacks: eaten quickly, tasty, satisfies hunger, and a pleasurable experience to consume. If we dig deeper into snack foods, there are subcategories (termed the Core 10 by that industry) like salty snacks, chocolate candy, and yogurt. We can also categorize snacks as healthy/unhealthy. With any of these categorizations, most people can identify the attributes of products in the category as well as name specific products and brands that belong to the category.

Consider a product like Soylent, a meal alternative that comes in liquid and powder form. It says it is complete nutrition accounting for 20% of a person's daily caloric needs.

- What's its frame of reference?
- Is it a meal or a snack?
- Does it fit into one of the Core 10 snack food categories?
- Is it a meal-replacement shake?

Until customers know what something is, they will struggle to evaluate it. Without the shortcut of an already-defined category to help customers evaluate a product, the company must spend time and dollars educating them about both the category and a product's characteristics. Educating is expensive and slow. Most startups don't have the resources to do it effectively.

Matt Johnson of GoKart Labs founded Kinly in 2008. Johnson had the idea that people would want a social media network just for their families. Through Kinly, families could share news, photos, events, and experiences in a safe, private way. What Kinly did especially well was signaling its category—"the Facebook for Families." (Kinly took on a different marketing debt that we'll discuss later, but they got the category piece right.) Anchoring the category with a well-known example (like Facebook) can be a helpful way to provide frame of reference for the potential customer.

Gil Sadis of Israel-based startup Licensario,[52] on the other hand, admits that one of the big mistakes it made on the way to failure was putting itself in a position of having to educate the market on what it was. Licensario described itself as "a cloud-based solution that solved the painful billing process of other *SaaS* companies." Most customers, especially SaaS companies, probably know what a cloud-based solution is, but what does a "painful billing process solution" do? In what category does it fit? Is it an invoicing system? Does it manage SaaS licensing agreements?

What Licensario did was to give SaaS companies a tool for testing product configurations and price points to optimize the combination for the SaaS company's customers and maximize revenue for the SaaS company. Even this explanation is a bit confusing. Ultimately, customers had no frame of reference to which to compare Licensario and ended up not moving forward. The venture failed.

A health IT startup, let's call it Startup Bravo, struggled with this as well. It began by offering a smartphone app that would connect a physician to a patient calling in after-hours, while also displaying key data from the patient's electronic medical record (EMR) on the smartphone screen. If you're not a doctor, you might think this idea seems pretty straightforward and interesting. However, for the first three years Startup Bravo struggled because, to doctors, its offering crossed three categories—after-hours call management, telephone answering services, and electronic medical records. It was part of each but not all of any of them, so doctors had a hard time evaluating it.

This lack of a clear category was a debt the company had to overcome. At that point, each sales call was very long—First, the company had to explain how it was like each of these three categories. Then, the company had to explain why it was different. Eventually, Startup Bravo focused on a single category, even though it contained only a part of its offering. This approach sold the product short, but prospective customers could understand it, so it was an entry point to the conversation. Once the company had formed a relationship, it expanded the customer's understanding to include the more complete product offering.

---

52   Gil Sadis, "The mistakes that killed my startup," *21ˢᵗ Century Geek*, August 28, 2017, accessed November 22, 2017, https://gilsadis.com/2014/08/28/the-mistakes-that-killed-my-startup/.

Not belonging to a clear and well-established category isn't insurmountable. It just takes more time, effort, and investment. It especially requires raising the appropriate financial capital to pay for market education. Educating the market is a slow process, so it's a debt that a startup may need to accept and plan to mitigate over time.

Navigation Plan: *Find a well-established category that is close to your offering and figure out which attributes define it. Then, explain your product's benefits over those attributes, and therefore over competitors.*

Weak Differentiation

The power of belonging to a well-known category is that customers automatically attribute characteristics that are common to all products in the category to the product. Marketers call these characteristics *points of parity*.

Remember that we established the following points of parity for snack foods:

- eaten quickly
- tasty
- satisfies hunger
- pleasurable experience to eat

That means when a new snack food enters the market, the company doesn't have to spend marketing resources educating people about the fact that the product has those four characteristics. Instead, the company just has to focus on what makes the product different. Marketers call these characteristics *points of differentiation (POD)*.

To compete, a company needs to have a simple and unambiguous reason why it is better. An effective POD isn't just unique; it also has to be important to customers. Finally, customers have to be able to verify that the product is different and better.

As a startup, Clif Bar faced a real challenge as related to its frame of reference. Founder Gary Erickson would take his bars to local athletic events and ask athletes to try them. When they asked what it was, he'd say, "an energy bar." The typical response was, "no, I don't like energy bars." The good news is that they recognized the frame of reference. The bad news is that they didn't like current options and had bad associations with that frame of reference. Fortunately, this perception also opened the door for Erickson's POD—a better taste because of ingredients that are more wholesome.

Let's revisit Soylent. Its marketing messages have included all of the following:

- food reformatted

- complete nutrition
- achievement unlocked
- better for you and the planet

None of these messages makes it clear why Soylent is better than all other products in its category. Customers are hard-pressed to list the reasons why Soylent is better than other snacks or meals, let alone whether those reasons are important to them. Startups have to make it easy for customers to know why they should pick them. Soylent is an interesting product for sure, but it will experience an ongoing challenge in the marketplace until it can quickly say to which category it belongs and what distinguishes it from alternatives.

As a counterpoint, let's look at Tide, the leading laundry detergent in the United States. It's a stain fighter. It promises to get the stains out of your clothes. If you have clothes that get dirty and stained, Tide is for you. That's simple and unambiguous. Tide has won the laundry detergent market-share battle with nearly a 40% share among a crowded market.

A quick review of directories that list startups, like Crunchbase, AngelList, and StartBase, shows that few startups can say, quickly and easily, what is the one thing that makes them better than their competitors. If you can't say why you are better, how will customers figure it out?

Many startups fear being too specific will make them less attractive. They are afraid that potential customers will eliminate them from consideration too early in the decision process. Here's where having a focus makes finding a POD easier. Startups should talk to target customers to find out how they make a product choice. Figuring out how the product can outperform the competition in that decision framework makes a good POD.

Here are some ripe areas to consider for an effective POD:

- Is there one benefit the product outshines on? Think FedEx and delivery in 24 hours.
- Are you faster or more efficient than everyone else is? How about Jimmy John's "Freaky Fast."
- Is there more variety? Consider Baskin-Robbins' 31 flavors.
- Is it the most convenient? Remember Amazon's delivery.
- Is it the least expensive? Think Walmart's Always Low Prices.
- Is it the best customer service? Consider Starbucks' customization.

These messages connect with the target customers. As targeting expands, so too can the PODs.[53]

---

53   For more ideas on possible PODs, see Kevin Lane Keller, Brian Sternthal, and Alice Tybout, "Three Questions You Need to Ask About Your Brand," *Harvard Business Review*, 80: September (2002), 80.

Navigation Plan: *In the beginning, startups should be narrow and focused. Make it easy for the right customers to figure out what the product offering does.*

Inconsistent Use

Becoming known for a specific POD takes consistent messaging over time. Big, well-known brands like Coca-Cola and Tide know this. However, it seems to be more difficult for startups to be consistent. First, startups are often not quite sure whether they have the right POD. They try one for a while, and, if they aren't getting traction, *pivot*. That pivot creates a debt of inconsistency—some prospective customers think the product does one thing and others think it does something else.

One SaaS startup, Startup Charlie, spent several million dollars over three years with a great variety of outbound marketing—trade shows, webinars, emails, etc. In that span of time, it described its POD in five different ways. It also had generated a database with about 80,000 potential customers who raised their hands for more information. This was really an amazing volume of leads. However, since these prospects raised their hands after hearing five different PODs, it was hard to know how to promote equally well to all of them. This startup then had to spend even more time and money figuring out which of these leads were still viable and re-qualifying their interest.

A second way this inconsistency happens is across messages—the website emphasizes one POD, the conference presentation talks about something else, and the startup's directory listings talk about another POD entirely. This inconsistency happens naturally because different people create each of these messages at different times.

One way that big brands create consistency is through documents called *brand books*. A brand book is a set of branding guidelines that specify what marketing messages should say about the product and how they should say it. Big brands also tend to have an approval process for communications. Decision-making is more decentralized at many startups. Startups can be more flexible and agile, but the cost is consistency of message both at one point in time and across time.

 Navigation Plan: *One way to combat inconsistency of message in the salesforce is to have a "pitch day" where the salespeople give their best pitches. Then, the group picks the one best pitch and everyone else adopts it. Inconsistency is likely to creep in again, but at least the startup has demonstrated that it wants everyone on one message.*

Let's come back to the startup Licensario, the SaaS pricing tool, in more detail. Even though it failed, its listing still appears in different startup directories. There is some consistency among them in that they have something to do with pricing, optimizing pricing, and billing. Other than that, it was not clear what made Licensario different and better:

- *AngelList.* The ultimate pricing tool for SaaS businesses.
- *Crunchbase.* Helps SaaS businesses to optimize their pricing plans, increase conversion rates and maximize revenues.
- *Gust.* The most flexible monetization solution out there for SaaS businesses that also optimizes pricing and increases conversions.
- *Start-Up Nation Finder (illist.co).* A technology that helps ISVs and SaaS businesses build flexible pricing models and sell their products.
- *StartBase.* Smart billing for SaaS companies. (After this statement appear four sentences to explain what that means.)
- *StartUpers.* A cloud-based solution that solved the painful billing process of other SaaS companies. (After this description appear two more sentences to explain what that means.)

 Lookout: *If a startup's listings are inconsistent, it suggests two possible problems. One possibility is that the founders might not yet really know what their POD is. The other is that no one is professionally managing the company's image. Even fast-moving startups should professionally manage their brand.*

A startup has to be more consistent than this for its customers, investors, and market to know what it does. Each time a startup describes itself differently or pivots messaging, it incurs marketing debt. While it is building assets like brand awareness and a database of leads, it won't be able to leverage those assets fully because the leads all think the company does something different.

Navigation Plan: *Picking a POD and sticking with it is the way to minimize this debt. Of course, that requires an in-depth understanding of customers' needs and competitors' offerings, followed by early message testing to home in on the best POD and then making sure that POD appears consistently in all messaging.*

In summary, the positioning process itself can create debt for startups. They need to quickly identify which existing category best describes their product so customers will have a frame of reference within which to evaluate their offerings. Then, they need to figure what uniquely differentiates them from the competition. Finally, they need to message that point of differentiation consistently across media and customers. Not having a clear market category for frame of reference, weak differentiation, and inconsistent messaging over time all undermine venture traction and create Marketing Ocean debtbergs that can sink the startup.

The Tactical Sea

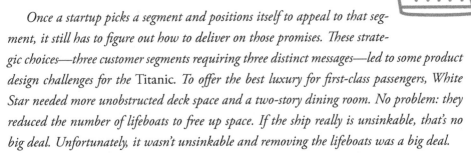

Once a startup picks a segment and positions itself to appeal to that segment, it still has to figure out how to deliver on those promises. These strategic choices—three customer segments requiring three distinct messages—led to some product design challenges for the Titanic. *To offer the best luxury for first-class passengers, White Star needed more unobstructed deck space and a two-story dining room. No problem: they reduced the number of lifeboats to free up space. If the ship really is unsinkable, that's no big deal. Unfortunately, it wasn't unsinkable and removing the lifeboats was a big deal.*

White Star needed to be able to wine and dine first-class passengers while minimizing costs with third-class passengers. To be able to deliver different experiences to different segments, the Titanic *had grilles—metal gates—that kept different classes of passengers in different parts of the ship. That might be okay for daily operations, but it was unconscionable in an emergency. Some grilles remained locked during the sinking, trapping the third-class passengers. It turns out that, under duress, it was operationally difficult to manage the emergency and take care of details like unlocking grilles. Ultimately, 61% of first-class passengers survived, but only 24% of third-class passengers did. Remember that there were twice as many third-class passengers as first-class. Ultimately, White Star didn't fulfill its promises to any passengers, but it inadvertently created disproportionate harm for the third-class passengers.*

Another debt the Titanic *incurred regarding tactical implementation related to the fact that, though being the "largest" ship was an easy-to-communicate point of differentiation, it also made the ship slow to turn. In the open sea, slow turning isn't necessarily a problem, but if you are about to run into a stationary and immovable object, slow turning can be a real hindrance. Even as the* Titanic *was leaving harbor for the first time, it came within two feet of hitting another ship due to lack of mobility created by its size. Ultimately, these marketing promises also caused product design challenges that contributed to the* Titanic's *sinking and tragic loss of life.*

Typically, marketers consider segmentation and positioning to be marketing strategy activities. Once the plan for these marketing strategies exists, startups still need to execute against these strategies through tactics. There are four major areas where startups incur marketing debts in the Tactical Sea:

- Customer Value Void
- Price/Value Mismatch
- Sales Process Not Scalable
- Incomplete Promotional Plan

Customer Value Void

In study after study, the number-one reason that startups fail is that they do not offer something new that better meets customers' needs.[54] This same factor is the biggest predictor of new-product failure as well.[55] The reason better-meeting-needs is so important is that people tend to behave in a consistent fashion. They need a sufficient incentive to change what's been working for them so far. For example, academic researchers estimate that families consistently buy about 150 products that account for about 85% of their total buying at the grocery store. Getting them to change this behavior requires something much better—more benefits, better price, or more convenient to access. As long as the current behavior doesn't create too many pain points, customers won't bother changing.

This factor is why one of the first steps of Strategyzer's widely popular *Business Model Canvas*[56] approach is to identify customers' pain points. This stems from the *Lean Startup* approach developed and advocated by best-selling authors Eric Ries, Steve Blank, and others. In the Lean Startup approach, the emphasis is to "get out of the building" (we talk about this more in Chapter 5) and interview potential customers and users extensively prior to developing a product. It's easier to get customers to adopt something that addresses their existing pain, so startups need to figure out what their prospects' existing pain is. When potential customers recognize they have a need, they are probably already interested in a solution to that problem.

Potential users may or may not be actively looking for a new solution. If they are already looking, this is great for the startup. That means that the prospective customers will pay attention to promotions that make them aware of the solution. Even if the prospects aren't actively searching for a solution, though, they will recognize and respond to promotions. On the other hand, prospects are likely to ignore promotions that talk about solving a problem that they think they don't have. Even if the audience

54   CB Insights, "The Top 20 Reasons Startups Fail," *Research Briefs*, February 2, 2018, accessed June 23, 2018, https://www.cbinsights.com/research/startup-failure-reasons-top/.

55   Kahn, Kenneth B, *The PDMA Handbook of New Product Development*. Hoboken, NJ: John Wiley & Sons, Inc, 2013.

56   See, for example, "Strategyzer and the Business Model Canvas," accessed July 28, 2017 https://strategyzer.com/canvas/business-model-canvas.

did process your promotion, it probably won't motivate them because they don't perceive it as relevant. A startup has a much easier time if it solves a problem that people already know they have.

Not meeting unmet needs is one of the reasons that the startup Quirky,[57] founded by Ben Kaufman, eventually failed. Quirky raised $185 million because it offered an interesting service—an invention platform. People could submit their own original inventions and have a path to get those inventions to market. Quirky got many submissions—thousands per week from its more than half-million users. The Quirky community voted on which ones were good, and Quirky built and sold the inventions that "won."

Unfortunately, it turns out there isn't a big enough market for cool inventions like water fountains for dogs, app-enabled egg trays, and bathroom mirrors that eliminate fog from shower steam. These were all cool inventions, but they didn't address pain points people were really willing to spend money to address. At the same time, it takes a lot of money to create a prototype and secure production quantities of new products. Ultimately, Quirky just couldn't make the financials work.

As another example, let's revisit Startup Bravo that crossed three frames of reference by offering a comprehensive communication system for healthcare providers. Unfortunately, this wasn't a pain point that these providers were prioritizing for their IT enhancements. A few early users appreciated the entire communication system, but most felt that it was an innovative option they wanted to look at "next year." When this startup focused on a communication problem that providers considered to be worth spending "this year's" budget on, it had greater and broader success. Focusing on just this pain point meant promoting only part of its product offering. The solution to this pain point was to *land and expand*: create the hook to land new customers and later expand its offering, once it had its foot in the door.

Unfortunately, the startup landscape is dotted with many other startups that had the same problem as Quirky and Startup Bravo. For example, Attila Szigeti of the European startup Rate My Speech[58] found that many people want to make their presentations stronger. However, they were unwilling to upload a video of their presentations so that others could comment and help them improve. In another example, Anthony Manning-Franklin wanted his Australian startup Gigger[59] to help bands both find talent they needed to add and be able to book themselves into venues more

---

57   Jessica Silvester, "The Rise and Fall of Quirky—the Start-Up That Bet Big on the Genius of Regular Folks," *New York Magazine*, September 13, 2015, accessed July 28, 2017, http://nymag.com/daily/intelligencer/2015/09/they-were-quirky.html.

58   Attila Szigeti, "Let it go, let it go…Sunset of my first startup: ratemyspeech.co," *Medium*, June 9, 2015, accessed July 28, 2017, https://medium.com/@aszig/let-it-go-let-it-go-sunset-of-my-first-startup-ratemy-speech-co-f79b1d72c482.

59   Anthony Manning-Franklin, "Post-Mortem: Gigger Rocked," *LinkedIn.com*, November 22, 2016, accessed July 28, 2017, https://www.linkedin.com/pulse/post-mortem-gigger-rocked-anthony-manning-franklin/.

easily. It tried to become the "Airbnb for bands." Manning-Franklin found out that the existing system of using contacts to get gigs worked well enough that bands would list themselves on Gigger but wouldn't actually book a gig through the app. They just saw the opportunity on Gigger and then went directly to the lead. Without the gig being booked directly, Gigger received no compensation.

Startups can't solve just any problem. They need to solve a problem that customers care about, want to fix, and are willing to pay to fix. Otherwise, the tactical debt they incur is too big to overcome.

> **Lookout:** *Startups need to understand the difference between "must-have" and "nice-to-have." Customers are looking for "must-haves." "Nice-to-haves" often don't address pain points worth paying for.*

Price/Value Mismatch

A startup has to offer the market something it needs, and then it has to get customers to pay for it. Pricing is one of the hardest decisions for both start-ups and larger firms. Price too low and there's not enough profit; you leave money on the table. Price too high and you can't get enough customers or build traction. Add in that many people see price as an indicator of quality. For those people, pricing too low indicates that your product offering isn't valuable. What is the target market willing to pay? This question can be hard to answer.

Typically, young firms set prices based on costs (assuming that they've figured out what their costs are) or on competitors' offerings. If a startup doesn't price above costs, its future is doomed, so it has to make sure it understands costs. Being aware of competitors is also a good idea. However, if the product offers more value than competitors' products do, then the price should capture that value above competitors' prices. Marketers call this approach *value-based pricing.*[60]

 Navigation Plan: *Customers might not always be willing to give all of the value a product creates to the manufacturers. Most startups end up splitting the value added with customers. Recognize that startups are unlikely to get pricing right the first time. Both pricing too high and pricing too low yield debts. Managing those debts and being strategic and intentional about pricing experiments are critical to limit the resultant problems.*

---

60   Andreas Hinterhuber and Stephan Liozu, "Is It Time to Rethink Your Pricing Strategy?" *Sloan Management Review,* Summer 2012, 69.

Startups need to start by answering questions about their prospective customers:

- What do prospective customers value about the product offering?
- How much are these improvements over the competitors' products or existing solution worth?
- What features of the offering do they view as "table stakes"—that is, which features must a product offer in order for the customer to consider it at all?
- Which are worth paying a premium?

While market research can answer some of these questions, monitoring customers' purchase opportunities is a better way. For example, experimenting with free versus paid trials can tell a startup whether potential customers are willing to "pay to play."

BitShuva Radio[61] is one example of a company that failed by not correctly matching pricing to value. This startup started as an accident. Founder Judah Himango wanted to be able to listen to Messianic Jewish music online, so he wrote himself an application. He shared in a blog how he did it, and suddenly people starting asking him to write a custom program for their favorite music type—Nigerian, Egyptian Coptic chants, etc.

The good news is that this is a focused *niche* (or customer segment) and the product addressed a pain point that the market knew it had. The bad news is that he wasn't sure how to price the product. He started low at $75 and gradually raised the price until people started saying, "No, that's too high." He figured out how his market valued what he offered, but only for the upfront fee. There were ongoing service requests that customers weren't excited about paying for. Eventually, this little business was taking too much of the founder's "free" time without compensating him, so, he shuttered the consulting part. Now, BitShuva Radio just plays music.

Homejoy[62] is another startup that failed due, in part, to pricing. Founders Adora and Aaron Cheung wanted Homejoy to be the "Uber of house cleaning" by connecting cleaners to people in need of a house cleaner. It was a nice explanation of the frame of reference.

They attracted $40 million in funding as they tried to scale. Then, they used a Groupon strategy to attract new customers at $19.99 per cleaning. The customers they attracted were deal shoppers who did not recognize the value that cleaning their house deserved, so they were not repeat customers. Homejoy changed its promotional approach towards people who were looking for good house cleaners.

---

61   Judah Gabriel Himango, "My startup's dead! 5 things I learned," *Debugger.Break();*, May 21, 2015, accessed July 28, 2017, https://debuggerdotbreak.wordpress.com/2015/05/21/my-startups-dead-5-things-i-learned/.

62   Sam Madden, "Why Homejoy Failed…And The Future Of The On-Demand Economy," *Techcrunch.com*, July 31, 2015, accessed July 28, 2017, https://techcrunch.com/2015/07/31/why-homejoy-failed-and-the-future-of-the-on-demand-economy/.

That change helped reduce the cost to acquire customers. Ultimately, Homejoy could not charge enough for each individual cleaning event to cover its own fee plus the cleaner's service fee. A startup has to be able to price above costs to be viable. To be fair, Homejoy took on several other hidden debts that contributed to its demise. Still, an initial go-to-market strategy of low pricing was one debt it could not overcome.

 Navigation Plan: *One tactical pricing approach startups can use to maximize sales is recurring revenue. With recurring revenue, a purchase moment becomes a revenue stream. Instead of selling each customer in each event, the startup turns customers into a revenue stream by spreading their buying over time. This is the classic idea behind a subscription model. Instead of ordering a box every time they remember they need one, people agree to a stream of purchases over time. Customers benefit by always having products they want. The startup benefits because it has a series of assured purchases. Recurring revenue offers more of a long-term opportunity.*

 Navigation Plan: *A second pricing approach is dynamic pricing, reflecting the time value of a purchase. When demand is high, sellers charge more. When demand is lower, sellers charge less. Classic examples of dynamic pricing are car rental rates, early-bird dinner specials, and surcharge pricing during peak periods for museums or entertainment. Find out what when customers value the product offering. Offer discounts at low demand times to increase demand. More startups should consider when to charge price premiums for their offering and likewise when to discount to incentivize buying.*

Sales Process Not Scalable

Landing initial customers who are in your backyard and maybe are friends, colleagues, or acquaintances is one thing. Selling halfway across the country or world to unknown hundreds or thousands provides a much bigger challenge. It's clearly important to get those first five paying customers in the founders' network. However, the real success is when the first customer the founders don't actually know buys.

There are startups where customers sign up online, and there is no need for a salesperson for direct sales. More typically, a startup needs to fine-tune its sales model to convert leads into paying customers. This sales challenge applies to both B2B and B2C startups. Some people might assume that only B2B startups have a salesforce challenge. However, just as many B2C startups have consumers who need someone to hold their hands through the buying process. Some B2C startups might assume that consumers will buy online. Those need to prepare for a more sales-laden approach if online buying doesn't happen.

The first step should be to seek out *channel partners*. Channel partners are organizations who sell, distribute, and service products created by another firm. For B2C firms, these tend to be retailers and wholesalers. For B2B, think about *buying groups* (an association that bundles purchases among its members to get volume discounts), *value-added resellers* (VARs), and manufacturers' representatives. A startup must consider who has access to groups of its target customers and think of ways to work with these partners to gain access to these customers. Selling to individual customers, one at a time, is arduous and time-consuming. A startup doesn't have that much time. Channel partners provide not only access to customers but also might help in the closing process.

Of course, in partnerships the partners earn some reward for helping to sell. Their cut factors into profitability. Founder Mei Xu of Chesapeake Bay Candle Company recognized early on that she wanted to work through retailers. The first retailer she focused on was Bloomingdale's—you'll recall that Bloomingdale's was the store that Xu frequented while she was working in New York. This was where she discovered that there was a gap in fashion-forward brands in the home department. However, since Chesapeake Bay Candle wanted to offer fashionable but affordable home goods, Target was a more logical partner than Bloomingdale's.

Likewise, founder Apoorva Mehta of Instacart quickly discovered that recruiting consumers one-at-a-time was a long and painful task. Mehta pivoted to targeting retailers, letting Instacart offer a new service to the retailers' existing customers. Instacart's sales process became scalable.

Once potential customers become leads, the next step is to convert them down the *sales funnel* (see the callout box). A sales funnel describes the process of converting potential customers into actual customers. The steps in the funnel can vary quite a bit depending on industry, brand, and target segment. Startups need to identify what their funnel looks like and measure how leads convert through each stage of the funnel.

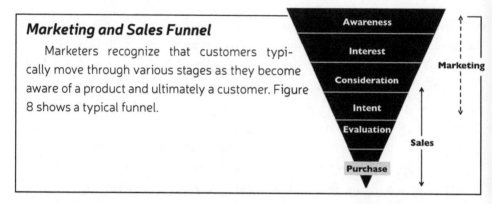

Marketing and Sales Funnel

Marketers recognize that customers typically move through various stages as they become aware of a product and ultimately a customer. Figure 8 shows a typical funnel.

First, the startup needs to understand the prospective customers' decision-making steps. Then, the startup needs an approach to move the prospective customers through each step. If 1-in-1,000 leads closes, that means the startup needs to use a lot of promotions to bring 1,000 times as many leads as it needs to the top of the funnel. That's a big debt to overcome. However, if the startup can improve its conversion percentage to 1-in-100, 1-in-50, or, amazingly, 1-in-10, then the startup will acquire more paying customers with less promotion expense. Figuring out a repeatable sales process that can scale across leads and effectively convert those leads to customers is an important priority for startups.

One accelerator we know established a rule that it won't fund a startup until the founders have sold to at least five customers directly. The accelerator wants the founders to demonstrate that they understand what value they create and understand the sales process firsthand. If the sales process is good, the startup then can make it repeatable with the accelerator's help.

Lack of a repeatable sales process is one of the factors that Outbox's founders Sukriti Agarwal and Kaushal Modi[63] attribute to its demise. This startup offered to pick up and digitize mail so people didn't have to deal with the paper. Outbox built a wait list, which was a great approach to see if there was interest in the market. When the service launched, about 10% of the wait list signed up. It was not a bad conversion rate, but not a great one either. However, once Outbox exhausted the waitlist, it could not figure out how to predictably generate new leads or close them. No new customers meant no future, and Outbox was not able to survive the scalability challenge.

Lastly, adding sales people is an expensive activity. One serial entrepreneur we know suggests you have to add sales people in sets of three because one will be excellent, one will be terrible, and one will be acceptable. At an average annual total cost of $200,000 per salesperson, three means funding $600,000 in annual expenses (including commissions). Even if the startup keeps those three salespeople for only a few

---

63   Anthony Ha, "Outbox Shuts Down Its Mail Digitizing Service," *Techcrunch.com*, January 21, 2014, accessed July 28, 2017, https://techcrunch.com/2014/01/21/outbox-shuts-down/.

months, that's still a $50,000 per month cash burn. Instead, most startups add sales people as they can afford them. This means a random assortment of capabilities and scaling dependent on cash flow. Again, the startup incurs a debt because it cannot maximize the opportunity in front of them.

 Navigation Plan: *Marketing debts in the sales arena start from relying exclusively on a direct sales approach, whether it's just a website or actual salespeople. Goal number one should be to find partners to help speed up the selling process. Still, most startups need salespeople to help close the deal. Therefore, you need to understand the ideal sales process and have a plan to add sales representatives to manage that process affordably. If not, the debt incurred here is not growing as fast as possible and wasted effort to finalize a scalable sales process.*

Incomplete Promotional Plan

Last but not least, customers need a way to find out about the product offering. Like the debt in sales, the debt that startups take on in promotion is usually one based on budget. Most startups add promotional investments as they can afford them (notice that we view promotions as "investments" and not "expenses"). *Promotions* include all of the marketing components associated with promoting a company and its products, such as the following:

- advertising—both inbound and outbound
- events and conferences
- digital marketing
- public relations
- email marketing
- sales promotions or discounting

Inbound marketing or *inbound advertising* is the first kind of promotion most startups try. Inbound seeks to attract people who are already looking online for your product solution through blogs, search engines, and social media. They find your online content interesting and come to your website. *Outbound marketing* or *outbound advertising*, on the other hand, relies on traditional media advertisements to help potential customers recognize that they have the problem that your solution addresses.

The logic for starting with inbound marketing is strong. It's typically less expensive in terms of actual dollars because the focus is on getting in front of people who are already online searching for the product offering. Then, a startup can offer a variety of content, mostly through the website, to attract, engage, and close sales. This approach takes more time and effort than budget, but it requires a few basics to be successful.

 Navigation Plan: *Here's how to begin inbound marketing. First, a startup needs a real website rather than just a Facebook or LinkedIn page. Social media listings are nice because they are essentially free, but the website should be the hub of inbound marketing efforts. It is worth investing in a good website. At a minimum, the website should be search engine optimized (SEO) on keywords that reflect its positioning or value proposition to help searchers find the product offering. Best practice is for the website to have a blog and a way to capture leads, such as a sign-up form. A customer relationship management (CRM) tool helps with the marketing automation to turn prospects in to leads and then in to closed customers. There are many other bells and whistles that a good website can have as well, too many to detail here.*

Most startups find that they cannot generate enough leads simply through inbound marketing. With very low brand awareness at the beginning, the most effective promotional tool is outbound marketing—the traditional advertising we tend to think of. Therefore, a startup should also have a budget for outbound marketing. This budget needs to be big enough to *break through*—stand out enough against competing ads—and get target customers' attention.

Lookout: *Many startup CEOs worry that their marketing personnel are mismanaging the startup's advertising efforts, inbound or outbound, if they don't see an immediate payoff. In fairness, a startup's overall spend is small enough that it would be difficult to "move the needle" right away. Early on, the cost of customer acquisition might be high, and awareness grows slowly. However, over time, this cost should come down through economies of scale and improved effectiveness, and the startup can realize a return on the investment in advertising.*

Before promotions can start, a startup needs to know where target customers get their information. Answering the following questions about the target audience is a good way to identify places to advertise:

- What magazines, if any, do they read?
- What websites do they visit for news?

- Are they on Twitter, LinkedIn, or Facebook?
- Do they attend trade shows and events?
- What influencers get their attention?

The goal of all of these efforts is to identify prospects, get them to raise their hands, and begin turning them into leads. Closing a sale might require the help of a salesperson, but a startup needs to know where their customers get information on new products so they know where to go to get prospective customers into the funnel.

The tactical implementation of promotions is the marketing iceberg that killed Kinly, the provider of a "Facebook for families" mentioned earlier. To get families to download and use Kinly, it needed a large promotions budget to reach out to everyday consumers. GoKart Labs funded Kinly internally. It never took investor funding. That meant it had a very small budget. It got a small network of families to download and use the app, but those few families were not enough to sustain it. Kinly would have needed millions of dollars to get this app fully distributed to its target market. Instead of solving that funding problem, Kinly ignored it. Eventually, without the budget for meaningful customer acquisition, the company had to fold.

Funding is typically tight at startups. Appropriately, the startup plows most of the money it gets into product development. It's critical to have a product that works and that adds value for customers. A great product is easy to promote, while no amount of promotions can save a bad product. It makes sense to prioritize getting the product right. However, customers still have to find out about this product. Unfortunately if you build it, they often still don't come. When startups don't create an effective plan for how they are going to promote their offerings, they incur a debt that can sink them. This funding might be able to wait until after the product is complete, but there needs to be a plan for funding promotions beyond a Facebook page.

In many startups, marketing is an afterthought to product design. In and of itself, this approach creates marketing debt that can challenge the company later. Even early on, the marketing function needs to act as a customer advocate, connecting product development to customers' needs.

Notice that the term we use is "marketing function." A startup doesn't necessarily have to hire a full-time marketer in order to accomplish the marketing function. However, someone in the company needs to make sure that the founding team is considering these marketing issues:

- Who is the target customer and how do we prioritize customer segments to target over time?
- What category does this product offering belong to in the minds of these target customers?

- What is it these target customers really want from a product in this category?
- How can we minimize their pain points better than competitors do?
- How do we get this product into customers' hands with a price based on the value the customer realizes from the product?
- How do we establish that value through appropriate pricing?
- Where do we find these customers and get them started in the buying process?
- Have we secured the funds to promote to and close sales with these customers?

Taken together, there are quite a few debtbergs in the Marketing Ocean that a startup needs to navigate successfully. Next, we'll provide some guidance about how to find those icebergs and get around them more effectively and efficiently.

Navigating Marketing Debt

At this point, it might seem like every decision related to sales and marketing creates some type of debt to overcome. How does a founder move the startup forward without taking on marketing debtbergs that will sink it? The first step is to embrace an experimentation mentality. It's hard to know in advance what is going to work best. Startups need to get used to identifying their key hypotheses and testing them, while recognizing the potential hidden debt that they could be creating.

Next, a founder needs to recognize that both sales and marketing play equally important roles in the venture's success.[64] There is a tendency in new ventures to prioritize the sales function—go get some customers signed up—over the marketing function. In reality, the priority needs to iterate between a sales focus and a marketing focus as well as between strategic planning and tactical implementation. In essence, an important role for marketing is to be a sales-enablement function. Figures 9 and 10 highlight an approach to this prioritization over the life stages of the new venture.

Embracing Experimentation by Stage

In the Human Ocean chapter, we suggested that there are four main stages of a new venture: Pre-Revenue, MVP (Minimum Viable Product), Launch and Early Growth, and Scalable Product and Business Model.

In the earliest stage, Pre-Revenue, both sales and marketing need to focus on strategic planning. At this stage, the marketing function needs to explore customers' needs deeply:

---

64   Kotler, Philip, Neil Rackham, and Suj Krishnaswamy, "Ending the War Between Sales and Marketing." *Harvard Business Review*, 84: 7-8 (2006): 68.

- How do they view current offerings?
- What pain points do they still have?
- Who makes the best target segment because they have these needs and are already looking for a solution?
- What are the underlying customer segments in this market?
- What criteria do they use to evaluate these offerings?
- What process do they use to find and evaluate alternatives?

The goal at this stage is to develop a hypothesis about the best target customers, a POD that is both unique and motivating, and an understanding about what product features will drive value.

Figure 9: Focus on sales vs. marketing by venture stage

In the next stage, MVP, the new venture should have a *minimum viable product* and begin to seek out early customers. A minimum viable product (MVP) is the most limited set of functionality that a customer would pay for. If product development goes well, at this point the startup sets an entry marketing strategy as a starting place.

Then, the focus moves more to sales with marketing providing support. Marketing still plays an important role tactically in beginning to create brand awareness to generate prospects and leads. However, these activities should help figure out the sales process. Those initial hypotheses now need to be tested. Now, the marketing function should be testing messages:

- Are the value drivers motivating potential customers to raise their hands?
- Which messages are more motivating?
- Where are these early target customers getting their information?
- Which media appear to be more effective?

Hand-in-hand with sales, marketing needs to ask questions to figure out what the sales process is:

- Has the startup identified the best target segment?
- What can help speed up or reduce leakage through the sales and marketing funnel?

Now is the time to figure out how to make sales and marketing scalable and repeatable. If the first target segment isn't responding as enthusiastically as expected, now is also the time to considering refining the target segment. Alternatively, the startup may need to enhance the product offering beyond being minimally viable. The new venture needs to make sure it is still adding value beyond competitors.

In the third stage, Launch and Early Growth, the focus in marketing iterates back to strategic planning. It's time to use the market experience to-date to finalize the product development plan for features to release over time (find more on this in Chapter 5), the initial target segment, a pricing model, key messages including the POD, and the best promotional approaches. The website and a CRM database should be in place. Developing plans for working more closely with channel partners is a priority.

In addition, there should be a plan as to which inbound and outbound tools to use. These are now stronger hypotheses, but these hypotheses still need continual testing, and the plans need refinement. What the next stage calls for is all-out implementation. Therefore, the startup should establish most hypotheses as a working model for going forward.

At the fourth stage, a venture should be moving into scalable implementation. The focus is primarily on tactical implementation in both sales and marketing. Of course, there is always room for adjustments to the strategic plan, but the focus should be on executing the strategy as fully as cash flows allow. Applying this approach certainly doesn't guarantee that the startup incurs no marketing debt— that's probably impossible anyway. Even so, a well-defined approach can help minimize marketing debt and provide mechanisms to help mitigate the inevitable marketing debt.

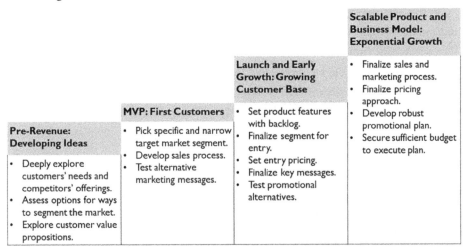

Figure 10: Critical marketing and sales activities by venture stage

Do More Market Research

Startups need to consider investing in market research that is more rigorous at an earlier stage in their life. Early on, there are so many ways to spend money and so little funding that market validation research is either not done or is done poorly. An ideal market research plan includes qualitative research to understand to which category customers believe this product offering belongs and explore the customers' decision-making processes. The startup should verify these insights by more quantitative research, most likely via a survey, to understand if the offering really has market potential. Finally, more qualitative research can deeply explore issues that came up in the quantitative phase.

Many startups rush through this research process. Instead of rigorous research, they ask a few people that they know what they think about the idea. Then, if they do some type of survey, they use a convenience sample of friends and family. These friends and family may or may not even be in the relevant target market. The outcome is the startup gets feedback that reinforces it has a good idea even when the idea might not generate enough value to cover costs.

Over the last ten years, the costs of market research have come down. Good data is less expensive than founders think. Here is a good place to reach out to local universities. They often have classes that can take on research as projects, or they might have a research group that performs outside research at a reasonable cost. Alternatively, running Facebook ads for B2C products and seeing what messages resonate is inexpensive. The key is to get objective input for planning.

Startup success stories often describe just how much effort founders made early to understand what customers want:

- Hetrick took his early TRX products to weekly "Liquidity Events" he hosted where he invited local athletes to try the products and help him develop workouts in exchange for their favorite libations. He used their feedback to rework the offering.

- Erickson took his early Clif Bars to athletic events, gave them away by the hundreds, and asked for feedback.

- Blake Mycoskie of TOMS brought a bag of early shoe products to Los Angeles and had women friends host focus group events where the women tried on the shoes and shared their ideas directly with him as to what they liked and disliked.

- Chesapeake Bay became a candle company because of customer feedback. Xu and her co-founder, David Wang, knew that they wanted to offer a fashionable home product. However, they didn't know what the product(s) should be for the US market. To find out, they started by taking about a half dozen different products to a gift show. Once they realized that over 90% of the orders they received were for fashionable candles, they knew they had an idea that the market wanted. This single event netted them $500,000 in orders. They formed Chesapeake Bay Candle to fulfill and expand this product offering.

- Gebbia started Airbnb by renting out his own spare beds. Once the platform was developed and Airbnb had the first listings, he was disappointed at the low rate of bookings. He realized that he needed to look at the business through customers' eyes more. To get that perspective, he traveled out to visit early listers and look at their properties as a renter would. He worked side-by-side with the listers to overhaul their listings to better showcase the properties and create more credibility. The result was increased bookings and better customer relationships.

The ability to get customer input is there, if a startup thinks creatively about how to get it.

Remember that we've described how to address marketing debts through an active sales and marketing function. We do not equate a function with specific hires. For some startups, it makes sense to hire these skills as full-time employees. In others, the founders themselves may have these skills. In yet others, the startup can outsource these skills. This decision overlaps with hidden debts on the human side—the

Employee Sea. It's not important what kind of employee brings this thinking into the startup. What's important is that someone is intentionally planning for sales and marketing from the beginning. You cannot just build an interesting product and assume that the startup will be successful. It takes careful and specific strategic marketing planning to help create that success.

The *Titanic* did identify something new that some customers were interested in—the most luxurious cruise from Europe to the United States. It managed messages to multiple target segments in two geographies reasonably well. However, overall, it failed to meet the customers' most important need—to arrive on the other side of the Atlantic Ocean safely. Just over 30% of the people onboard survived. While the *Titanic* took on significant human and *technical debt* that clearly contributed to its demise, it also took on marketing debt that not only helped sink it—it increased casualties as well. While marketing debt is inevitable, managing it minimizes the likelihood of sinking on the maiden voyage.

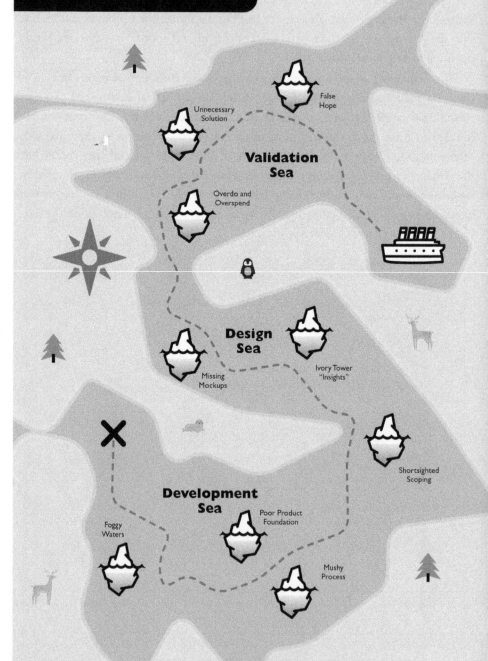

THE TECHNICAL OCEAN

False Hope

Unnecessary Solution

Validation Sea

Overdo and Overspend

Design Sea

Missing Mockups

Ivory Tower "Insights"

Shortsighted Scoping

Development Sea

Poor Product Foundation

Foggy Waters

Mushy Process

CHAPTER 5

THE TECHNICAL OCEAN

"If the art of shipbuilding were in the wood, ships would exist by nature."

–Aristotle

"And so castles made of sand fall in the sea eventually."

–Jimi Hendrix

*E*ven though the human and marketing issues with the Titanic *clearly contributed to its sinking, let's remember that it was the engineers who set out to design a "practically unsinkable ship" and ended up permanently redefining the word "titanic" as a synonym for "failure."*

Who were these engineers? Was this a human debt of substandard employees in the wrong role? Not exactly. Joseph Bell, a native of Cumbria, England, was the chief engineer on the Titanic. *He joined White Star Line in 1885 and served on a number of its ships. In 1891, when Bell was just 30, White Star appointed him the chief mechanical engineer of the* Coptic. *After successfully completing that project, he moved on to lead the design of the* Olympic, *whose construction started at the same time as the* Titanic. *Bell helped launch the* Olympic *and then received the* Titanic *as a project. As the chief engineer on the* Titanic, *he was in command in the engine room that fateful night when he received the order to "back all over" (reverse). Unfortunately, he received that order too late. Regardless of what Bell and his team did, the ship was going to sink. He stayed, manning the engines until they exploded, trying to buy time for passengers to evacuate. Ultimately, in part due to technical failures on his team's part, he went down with the ship along with the captain and other crew and passengers.*

Once White Star had decided it wanted the Titanic *to be the largest and most luxurious ship on the seas, it had a number of engineering and design challenges to overcome. Planning to build three of the largest ships ever, and two at the same time, magnified the challenges. Finally, the* Titanic *was to be the heaviest of the three boats due to her luxurious accommodations. To get the* Titanic *in the water and through her maiden voyage successfully, White Star needed to complete all the following tasks:*

- *Build two shipyards with servicing equipment to manage the height and depth of the ships*
- *Scale up a relatively new technology in steel welding*
- *Develop a propulsion system, including multiple inverted reciprocating steam engines, to power a low-pressure turbine that controlled the propellers*
- *Design those engines to maximize power output while minimizing fuel consumption*
- *Build in an internal power plant to maintain electrical power throughout the ship*
- *Design a new approach to manage leaks or breaks in the hull in order to make the ship unsinkable*

From a product development perspective, that is a lot of work for the engineers to get right.

The Technical Ocean debtbergs are easiest to identify in software-based products. Much of our discussion in this chapter notes the particular challenges in software development. However, the concepts apply equally to physical, biotech, and other products with a highly technical development component. As such, we recognize that these concepts can apply to both developers of software as well as product engineers.

We must admit that developing new products is not easy by any means. Our goal in this chapter is to raise issues to help a *startup* avoid being swamped by *technical debt*. Ward Cunningham coined the phrase "technical debt" in 1992[65] to describe development projects that start with a mindset of "quick and dirty" instead of "get it right the first time." For startups, the phrase describes the scenario when a technical development project relies on so much rickety, just-get-it-done-or-our-startup-dies architecture that each new product change triggers cascading bugs and problems.

Sometimes, the engineer is culpable for technical laziness or just doesn't know how to build a foundation flexible enough for the changes that a startup inevitably encounters. However, just as often, engineers unfairly get the blame for failing to recognize technical requirements that an entrepreneur took for granted. It's hardly fair to blame the engineer when the captain shows up with an outboard motor for the bamboo raft and can't believe the engineer didn't understand that the original requirement of "it just has to float" also contained a silent "and go sixty miles an hour!"

---

65   See Ward Cunningham, "The WyCash Portfolio Management System," *OOPSLA '92 Experience Report*, March 26, 1992, accessed April 18, 2018, http://c2.com/doc/oopsla92.html for one of the first appearances of "technical debt." Martin Fowler, of leading software developer ThoughtWorks, published a good discussion of technical debt on October 1, 2003 at https://martinfowler.com/bliki/TechnicalDebt.html.

Succeeding in a startup should not require technical heroics, despite folklore and popular stories to the contrary. Modern navigators know that the best way to survive is never to run into the debtberg in the first place. Navigating through the Seas in the Technical Ocean is almost never a linear journey.

Welcome to the treacherous, scary Technical Ocean. Like the other Oceans we've been sailing through, the Technical Ocean contains three Seas:

- **The Validation Sea**—Build the right ship
- **The Design Sea**—Plot the right course
- **The Development Sea**—Stay on course

The Validation Sea

The process to build the Titanic started with many assumptions, as most new-product building processes do. Most were commonplace and harmless, like the assumption that people would like to travel in style and still get to their destination quickly. White Star Line had tested that assumption in years prior with ships like the Olympic. *However, other assumptions were untested—especially those that related to size and safety.*

For example, the design team assumed that the captain would always have plenty of time to steer around an iceberg, and so avoiding it entirely would be an option. The design team had not considered the possibility of a glancing blow when they designed the ship. In addition to the amount of forewarning, avoiding an iceberg also depends on the turn radius and responsiveness of the ship. Unfortunately, the crew did not spot the iceberg until it was about thirty seconds from impact. The large ship and steam-powered turning mechanism required at least that much time to engage the rudder and even begin turning or reversing. There was no chance to avoid a collision.

Second, when the iceberg ripped open not only one but at least six compartments, the ship began filling with water quicker than anticipated. The new design called for keeping sixteen compartments horizontally watertight, which it did. Unfortunately, though, the water in the six compartments that did suffer damage made the ship list, which caused water to move between compartments, over the top of the bulkheads and into the undamaged compartments.

This shifting water caused the bow to sink, which raised the back of the ship, with the engines and propellers, out of the water. The stress across the middle caused the Titanic *to rip into three pieces. Engineers had expected the new watertight compartments to allow the* Titanic *to stay afloat for days if damaged. Instead, filled with water, they caused it to sink more quickly. Had the* Titanic *engineers validated their assumptions and considered a glancing blow and listing, the story might have ended differently.*

New ideas don't exist in a bubble. To succeed, a new product idea needs validation at every stage of development. A startup needs to understand the full picture of its product and market: What reasons do customers have to buy this new product? What does the product or service need to include in order to satisfy those reasons? If the startup isn't asking these questions continually, it is bound to sail off course.

Validation is the early step of making sure that the product you are building actually addresses a pain point that customers feel. Sometimes this is called "*product/market fit.*"[66] Icebergs in the Validation Sea relate to the Customer Value Void iceberg in the Marketing Ocean. They are the technical and product-related side of this debtberg. Think of the two as the yin and yang of product/market fit. The iceberg drifts in the Validation Sea include:

- False Hope
- Unnecessary Solution
- Overdo and Overspend

Bulgarian entrepreneur Ivaylo Kalburdzhiev learned about Validation debtbergs the hard way after launching his startup KOLOS. He loved playing racing games on the computer and wanted to create a new accessory. His idea was to develop an accessory for people to use while playing racing games on a tablet computer. The accessory would clip the tablet into the middle of a steering wheel so the player could have a more realistic driving experience. Similar devices already existed that turned smartphones into steering wheels, and Kalburdzhiev figured that tablets were the next natural step.

He did his competitor research and, sure enough, there was no competitive product for tablets. Before getting any customer feedback, Kalburdzhiev took out a loan and started building a prototype. After running through that first loan and joining an accelerator, he launched two crowdfunding initiatives—Indiegogo and Kickstarter—that both failed. Ultimately, he discovered that people agreed that a tablet steering wheel was a cool idea—just not one that they wanted to pay for. The whole concept was a "*nice-to-have.*" It did not solve an actual problem people were willing to pay for. If Kalburdzhiev had sought negative feedback from customers early in design, he would have saved himself $50,000 plus three years of hard work.[67]

---

66   See more detail on the background of "product/market fit" on venture capital firm Andreessen Horowitz's blog—Tren Griffin, "12 Things about Product-Market Fit," accessed April 18, 2018, https://a16z. com/2017/02/18/12-things-about-product-market-fit/.

67   Ivaylo Kalburdzhiev, "Kolossal failure: 10 lessons I learned from burning through $50,000 on a hardware project that bombed," *Tech.EU*, April 16, 2015, accessed April 18, 2018, http://tech.eu/features/4346/ kolos-kickstarter-story.

False Hope

Like any captain starting on a new voyage, founders are enthusiastic about starting a company. During this stage, it's easy to let excitement propel a startup forward. Entrepreneurs need to be wary of the False Hope drift. Getting caught in this drift could leave a founder building a product based on assumptions, rather than validated facts, about customer needs and wants.

It's easy for entrepreneurs to have false hopes. Today, society heralds founders as the heroes who are creating jobs and changing the world. Parents, coworkers, and even strangers, naturally want to support them and encourage their creativity. Just watch a few episodes of *Shark Tank*—most of the entrepreneurs have never heard that they don't have a great idea.

Many entrepreneurial education resources now advise startups to validate their solution with potential customers. Founders love "the solution" so much they devote their lives to building it, and so it is the first thing they want to discuss with potential customers. Unfortunately, going to the customer with a solution in hand often cuts off the most critical information entrepreneurs need to collect about the problem. Instead, startups should ask these questions even before talking directly with potential customers and developing a solution:

- Does the problem currently exist?
- Do customers recognize the problem?
- Is it important to fix?
- Is there a valid or "good enough" solution currently?

When a startup goes to customers to talk about a problem the customer hasn't already identified, just the process of asking for feedback creates the problem in the minds of the customers in a way that reflects the way the founder thinks about it. Coloring the customers' thinking about the problem like this naturally creates bias in the customers' feedback.

The route to honest input requires the founder to spend a lot of initial time exploring the context around the problem and understanding how people currently solve it. This process takes time but provides valuable insight, not only into the perceived and real magnitude of the problem, but also about solutions that already exist. False hopes often grow on premature assumptions that skip this step.

After thoroughly understanding the problem, it's time to get customer feedback on the proposed solution. Oftentimes, at the beginning, founders only want to hear positive feedback. This may be good for their egos, but it won't help in the development of their products. Instead, founders need to ask people what confused them, what they don't like about the product, and what made them put the product down and stop using it. A startup should want to eliminate any pain points its product introduced to the problem before moving the product forward.

Tesla co-founder Elon Musk is a huge advocate for seeking out negative feedback. In fact, when his friends purchase a product of his, he asks that they refrain from telling him what they like and instead focus on what they don't like.

 Navigation Plan: *Hide the solution until you've exhausted conversations about the problem. Seek out negative feedback. An entrepreneur has no better friend than a devil's advocate. Pitch to someone who will give honest critiques.*

As the saying goes, "If you want advice, ask for money. If you want money, ask for advice." To avoid hitting the False Hope debtberg, serial entrepreneurs know a different maxim—after getting positive feedback, and building the prototype to the prospect's satisfaction, they ask for a (non-binding) letter of intent to purchase. Then the *real* feedback begins! Signing your name to something, even something non-binding, is a way of giving your word, and most people want to honor their word. Asking potential customers to sign an agreement triggers an entirely different set of mental pathways, and you might find the response begins with, "Oh! Um, I meant this product would be great for *other* people *like* me. I wouldn't actually buy it because…"

Lookout: *If startups have a lot of "great conversations" and leads, ask them to get letters of intent from potential customers, including a suggested price.*

 Navigation Plan: *If your startup has great first sales meetings and then stalls in the middle of the sales funnel, you might be seeing evidence that you reveal the solution too early to prospects. The key is to understand the prospects' problem first and be sure the solution is a fit for them.*

Let's consider an example where making sure that a problem really exists is an important first step. An entrepreneur for Startup Delta (we'll use a fictitious name to protect this entrepreneur) was sure that customers would love his "broadly applicable" product at $14.99 per month. It wasn't clear whether anyone wanted the problem that the product addressed solved at any price point. So, he headed out to get feedback from friends and family about the actual problem.

A week later, he came back with great news! He had twenty friends and family who all said they would buy the product. Possibly one or two were a "maybe" but everyone else was all-in. An Internet search revealed a competing product that solved about

80% of the entrepreneur's proposed problem and would do for only \$4.99/month. While our fearless entrepreneur was undaunted by this competitor, he reluctantly agreed that his customers would likely buy the cheaper option to solve their problem. He went back to his potential customers to find out.

A few weeks later, he came back and admitted that *not even one* of the twenty friends and family who had said they would buy his product would buy this competing product, even at one-third the price of his solution. Either (A) the small amount of functionality that his solutions offered over the competition was the deciding factor in whether they purchased or (B) the twenty people he talked didn't really need the problem solved at any price, and had just told him they'd buy his product to support his entrepreneurial dream.

After a short discussion, he finally admitted to himself that his product's small advantage over the competition probably wasn't enough to convince people to purchase, especially at three times the price. This kind of honest validation is hard. It can yield bad news, but it saves launching a ship doomed to sink from the start.

Some startups use the approach of fielding a *crowdfunding campaign* to validate market interest. A crowdfunding campaign lets a startup describe a product to people who might want to contribute to the product's development. If the product description fails to inspire users, then it won't receive their funding. This approach can be a good way to test the market in terms of solving a problem, identifying features, and establishing a price point. However, successful crowdfunding can generate its own debtbergs in the Development Sea. See the callout box for more details on some of these challenges.

Kickstarting to Success?

Kickstarter is the most popular and best-recognized crowdfunding platform for products and "rewards." However, studies suggest that in as many as 84% of the top-funded Kickstarter projects, backers did not deliver the promised goods on the original timeline.[68] Moreover, 9% of Kickstarter projects never deliver rewards to backers[69] at all. It turns out that actually developing the product and getting it into the hands of backers is harder than many entrepreneurs anticipate, often due to technical debt.

The reasons for these delays include the following:

- *Manufacturing obstacles.* Jake Bronstein created a new company, Flint and Tinder, to offer men's underwear made in the United States. He had expected to sell 3,000 pairs and bought that volume of elastic. Surpris-

---

68 Julianne Pepitone, "Why 84% of Kickstarter's top projects shipped late," *money.CNN.com*, December 18, 2012, accessed April 18, 2018, http://money.cnn.com/2012/12/18/technology/innovation/kickstarter-ship-delay/index.html.

69 *Kickstarter.com*, "The Kickstarter Fulfillment Report," accessed April 18, 2018, https://www.kickstarter.com/fulfillment.

ingly, he sold 23,000 pairs of underwear. That meant he needed more supplies. Unfortunately, the elastic manufacturer needed several extra months to produce that much additional elastic. This delay and other problems in the manufacturing process drove his costs up. As a result, he made no profit on that product.[70] Flint and Tinder eventually sold to Huckberry and the brand exists today, but avoiding technical debt could have resulted in a much better outcome for Bronstein!

- *Changes in design specifications.* Haje Jan Kamps shared that, for his device Triggertrap Ada, design specifications changed dramatically once development started. He built the Kickstarter campaign (and its pricing) assuming that the device would use a lower-end microprocessor. As the design process progressed, he discovered he needed a more expensive microprocessor, which was bigger and had different functionality. Re-designing for the new microprocessor incurred time and cost delays.[71] Of course, that change also required more "tooling"— the metal fixtures and components for manufacturing the parts of the device. These changes to the specifications caused startup and ongoing costs to be higher than expected. This meant that pricing would be much higher. Investors were not willing to support the higher price, the campaign failed, and the company folded.

- *The high cost of small-volume manufacturing.* Many crowdfunding campaigns make assumptions about costs. However, sometimes per-unit costs are much lower for volume manufacturing, than for small runs. After the campaign hits its goal, it's not uncommon to discover that making a small number of items, say 3,000 instead of 300,000, costs much more per unit. Numerous crowdfunded campaigns have ended with the budding entrepreneur having to use their own funds to finish production. They actually lost money by offering the product.

- *Shipping challenges.* Crowdfunding campaign initiators have affectionately named this scenario "Shipocalypse." Even if manufacturing goes smoothly, the logistics of shipping are still complex—from figuring out which carrier to use, to choosing packaging, to packing the boxes, to printing labels, to sorting and delivering to the carrier. When you sell 23,000 units instead of 3,000, the shipping challenge expands proportionally.

70 Alyson Shontell, "How Raising $291,000 On Kickstarter Nearly Killed Underwear Startup Flint And Tinder," *Business Insider*, December 18, 2012, accessed April 18, 2018, http://www.businessinsider.com/flint-and-tinder-jake-bronstein-kickstarter-2012-12.

71 Haje Jan Kamps, "How Triggertrap's $500k Kickstarter campaign crashed and burned," *Medium*, March 1, 2015, accessed April 18, 2018, https://medium.com/@Haje/how-a-half-million-dollar-kickstarter-project-can-crash-and-burn-5482d7d33ee1.

Unnecessary Solution

Validating the problem and initial envisioned solution is still not enough. The startup still doesn't know that this product is necessary. The nagging question to explore is *why now?* Why has no one solved this problem already? The answer is rarely "no one ever thought of it before." Even more importantly, often you can find others who attempted—and failed—to solve the same problem with a similar solution. Their failure might mean they were bad entrepreneurs, but more likely, the problem was hard to solve or didn't need solving. A startup should make the effort to learn what its predecessors paid blood, sweat, and tears (as well as dollars) to learn.

 Navigation Plan: *Examine the history, supply, demand, and market validation of your idea. Use history and past attempts at creating a product similar to yours to help inform you and validate that this is the right time to launch your startup. Is the solution necessary now?*

A surprising number of entrepreneurs look back at their failed startups and synthesize what they learned from the failure. If you can find a "this is why I failed" post from the old founder, you can often validate assumptions that might have cost months and tens of thousands of dollars to do yourself.

 Navigation Plan: *Check out some lists that aggregate these failure stories: productgraveyard.com, startupgraveyard.io, and autopsy.io. Startup monitor CBInsights.com both analyzes startup postmortems and aggregates lists of postmortems.*

Once the startup has answered the question of "why now," it's time to start thinking about competition. No market is stagnant. Customers and competition are constantly evolving and changing. It is essential to a company's success to understand the marketplace and competition and to stay updated with the changes going on. It's tempting to look at a few of the largest competitors and focus on them. However, no product, service, or firm is too small or low-tech to ignore. Anything the market uses currently can become—and should be treated as—competition.

Many startups are convinced that "no one is doing what we are!" However, if the problem the startup solves is a real problem, then customers are already addressing it in some shape or fashion. The competition isn't just composed of similar solutions; competition includes all of the alternate problem solutions, including the dreaded "ignore it!" Lack of direct competition does not mean competition does not exist in an indirect form.

Navigation Plan: *When doing the validate-the-problem part of the interview with prospective clients, be sure to ask, "How are you currently addressing this problem?" (Better yet, observe them solving the problem.) Maybe the participant isn't solving the problem at all, or maybe they're using a very simple tool, like a spreadsheet or a notebook, instead of an app or software program. Look at all of these options and understand the implications of leaving the problem unsolved.*

Here's a great follow-up question: "Is your current solution the best one you know about, or is there a better solution out there? If there is a better solution, what is keeping you from buying or using that alternative?"

Overdo and Overspend

When it's time to start building the product, some founders can fall into a trap of wanting to develop every feature in version 1.0. The founder may start to throw money at design and building out a complete product. These mistakes waste time and money that the startup could spend more efficiently elsewhere.

While designing the foundation and content for a startup, the founder is bound to run into areas of conflict and *uncertainty*. Common examples include the following:

- Should the app have a sign-in feature?
- Should the welcome screen contain more copy than images?
- Will users hold the device in the right or left hand?
- How big is too big?
- Which feature is more important: lightweight or carrying capacity?

These are difficult decisions that can affect the bottom line. It can seem like a good idea to test whether to go with one decision over the other as part of the validation process. However, testing each and every decision with a developed product, even an *MVP*, can become paralyzing. There are always more tests you can do.

A/B testing is a common way to solve design conflicts (see the callout box to learn more about A/B testing). Though A/B testing is rigorous and effective, it can also be the most expensive way to make a design choice and can be overused.

A startup can do a much cheaper analysis in the validation phase by thinking through the outcomes and involving the customer in providing feedback—a deep thought experiment—as opposed to overspending on a functional widget. A thought experiment considers the outcomes of both A and B, and then chooses which has a better or more measurable outcome. Sometimes, a startup and its engineers can reach agreement in fifteen minutes, while an A/B test can consume fifteen days and considerably more resources. Even if the thought experiment doesn't conclude with an answer, it often exposes the testable facets of the issue in a way that shortens or improves the efficacy of an A/B test. Startups should only consider using A/B testing when the difference in results justifies the time and money investment.

 Navigation Plan: *Try talking out both options in an A/B test, comparing the results of one idea over the other. With some thought and insight, you might be able to make the right decision without having to run a physical test and gather the results. Use A/B tests with customers selectively as part of design, not validation.*

A/B Testing

A/B testing, also called split testing or bucket testing, is an experiment between two variants to see which performs better. These variants could be two different product features, two different shapes, two different colors, two different webpages, two different displays, two different subject lines in an email—you get the idea.

You can even use A/B testing to pick between two alternatives approaches. For example, does leaving the house's thermostat on at a lower temperature when you are out of the house in the summer save more money than turning off the air conditioning? Testing these alternatives requires running a multi-day experiment, across different houses, at different outside temperatures while measuring energy consumption. That's a rigorous testing process. So, first make sure that the alternatives you are testing are worth the effort. Then, decide on the right performance metric. Finally, fairly test each alternative against that metric. Move forward with the one that performs better.

Best practice is to have a hypothesis that you are testing. In our example, the hypothesis might be "turning the air conditioning off saves more money because you use less energy to re-cool a home than keep it cool continuously." Testing a hypothesis gives a startup a way to learn facts about what matters in different situations. The startup can then use this new knowledge to generate new hypotheses and run more experiments. The value of A/B testing is both finding an answer in an uncertain situation and learning about market needs and preferences.

A/B tests can provide powerful insights, but they are time-consuming and can be expensive. Startups need to use A/B tests appropriately, at the right stage of development, to have the best payoff.

Lookout: *Be wary of startups with countless planned and executed A/B tests.*

Validation can also yield additional benefits. Through validation, Joe Gebbia and Brian Chesky of Airbnb learned that a key pain point with people offering accommodations on their site was knowing how to market their properties. As a result, Airbnb built features into the platform to capture and share best practices over time. Apoorva Mehta of Instacart learned from early validation to arm his "shoppers" with tools to do their jobs more efficiently and effectively. The shoppers needed maps and guides to the stores to speed up finding items on the list, so building those things into the app improved shopper satisfaction. Validation research not only can limit False Hope, Unnecessary Solution, and Overdo and Overspend icebergs—it can generate insights that allow for a deeper understanding of the problem and lead to additional *points of differentiation.*

The Design Sea

Many scholars believe that the crash itself could have been far less deadly if the engineers working on the Titanic *hadn't made negligent errors during the design of this massive ship. The design was left to Alexander Montgomery Carlisle and the chief engineer of the* Titanic *project, Bell. The problem facing Bell and his team was a large one. Ships of this size and complexity were at the forefront of technology. There was very little outside knowledge or prior experience from which to draw.*

The team spent three years building the Titanic *in Belfast, boasting that their technology helped devise a ship that was practically "unsinkable" thanks to a system of watertight compartments and electronic floodgates. Naturally, people were relieved and excited by this premise, as icebergs that could send the ship to the depths often plagued the journey across the North Atlantic. The idea was that if one of these ice behemoths punctured the ship, the compartment would seal off and the* Titanic *would be able to make it to shore safely. "Error proof!" declared the engineers.*

There were sixteen "watertight" compartments on the Titanic. *The ship could stay afloat with four, at most, of the compartments flooded. These compartments were protected by bulkheads, which were watertight walls in between the compartments. The theory was that in the event of a tear, these walls would've been able to contain the water. However, the walls didn't go all the way up to the ceiling. This is the critical design flaw of the* Titanic. *The compartments were only watertight when the ship was horizontal. When water stormed into the* Titanic *after it hit the iceberg, it filled the front of the compartment and its weight caused the compartment to lean and spill over the tops of the walls—something the engineers of the* Titanic *did not account for. This filled the ship with even more water and sped up the sinking process.*

The Physics of Size versus Speed

Physics and competition help us understand why the White Star Line shifted from speed, its differentiator in the late 1800s, to size. Cunard, the rival line, was challenging White Star on speed. As ships get faster, the power demands increase at an exponential rate. Above 20 knots per hour, (about 23 mph) the incremental cost and power requirements grow substantially faster than the improvement in speed. As profits—or lack thereof—were already a concern for White Star, it shifted to size and luxury as its competitive advantage. This shift had unanticipated consequences for ship design and development.

The problem that White Star's design came up against was the Froude number. The Froude number is a ratio that suggests boats run at a speed of the square root of their length. Moving boats create a wave crest at the bow and trough at the stern. The longer the boat, the longer the wave crest at the bow. This wave functions as a wall of resistance. Sufficient power is required to get the boat over the hump in the resistance curve it creates. That became the engineering problem White Star had to solve—powering the *Titanic* over its resistance curve.

It's hard to anticipate all of the possible outcomes of a design. However, an important part of design has to be to imagine the unimaginable. What are all of the ways that the design could fail, or at least not meet customer needs, in actual use?

At this point, a startup has some solid facts and customer input from the initial validation process. Now it is time to lay down some solid visualizations and work through design parameters of the idea before starting down a path from which it cannot return. Unfortunately, this process creates its own debtbergs. The iceberg drifts in the Design Sea include:

- Missing Mockups
- Ivory Tower "Insights"
- Shortsighted Scoping

Missing Mockups

Design is crucial to the success (and eventual monetization) of the product. Strike that—*good* design is crucial to success. Now comes the early work of figuring out what to build. The next step is to prototype and test.

Can the startup design a product that is going to work as a solution to the problem? To do this, the startup has to turn those ideas into reality. It has to get its ideas sketched onto paper—design plans, wireframes, and sketches—or built into a prototype. All of these, but especially wireframes, are blueprints of what the product will include. A startup must generate blueprints so that everyone understands the product while they're building it. Some prototypes of physical products might include quite a bit of duct tape, Styrofoam, and/or poster board. Rough prototypes or mockups are an efficient way to brainstorm, get feedback, and get everyone on the same page.

Think of building the first bicycle. Based on validation, customers might have understood the basic idea and encouraged the founders to build an early working version to test. As a function of their feedback, the startup might have chosen to go to an MVP with two wheels, a single gear, and a way to drive power from the pedals to the wheels. This might be the minimally viable path to market to get further feedback. Sweet! However, by showing a visual mockup or a prototype before taking this expensive step, the founding team might have learned that nobody could get enthused about a bike that did not have something to sit on (saddle) and a way to stop the bike (brakes). A prototype or sketch would have yielded additional necessary insight to get to a real MVP—and avoid some accidents in the process.

 Navigation Plan: *Startups should avoid going straight from a back-of-the-napkin concept to MVP. A mockup or wireframe is an important intermediate step.*

In the software world, founders often rush to a fully developed and technologically enabled product, even if the product is minimally viable. A preferred shortcut to full software product development is to build a hyper-thin frontend and manual backend—it feels like software to potential customers but in the back, a living, breathing human is doing many of the functions, often supplemented with off-the-shelf software tools. Think of it as a "low-resolution" initial solution.

While this may seem like tedious and slower work up front, it gives a startup a way to figure out how to make the product work. It can add and subtract features and benefits at little cost except effort. This effort pays back many multiples in time and money saved in not building unnecessary features. Furthermore, the startup can build necessary features with far less iteration. For other kinds of products, this might be a three-dimensional prototype with minimal-to-no real functional capabilities. It looks like the planned product without necessarily working.

Mei Xu did this kind of an experiment when trying to decide which home design product to launch. Rather than securing full-scale manufacturing for multiple products, she simply took some samples of five different products and tried to sell them at a gift show. Candles won, hands down—and Chesapeake Bay Candle had its signature product. Direct customer feedback helped to select the right solution. However, these were just basic versions. Once she knew candles were the right choice, Xu then had to decide what kinds of candles and develop her specific product line in terms of looks, scents, and colors, and secure manufacturing to scale.

A few years ago, an entrepreneur for a company we'll call Startup Echo wanted to create an application that would detect where severe weather hit and then immediately make automated phone calls asking if folks needed help with a tarp, roofing, etc. The idea was to generate leads for roofing companies in the following weeks. He had already spent $200,000 working with university professors and software developers on complex weather algorithms before even starting the automated phone system to call people once the weather system detected an area with potential damage.

By the time he was ready to start building software, the entrepreneur was out of cash. After we heard his *pitch*, we had a conversation like this:

Us: "Have you tried just looking at a weather map for a big line of "red" storm clouds and then calling a few dozen people in that area once the storm has passed and asking if they had house damage and needed immediate help?"

Him: "What would I do if they said yes?"

Us: "You could Google a roofing company in the area, call them, and ask if they wanted a lead."

Him: (Silent for a while, his face growing as red as a storm-filled weather map) "Why the f*** didn't anyone tell me that a year and $200,000 ago?!"

This entrepreneur could've saved a lot of time, money, and headaches by doing the process manually first and then building an automated tool once he figured out whether people actually wanted the service. Missing the mockup caused a giant iceberg to evolve.

Just remember that early mockups or wireframes will not be beautiful or complete. The first mockup is never as good as the product the founder imagines in her head. Early iterations should be rough or rudimentary, in part to avoid Overdoing and Overspending on design at the beginning. Moreover, a wireframe is typically just a very simple visualization of what could be. It just isn't that interesting to look at. Wireframes are good for making sure everyone is on the same page and avoid wasting effort in creating something no one likes.

 Navigation Plan: *Expect compromises. This is natural, and it's important not to let this stage leave you feeling defeated. Accept that early designs will be incomplete and not aesthetically pleasing.*

Wireframes 101

Wireframes are the digital equivalent of architectural plans. They are typically black-and-white and capture a software product or website. All of the information appears in a linear format with a logical flow. Typically, wireframes have a good bit of information, but are plain to look at. Check out this typical wireframe template for a website. It's really just a map of what a product might include.

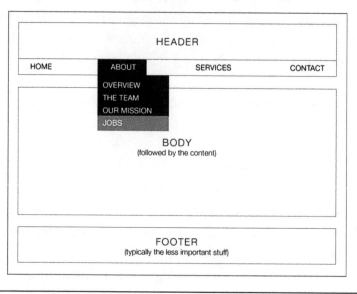

Ivory Tower "Insights"

When sailing through the Design Sea, it may be tempting to remain in the captain's quarters with the maps laid out. However, there is danger in remaining too far removed from the activities of the people sailing the ship. When traveling these waters, it's important to step away from the post to collect feedback from the people who are actually using the product.

After going through the trials of validation and design, it can feel like a waste to spend multiple days out of the office conducting tests and seeking feedback on those designs. Some might think it would be wiser and more efficient to spend hours in the captain's quarters, revising the imperfect design. However, this is a fatal mistake—at this stage, founders don't gain insights from the ivory tower, looking at or imagining user experiences from afar.

In the Validation Sea, we cautioned startups against A/B testing every aspect of the product. Instead, we suggested conducting thought experiments. However, being thoughtful about design can get a startup only so far. The design phase is a good time to seek customer input, and having a tangible representation of the design is crucial. While not every design choice requires an A/B test, taking the time to go into the field with design A and design B can be incredibly powerful.

When a design team comes on the scene, it can be easy for the founding team to step back and let the professionals do their work. However, not being involved in getting feedback directly from potential clients about the wireframes and prototypes risks not hearing and understanding the feedback firsthand. Startup founders cannot rely on others to do the testing for them and report back. Letting someone else experience customers' reactions is like the children's game of "telephone." What ultimately gets back to the startup could be very different from what customers actually said. The challenge, of course, is to be able to sort through the feedback, understand what's critical to incorporate, and avoid *pivoting* too frequently. This understanding is easier to develop when the startup hears the feedback firsthand rather than through others' interpretations. Understanding why A beat B, and how customers use both, is more important than just learning which version won in an A/B test.

Randy Hetrick of TRX frequently shares that he had at least fifty variations of his design before he homed in on the final product. That means he took at least forty-nine different versions of the product out to customers and "rejiggered" it each time until he got it right. Some of these re-jiggerings were relatively minor, such as to get the grip and adjustability of the TRX product right. In addition, these versions were not time-consuming or expensive to make since he made the changes himself. Importantly, he also did that testing personally so he could see firsthand what wasn't working. You have to appreciate Hetrick's persistence, even as you hope your own product doesn't needs forty-nine versions to find a "better than others" version.

 Navigation Plan: *It is critical to the success of a startup for you to leave the office and go to the users! Schedule testing during the pre-launch phase because that's when the feedback is most important. Find ideal users and then ask them for their opinion as they go through the designs. Having fresh eyes on a project helps best show where the product's usability needs improvement. From this information, it's possible to make updates to the product before it goes live.*

Founders should expect to stay close to the product and customers through the design process, even if a design team is in place. This limits the icebergs due to false or inappropriate insights from being too detached from user experience—there are few real insights from the ivory tower at this stage.

Shortsighted Scoping

Now that the startup is actively seeking customer input, it needs to make sure it is evaluating that feedback and planning appropriately with it. Rather than overreacting to every piece of customer input, a startup needs to think about how today's decisions will affect the future course of the product. Scoping design decisions must factor in not just short-term and reactive adjustment but also long-term goals and product direction.

In the initial design brainstorming sessions and with mock ups, it can be easy to get excited about small changes and feedback. It feels natural to take in feedback and redesign the app, webpage, or product prototype. Beware—these quick reactions grow design debt in the first few months. In the best-case scenario, the design specifications for the MVP have already been set from the validation phase. Not hitting the Missing Mockups iceberg can help.

Feedback here can provide minor tweaks to the MVP, but more likely will help scope the longer-term development plan. It's better to move forward with a less-than-perfect product than to keep iterating through designs until the product is absolutely perfect. An oft-repeated shorthand for this is "Done, then iterate!" instead of the problematic "Iterate until done!" In other words, continuous iteration can feel like failure because the output isn't exactly as envisioned. However, it's better to get it to 90% of what you want it to be and call it done than to spend hours agonizing over perfecting that last 10%. Without customer feedback, those hours could be wasted on perfecting something that didn't need the extra work.

Navigation Plan: *Once you've developed mockups and are receiving customer input, sort out the feedback that requires changing the MVP from the feedback that provides scope for long-term development. Avoid making major, drastic changes to the MVP unless they are critical for launch.*

Often, startups have an assumption that users will interact with the platform using only one type of device (such as a smartphone) when, in fact, they typically use it on another (like a desktop computer). The device where users use the product matters. A lack of appropriate scoping of necessary features at the right stage can lead to both overdevelopment and a lack of design incorporating critical elements.

For example, let's consider Startup Bravo, the health IT startup that we talked about in the Marketing Ocean Chapter. It was having good success with a mobile communication platform for physicians and care teams. The development team initially assumed that users would interact with the product through a mobile phone platform, so it created a robust design for smartphones. In early trials, however, it became evident that nurses using the platform for scheduling and notification rather than patient communication were primarily doing so on a desktop computer. In fact, nurses rarely used mobile phones while on shift. Moving some features to desktop computer-only and others to desktop-and-mobile phone simplified the design for major components of the launch system.

Mobile phones themselves are an interesting example of change in user experience. Originally, mobile phones functioned only as phones (and bad ones at that). By the year 2000, the first camera appeared in a mobile phone. Dial forward four years and in the third quarter of 2004, two-thirds of mobile phones purchased had a camera onboard. By that time, cameras on phones outsold actual standalone cameras. Now, smartphones have much of the functionality of a computer (even though they are still not great phones).

Anticipating how a product might break is also important. Airbnb discovered the pitfalls of shortsighted scoping when, in 2011, a guest who booked the space through the platform trashed a host's apartment. The company had not planned for such an incident. Unsurprisingly, the story hit the front covers of the *New York Times*, *Wall Street Journal*, and *Financial Times*. When it happened, Jonathan Golden, former Director of Product, said, "it created a media firestorm with many predicting the end of Airbnb. We had never encountered such an existential crisis." [72]

Listings made through Airbnb dropped precipitously. It was crucial for the company to restore trust and credibility with its hosts. Golden described how Airbnb approached its *strategy*: "assembling a small team of five, we spent the next two weeks fully operationalizing a program that involved legal, marketing, product, and operations." Airbnb decided to offer the hosts insurance of up to $50,000—despite having no insurance company at the time—by self-insuring, even though it meant assuming up to $500 million in exposure.

The plan worked. After only a few claims, they eventually found an insurer and stabilized trust, allowing them to increase coverage to $1 million. By responding quickly, Airbnb was able to maneuver around its iceberg and resume navigation. However, a lack of anticipation of how the product might break could have sunk the ship.

Solid design incorporates a deep understanding of the *user experience*—not just all the things that users might want, but also how things might go wrong. User experience (often referred to as "UX") relates to how a person feels when using or interacting with a product. In software, this can include the product's ease of use, the level of frustration it creates, or how aesthetically pleasing it is. When considering UX, it is important to consider how the users will utilize the product in the course of their daily

---

72   Jonathan Golden, "Lessons Learned Scaling Airbnb 100X," *Medium*, August 15, 2017, accessed April 18, 2018, https://medium.com/@jgolden/lessons-learned-scaling-airbnb-100x-b862364fb3a7.

lives and the platform on which they will use it. The key with UX is to put the product in users' hands and watch what they do. Customers often do completely different things with new products than we expect—and the more disruptive the product, the more likely unanticipated uses are.

 Navigation Plan: *Envision how your design will respond to different platforms or circumstances. It is much simpler to create a responsive design from the start, ready for potential issues, than to try to improve an inflexible design that only works in one specific instance or on one device.*

Think through various scenarios the user could experience when using your product—and be sure not to avoid the negative ones. Are there any areas that might be confusing? Is there potential for someone to use your product maliciously? Are there weak spots that might expose your user to harm? It's better to think about these questions when designing the product than when disaster strikes—you'll have much more time to think through a solid solution.

The best teams in the world know that wireframes are great for testing concepts, but nothing gets a team learning faster than real customers using real software do. To get there as fast as possible, the team builds an *MVP*. The MVP, or minimum viable product, is the smallest thing that delivers value to the customer. It's important for a startup to start small and add to the product over time so that it can collect and adapt to feedback. The idea of an MVP is not to cut corners everywhere; it's to simplify to what's critical. Milton Glaser, one of most celebrated American graphic designers, who won both a Fulbright Lifetime Achievement Medal and a National Medal of Arts, noted in an essay titled *Ten Things I Have Learned*: "Less isn't more, just enough is more."[73] It's okay to do less. Just do less exceptionally well and not with shoddy design.

Roger Ehrenberg, COO of failed Monitor110, attributes that startup's demise to spending too much time trying to get the product perfect before putting it into customers' hands. Monitor110 intended to be an investor news aggregator. Co-founder Jeff Stewart was the technology lead for Monitor110. Although the founders said they wanted to "release early/release often," when it came time to put a product in front of customers, they got nervous that they would look stupid in front of Wall Street and hedge fund customers if not everything worked perfectly. They also had appeared on the cover of the *Financial Times*. To them, this extra attention only made them want to have the perfect product even more.

They worked for three years trying to make the perfect product leveraging the latest technology. However, technology is constantly evolving. As soon as they thought they

---

73   Milton Glaser, "Ten Things I Have Learned: Part of an AIGA Talk in London," *MiltonGlaser.com*, accessed April 18, 2018, http://www.miltonglaser.com/milton/c:essays/#4.

had the perfect product, it needed new enhancements. Three years and $20 million later, they had an unwieldy design that didn't produce great results for customers. They needed to make a major technology pivot to a simpler approach for user experience, but it was too late and Monitor110 folded instead. Ehrenberg notes that if they had put an early version into customers' hands, they probably would have been successful.[74]

 Navigation Plan: *Strike a balance. Make sure you are incorporating features that are necessary to solving the core problem without overdoing it with added frills.*

Moving a product idea from Validation to Design is hard. Expectations are high. Seeing early prototypes is typically underwhelming and possibly disappointing, but a necessary step to avoiding Missing Mockups. The purpose of the Design phase is to plot the course of the product as it moves into development. Being down in the trenches, meeting customers face-to-face, seeing how they use the product, and giving them permission to try to break it yields important insights about what is critical for launch. These steps also help lay out a development plan to carry the new product from launch to growth, avoiding the Shortsighted Scoping drift. Investing time and effort in design can help a startup head into Development with full sails and avoid misleading insights from the Ivory Tower and debtbergs created by Shortsighted Scoping.

The Development Sea

Product development means actually building out the product. For the Titanic, *the build-out took longer than White Star expected and longer than it had for the Olympic. In fact, some people believe that if the* Titanic's *build-out had been on schedule, it might have avoided the iceberg season altogether when crossing the Atlantic for its maiden voyage. This build-out was both long and fraught with peril. Imagine a ship standing 104 feet tall being ensconced in massive steel plates. It was hard to make sure every one of the nearly 15,000 workers was in the right place at the right time. Before the ship even entered the water, 246 injuries occurred with twenty-eight that were described as "severe" because of severed arms and crushed legs. Six workers even died during construction. Process-wise, this was a complex development task.*

Part of the tragedy of the Titanic *began with the lack of raw materials to implement the design and build three large ships almost simultaneously. Building three mammoth vessels required a huge amount of steel plates, wood, and rivets. Rivets are the bolts that*

74 Roger Ehrenberg, "Monitor110: A Post Mortem," *Business Insider*, July 19, 2008, accessed April 18, 2018, http://www.businessinsider.com/2008/7/monitor110-a-post-mortem.

hold together two pieces of metal. Think of them as the glue that holds together the different pieces of the Titanic. *It was important that the rivets were made of steel, as steel is an alloy that is much stronger than a pure metal like iron or silver.*

Shipbuilder Harland and Wolff needed more than three million rivets, but there just weren't that many steel rivets available. Instead, the shipyard had to use a combination of steel and slag rivets. Slag is the scrap metal collected from the making of steel. Slag's imperfections made the rivets more fragile and prone to damage. This meant that the foundation of the Titanic *was of poor quality in places. On that fateful night, the rivets tore, contributing to the ship flooding quickly. Better rivets would perhaps have kept the* Titanic *floating long enough for rescuers to arrive.*

The availability of high quality raw materials was not the only development challenge. Halfway through the build, White Star learned that the market was stronger for a grander ship. During construction, J. Bruce Ismay decided to create a more dramatic entryway, double the height of the ballroom, and expand the promenades for the first-class passengers. These changes required the designers to lower the bulkheads—a technical debt that allowed the water to spill over the lowered bulkheads when the ship shifted. These changes also resulted in reducing the number of lifeboats on board. While the number of lifeboats exceeded the accepted safety standard at the time, it would be enough only if packing passengers into the lifeboats was optimized. It left little room for error on the part of the crew. Under duress, of course, is when people are most likely to commit errors, unfortunately. This combination magnified the catastrophic loss of life.

It might seem that, since we put this Sea after the other two, product development comes only after concept validation and product design are complete. Actually, the best startup teams are continuously validating, designing, and building as they go. During any new product launch, whether a software, medical, physical, or other kind of product, the members of the team should do the following:

- learn more about their own capabilities and theories
- discover what they guessed wrong about or learn more detail about market need
- realize the market itself is changing as time passes

That said, while Validation and Design are about building the right ship and plotting a course, Development happens when the startup has settled on the initial product it will sell. Staying on course with the original product design or strategically deviating from the initial plan: either choice create its own type of debtbergs.

The core navigation goal while in the perilous Development Sea is not to allow the changes driven by all the learning that will inevitably occur to sink the startup. The three iceberg drifts in the Development Sea include the following:

- Mushy Process
- Poor Product Foundation
- Foggy Waters

Mushy Process

The startup has validated that the product fits the market, and the design team has produced an MVP to get customer feedback. The solo designer or outsourced resource has a good mental map of next steps.

Then the real world hits. There is a big demo for a tradeshow, or one make-or-break customer that the startup desperately needs who is demanding unique features. The brilliant developer, knowingly or unknowingly, takes a few shortcuts to hit the deadline. Then the next deadline shows up....and the next. When the real journey to product/market fit ends up taking twelve, twenty-four, or even thirty-six months, adhering to sound development practices and remembering hoped-for product development changes becomes difficult. The inability to stay true to a rational process for product fixes and development starts to cause leaks in the ship from icebergs of increasing size.

Even if there is a single engineer, a startup needs to follow good practices to avoid incurring serious technical debt that will cause their ability to react to the marketplace to grind to a halt:

- The startup should maintain a continuously ordered list of user stories and features. (In software development, we call this list a *backlog*—an ordered list of everything the company knows should be in the product. See the callout box below for more on backlogs.)
- Even though they may change, major milestones can and should be ballparked on a timeline.[75]
- The team should use one of the many team tools for managing backlogs, items in progress, and completion of Agile product development activities.
- In a software development world, the startup team must build a process that incorporates testing, peer review, and automated code quality tools *and* must review the results every single cycle. There are many parallels to these processes for physical product development or perfecting an innovative service.

---

75   Brett Harned, "The How and Why of Using Milestones in Your Project Plan," *TeamGantt*, February 14, 2017, accessed April 18, 2018 https://www.teamgantt.com/blog/the-how-and-why-of-using-milestones-in-your-project-plan/.

In 1981, the Hyatt Regency Kansas City hotel experienced the consequences of a poor building process when two hanging walkways collapsed—killing 114 and injuring 216. Upon investigation, an architectural engineer discovered that there was a change that appeared to be minor to the original design plans. In the original design, both walkways attached to the same continuous-threaded rod from the ceiling. The rod was long, and a nut needed to be threaded almost the entire length of the rod to secure it. To avoid spinning nuts twenty feet up the threaded rod, the builder decided to cut the threaded rod into two and hang the lower walkway from the upper. This meant the upper walkway now had to support its own weight and the "not-designed-for" weight of the lower walkway. In the courtroom, it was unclear whether someone made a mistake during the required inspections or a Mushy Process allowed the change to slip through without the necessary reviews and sign-offs. This development iceberg had a tragic outcome for many.[76]

Backlogs and Sprints

A backlog starts with all of the features to build into a software product. The team then breaks each feature into manageable steps called backlog items, and assigns the backlog items to product release dates. This allows everyone to get both a high-level view of what needs doing, as well as the specific steps it will take to get there.

By dividing features into backlog items, project managers are able to create *sprints*—work cycles (typically fourteen to thirty days long), that focus on iteration. This is part of the *Agile software development methodology*.[77]

Say your team has a two-week sprint cycle. At the beginning of the cycle, the whole team collaborates on determining the most important backlog items, and the development team commits to getting them done. In exchange for the commitment to get them done, the rest of the team agrees not to throw in new requirements or changes during the sprint. This prevents demoralizing direction changes. The end of each sprint cycle creates a great opportunity for incorporating customer feedback, reprioritizing backlog items, and showing off actual working product features.

 Navigation Plan: *When entering the development phase, consider visiting a few teams that are multiple years into iterating their products so you can take notes. Make the commitment to a process even when it might feel slower or more painful upfront.*

---

76   The Engineer, "Hyatt Regency Walkway Collapse," *Engineering.com*, October, 24, 2006, accessed September 5, 2018, https://www.engineering.com/Library/ArticlesPage/tabid/85/articleType/ArticleView/ArticleID/175/PageID/199/Default.aspx.

77   See Ries, Marcus and Diana Summers, *Agile Project Management: A Complete Beginner's Guide To Agile Project Management.* CreateSpace Independent Publishing Platform, 2016.

The painful reality of lurching towards a better product (and the changes required along the way) is why solid foundation and structure are critically important. When it comes time to make updates based on what the team is learning—in addition to the real world changing over time—updates have to be possible without causing a problem that will sink the ship. This requires a process to capture learnings from existing users, as well as to plan changes and new additions to product features. Communication internally is critical here—often the development team is detached from the actual users of the product. A solid process allows for learning across members of the startup.

 Navigation Plan: *Make sure all major features and tasks are on some type of list or backlog and that you spend the effort necessary to order and reorder that list.*

Lookout: *Engineers, and even founders, sometimes end up working first on the most challenging technical feature or the one that is most interesting to them. Watch for signs of this and help prioritize mission-critical development, even if it is not the most fun development task.*

The last night the Titanic *stood as a functioning ship, the lack of a proper system for handling information caused huge problems for the crew. On the night of the crash, at around 9:40 p.m., the* Titanic *received a message from nearby ship the Californian. During this time, the senior wireless officer, Jack Phillips, was desperately trying to send out hundreds of messages from ship passengers. As a luxury liner, the* Titanic *wanted to make it easy for passengers to share their excitement with friends and family. The telegraph was a new system for doing so, and passengers were eager to try it.*

At the same time, an operator from the Californian was trying to tell Phillips about dangerous icebergs approaching. The Californian's messages were interfering with Phillips transmissions and Phillips was getting frustrated. He sent the Californian a message back: "Shut up! Shut up! I am busy." The Californian cut off transmission with the Titanic *to prevent further message interference. This ship was less than an hour away from the* Titanic *but there was no way to communicate between the two. Later in the night, the captain of the Californian would not notice the* Titanic's *distress signals until after it was too late to help. The new technology combined with a mushy process for prioritizing and sharing messaging was a contributor to the* Titanic *disaster.*

Poor Product Foundation

A codebase or a mechanical design can become so filled with technical debt that building on top of it is about as easy as building a penguin pyramid on top of rain-slicked iceberg. (For those who have not had this experience, it is really hard).

One specific iceberg that occurs is that engineers can become so focused on building a product feature quickly that they fail to create a plan to test the quality of the work. In software development, most modern programming languages provide support to incorporate testing into actual code as the product is being developed. This is absolutely critical because, as the product complexity increases, each new change has the potential to cause the growing list of prior features to fail. Building tests for each feature as you go means that every time the team develops a new feature, it can run the prior tests—usually in an automated fashion—to ensure the old features still work. In a world of cloud-based software (*SaaS*), where everything is supposed to "just work 24x7," using built-in, automated testing is essential if an engineering team is to have any chance of delivering on that expectation. Plus, because the complexities of the feature are top-of-mind when the engineer is writing the test, it costs much less to build the testing simultaneously than it would be to come back and try to wedge it in later.

 Navigation Plan: *Create a process for peer review. When engineers review each other's work before releasing it for production and distribution, there is the double benefit of cross-learning and the prevention of bugs. Perhaps even more important is that engineers tend to build far better features when they know for certain that a fellow engineer is going to see their work!*

Two days after its launch in 1854, the RMS *Tayleur* ("the first *Titanic*"), another full rigged clipper ship chartered by the White Star Line, got stuck in a storm. That storm ended up being terrible timing to discover that the rudder (used for steering the ship) was too small for the boat—making it hard to turn. On top of that, the rigging (the system of ropes used to support a ship's masts) wasn't working. Typically, ropes need to be pre-stretched before field use, but the ropes were not pre-stretched, resulting in too much slack and difficulty in controlling the sails. In an attempt at control, the crew dropped both anchors, but the ship ran aground. Had the crew run tests or had a series of task reviews in place, the ship likely would have had a different fate. Of the 650 aboard the *Tayleur*, only 280 survived.

Let's focus on software development for a minute because writing a large codebase is a beast unto its own. The more code you add, the more out of hand it can get—especially if there is only one developer.

Imagine this common scenario: The founding team keeps asking the developer for updates. They get the gist of what's going on, and they're happy. Then development output plateaus, and the founding team attributes the slowed productivity to the growing product. The team hires another developer. However, this new developer can't make sense of the codebase.

There can be a huge barrier to entry for a new developer when code becomes so complex that it's really only understandable by the first developer. When progress becomes more important than process, the product's code can collect inefficient, unnecessarily complicated code. This contributes to a Poor Product Foundation.

 Lookout: *If your engineer has the view that no one else is able to work on the product, it may be time to start looking for his or her replacement. Make the transition before you have insurmountable debtbergs weighing down your startup!*

Navigation Plan: *It turns out that developers almost never do a great job of documenting code. However, when you have built-in testing that came from peer review and automated code quality tools, that codebase becomes profoundly more readable by future developers joining the team.*

Audrey Ledoux, founder of startup Spinvite,[78] highlights the development mistakes she made in the Poor Product Foundation drift. It was 2014 and Spinvite wanted to be an app that showed what events all of your friends were attending. Rather than emailing/texting or pulling information from multiple social media sources, friends would join the app and list activities they wanted other friends to join. To minimize her costs, Ledoux outsourced all of the development work. After launching the app, Ledoux learned that most outsourced developers care more about being paid than making you the perfect product. She'd never done any product testing; she did not know how to quality-check the product she received.

She describes the development process as having these steps:

1. Sketches
2. Prototype
3. *Alpha testing* (first internal customer)
4. *Beta testing* (first external customer)
5. At the app store

---

78   Audrey Ledoux, "Spinvite—The Party's Over: A Post-Mortem," *AudreyLedoux.com*, March 4, 2018, accessed April 18, 2018, https://www.audreyledoux.com/single-post/2017/09/12/Spinvite---The-Partys-Over-A-Postmortem.

Notice what's missing: second, third, and 123rd beta tests, quality checks, continuous updates, and fixes. She ran out of money before the real testing and correction phase got started. Along the way, of course, timelines slipped and the product got way behind schedule. Spinvite released a pretty but not very functional beta version, but never moved to a scalable and usable app.

When development accelerates and changes become more frequent, planning to have more than one engineer on the project becomes critical to have them test each other's work. As volume of use increases with more customers and more functionality, *load testing*, or testing the maximum functional capacity of the system, becomes paramount to avoid the Poor Product Foundation drift. This includes a plan for how to integrate new members into the development team.

Lookout: *The more people on a project, the faster the process of building should be. If adding development resources is not increasing output at the expected rate, a startup could be suffering from Poor Product Foundation icebergs.*

Product companies have their own forms of technical debt. As TRX began to take off, Hetrick faced a supply challenge. At the beginning, he made all of his inventory by hand. As sales took off, Hetrick had to move beyond buying strips of fabric and sewing finished product himself, so he contracted with a manufacturing firm to meet demand.

An early lot of inventory came in for distribution to customers. Anxious to test the product and get revenue in the door, Hetrick relates, "We hooked up the suspension trainer and leaned back, and the handles just cracked like potato chips." Randy and colleagues had to go back to making the product themselves in order to meet orders that had already been placed. This was a costly problem in dollars as well as time for TRX—but nowhere near the magnitude of iceberg that a wrongful death lawsuit and product liability claim would have resulted in. Through quality control and testing, albeit manual, Hetrick avoided a ship-sinking event.

There can be a push or preference to be in control of the entire development process. It's common to want to have all the work done in-house. After all, isn't that the only way to make sure of a sustainable and trustworthy product? In fact, subcontracting to outside sources can be viable and even necessary to scale. A startup needs to be willing to bring in some outsourced work (to avoid the Reactive Employee Resource Type drift in the Human Ocean).

The big concern about outsourcing is "quality fade" as these vendors try to improve their margins and cut quality, as happened with Hetrick/TRX, or subcontract to companies with lower standards. If a startup moves to outsourcing, it still needs to enforce its quality standards. It needs to manage these relationships proactively, applying the same standards as it uses on itself, or it will incur unnavigable technical debtbergs, with failed products leading to disappointed customers and even injuries and lawsuits.

 Navigation Plan: *Consider what aspects of development work to out-source and when, making sure to include minimum quality standards in any outsourcing contracts. For software development, skilled buyers know that the use of automated code quality tools and trusted internal or part-ner resources for peer review can make an enormous difference.*

Foggy Waters

Congratulations, you have a few customers or users and your product is off the ground! A startup finally gets momentum, and customers are increas-ing in number and value to the firm. For a founder, it's hard not to relax, have a beer, and bask in the glory of a newly released product. However, this is only the beginning.

So many startups that make it through the early, treacherous waters of launch end up foundering at the discipline required to operate continuously. More and more of the *venture's* activity migrates out of the direct sight lines of the founding team, even if the team is not locked in the Ivory Tower. During this stage of a company, it's import-ant to keep the hunger and enthusiasm that was there at the beginning. Easing up now could diminish all of the hard work put in.

Now the team has to grow and fully develop the product. Technology changes every day, and startups have to keep up with customer demands and head off emerging competition. Startups can't allow service interruptions, but ensuring that monitoring is in place *and* that the process for responding to alerts always works are tasks that tor-ment a shockingly high number of startups at this phase. This is where the team often gets so busy that they forget to "be the customer" and use their own service with fresh eyes from time to time. This can result in embarrassingly basic oversights on customer experience. It is a particularly bad time to lose sight of customers and the development plan in Foggy Waters.

The Chesapeake Bay Candle founders learned the hard way that you cannot relax once the product launches. Early on, they secured distribution in Bloomingdale's, Nordstrom, and about 3,000 boutiques. It sounds great, but Xu knew she needed a big-box merchandiser to be really successful.

It took her over a year of calling the buyer at Target every week to get a meeting. For that meeting, Xu innovated new colors and fragrances specifically to address the needs of the Target customer. At that meeting, she secured a contract that would require building a new factory in China, finding new distributors, and putting an inventory management system in place. Xu never expected to walk out of her first meeting at Target with a $3 million contract. She says, "I was completely caught off guard."[79] Instead of being able to bask in this accomplishment, Xu quickly had to build the capabilities needed to complete this contract. That meant building a factory, making the candles, and importing them back to the United States in time for the upcoming shopping rush. She did and Target turned into an $8 million annual customer—that's a lot of $10 candles.

Notice that Chesapeake Bay Candle innovated the product after it launched. So too will most startups. Products need constant innovation and evolution. The development plan and process has to account for these future innovations. Planning for these changes gives a startup the ability to take a longer-term view. For example, most new pharmaceutical products have a development plan to take the product from launch through the entire patent life—on average, that's a twelve-year[80] planning horizon.

 Navigation Plan: *Include product evolution ideas on the development plan or backlog. Make sure the development team is planning for next-generation products well before launch. Differentiate between new features in an existing product versus new product offerings.*

As the company grows, it remains important to monitor how customers actually interact with the product. That is not just a design challenge! Many startups invest a lot in Google Analytics to see who's coming to their websites; however, they fail to invest in actual app analytics, customer use metrics, or in-market customer monitoring. Even if these metrics do exist in the product, the startup may not be monitoring and evaluating them. The company flies blind until it finds something that can measure how long people are spending with the product, what features they use, and what features they don't use.

After launching a new prescription drug, one pharmaceutical company wondered how long patients were taking their prescriptions. The company worked with a drug store chain that called customers one, two, and three months after they'd picked up their new prescriptions. The feedback they got was shocking—20% of patients bought the prescription but didn't take the drug at all. At the end of the second month, 80% of patients had stopped taking the drug. The number one reason for stopping was

---

79   Lindsay Blakely, "How We Landed on Target's Shelves," *CBSNews Money Watch*, January 11, 2011, accessed April 18, 2018, https://www.cbsnews.com/news/how-we-landed-on-targets-shelves/.

80   Most patents last for twenty years after invention. However, the average pharmaceutical takes eight years to arrive on the market, leaving only twelve years of exclusivity from the patent.

price. The company began actively managing sales *promotions* to encourage its customers to continue using its products. Landing the customer is not enough—tracking interaction over time and understanding the lifetime value of a customer becomes necessary to avoid the Foggy Waters drift.

Monitoring customer usage has multiple benefits. First, it provides feedback for continuous product improvement. It also points out opportunities to improve the customer experience. Finally, it identifies ways to improve customer retention. The average smartphone user has downloaded nearly 100 apps to their phone. However, they tend to use only nine per day and thirty per month.[81] These statistics have been fairly stable for the last few years. Consider how better understanding customer usage could improve the chances that any one app gets better utilization.

Monitoring customer usage can even shine a light on whether the entire business model is viable. Juicero secured $134 million in funding to build an Internet-connected device to squeeze its packet of high-quality diced fruits and vegetables.[82] Founder Doug Evans aspired to be the Keurig of smoothies. The connectivity element tracked inventory and monitored freshness. The device originally retailed for $699 to $1200, depending on whether it was for personal or business use.

After customers got the device and the juice packets at home, these early adopters discovered that they could just squeeze the packets by hand. (It did not help Juicero that *Bloomberg* published this fact.) They also realized they were not too concerned about the automated inventory monitoring and freshness features of the expensive device. Juicero tried some fixes—reducing the device price, only selling juice packets to people who had bought the device—but it was too late. Juicero had over-engineered the product and didn't monitor what people were doing with it. Juicero shuttered after its product was in the market for only sixteen months.

 Navigation Plan: *Put tracking in place to monitor user activity. This feedback has multiple benefits for product development and long-term strategy.*

Let's take a step back. Nothing has changed from the beginning of this process. The customer should continue to be at the center of the startup's product design. To gauge customers' reaction, a startup needs customer service people, in addition to customer analytics, to pass customer input to product development. Having your finger

---

81   Sarah Perez, "Report: Smartphone owners are using 9 apps per day, 30 per month," *Techcrunch.com*, May 4, 2017, accessed April 18, 2018, https://techcrunch.com/2017/05/04/report-smartphone-owners-are-using-9-apps-per-day-30-per-month/.

82   Sam Levin, "Squeezed out: widely mocked startup Juicero is shutting down," *The Guardian.com*, September 1, 2017, accessed May 5, 2018, https://www.theguardian.com/technology/2017/sep/01/juicero-silicon-valley-shutting-down.

on the pulse of customer support issues also allows the team to have an advanced warning when dissatisfaction is mounting.

No captain would skip lookouts, waiting until he hits an iceberg to begin steering. However, you'd be shocked how many startups launch with a "strategy" to let the crashes happen and let the screams of passengers (or customers) be their warning system. Alternately, they take the time to install an amazing automated warning system, but then don't assign anyone to look at the control panel.

Monitoring customer service can give a startup a couple of quick wins in addition to identifying what parts of the product are broken. Commonly asked questions of service people can translate into frequently asked questions (FAQs) documents or a page on a website for users to help themselves. For example, TurboTax has an online community where people can ask questions. Given the number and variety of questions it's already answered, TurboTax can show customers the most commonly asked questions and their answers. This capability makes customer service proactive rather than reactive. It can also lead to increased sales. A recent study from Zendesk notes that 62% of B2B customers and 42% of B2C customers purchase more after a customer service encounter.[83]

Development is the most long-lasting Sea in the Technical Ocean. This is where the hard work of creating a product comes together. This is where planning for the future happens. This is where the need to manage continuous improvement appears. It's critical to set up a development process that plans to incorporate more than one person, keeps tracks of changes, and uses the team to prioritize changes. A startup needs a quality control and testing process to make sure the product will actually work—whether it's developed completely in-house or outsourced—to avoid a Poor Foundation and Mushy Process. Finally, the development plan also needs to have a long-term perspective based on continuous improvement and customer feedback to avoid the perils of Foggy Waters.

Navigating Technical Debt

The Technical Ocean is where product/market fit comes to life. To launch and scale, a startup needs to be able to build and iterate on its product without building insurmountable debt. While there are specific navigation tips spread throughout the chapter, here are three higher-level suggestions for navigating in this treacherous Ocean. They include:

- Plan the Plan
- Make It a Team Sport
- Test, Test, Test

---

83 Dimensional Research, "The impact of customer service on customer lifetime value," *Zendesk.com Library*, April 2013, accessed April 18, 2018, https://www.zendesk.com/resources/customer-service-and-life-time-customer-value/.

Plan the Plan

The art of shipbuilding is not in the wood. Products don't emerge from raw materials, and don't evolve without intentional planning. Code does not naturally evolve into software. Furthermore, a product is not a company. Building the right ship, plotting the right course, and staying on that course should all be parts of a comprehensive plan.

Two levels of planning are helpful to map out early in the startup journey. The first, product-focused plan lays out the entire workflow of the customer experience and how it will evolve over time. To start, there will be a lot of gaps in information, particularly about later stages in the journey—but placeholders should identify these gaps, with part of the plan being when, how, and who will fill in the gaps. Think of a placeholder as a slide deck with some slides that have titles but no content—they are holding places for information to be filled in later. Initially, this might involve just three buckets: what happens before the customer starts using the product, what happens during, and what happens after. Obviously, this plan will become a lot more detailed as the startup gains insights into the customer journey.

At this stage, founders can start asking questions like the following:

- At what points in this plan are we ready to move from concept to wireframe/prototype to MVP to a developed product?
- What are the assumptions we are making about the customer journey and pain points, and where they are coming from?
- How can we initially validate these assumptions and develop a deep understanding of the customer experience?
- At what point do we expect to have a solution to offer?

Remember to start with the problem—don't lead with the solution.

An easy example of the planning process is website design. When founders have an idea, they often secure the domain name they think might represent their startup name. It is a holding place—the website is not active. As the concept moves forward, the founders might start to think through what a website will look like and what functions it will have. At some point, the startup formalizes the concept in a wireframe that maps these ideas—but the website is still not live.

In this analogy, a product in MVP is like a website that is live but has a few active pages and limited functionality. It makes the startup seem "real" to customers and outside stakeholders. As the startup moves forward to multiple customers, the website becomes a central hub for communication, and needs to be more robust. The website, though, evolves over time as customer and communication needs change, features are added, and new products developed. The product evolves similarly.

Planning the plan for the evolution of the company in tandem with the technical plan is important as well. See the Strategy Ocean for more on how this product plan to navigate the Technical Ocean should parallel the startup's plan for navigating the Human and Marketing Oceans as well.

Make It a Team Sport

Many startups begin with one engineer, or an idea and an outsourced engineer relationship. This is not bad initially, and may get the startup to a wireframe or even MVP in a cost-effective way. However, there's a perverse incentive for solo engineers to remain solo—to avoid embarrassment when someone new sees the shortcuts they took in product development. Even more so, an engineer who is not a founder might want the job security. After all, the engineer controls the product.

As technical debt mounts, though, the founding team may decide it is time to switch players and bring in a new engineer. This is often the moment that finally brings the emerging icebergs to light. Get a few beers in a group of startup CEOs, and many will vividly recount that horrible day and time when their new product development manager started a conversation with them like this, "Well boss, we learned a lot from the first version, but unfortunately we need to start over…"

By the time development really kicks in, the startup needs to avoid the Mushy Process drift. A process can't be followed if there isn't a team in place to follow it. Often, if founders have never hired or recruited a developer for the team, they won't know what to look for. The person doing the hiring may have little-to-no background on the technical requirement for the job—in software, this might be system architecture, responsive design, or using current tools. The person is stuck looking for an awesome engineer who can "do it all," but can't tell the difference between one who thinks he's awesome and one who actually is.

How do you address these issues? Development has to be a team sport. Initially, all the founders should be working closely with the development team to be on the same page to communicate features and objectives and build the technical plan. As the company moves to an MVP, it may be time to add development resources. A startup can accomplish this by outsourcing development tasks or hiring a coder, but eventually should plan to hire an internal CTO who both codes and guides development. This team will grow over time, but at least one founder should continue to engage in the development process, and the whole company should be aware of features, problems, and technical plans through early growth.

Test, Test, Test

Testing occurs at many levels, and can help avoid many of the debtbergs in the Technical Ocean. The first testing begins with assumptions about the pain points customers face, parts of the customer journey and experience, and available solutions. Systematically test those assumptions in the validation process. This avoids icebergs in both the Technical and Marketing Oceans.

Testing then occurs multiple times in designing a solution. Startups should systematically gather feedback as early as the prototype or wireframes and then as the concept evolves to an MVP and beyond. Continue to test and validate assumptions about how, when, and why the customer uses the product.

Testing goes beyond assumptions and customer feedback. It has a technical, product-facing side as well. For software, the core of the process that DeveloperTown uses to help clients develop scalable technology and avoid the big icebergs of Mushy Process involves three aspects:

- testing code (via coded, built-in tests that automate the process)
- grading code (with automated grading as a metric for robustness of the code)
- using peer review (with mutual respect and egos in check)

These three tasks reinforce Making It a Team Sport. There are equivalent tests for physical products, especially as the venture grows and outsources components. Have a way to identify quality fade in this stage through random or systematic inspection.

Startups by Stage

In some ways, the Seas in the Technical Ocean look like they are sequential. In reality, they are iterative. Each new piece of information acquired or product development milestone reached usually calls for revisiting assumptions, adding design elements, and updating the development plan. Let's revisit the four stages of a startup to explore how the relative focus and priorities of three Seas vary by stage: Pre-Revenue, MVP, Launch and Early Growth, and Scalable Product and Business Model.

Pre-revenue, the focus is primarily in the Validation Sea. A startup needs to spend time and effort here making sure any investments in product development will be valued by the market. This is the time to expand on lessons learned from avoiding Customer Value Void from the Tactical Implementation Sea in the Marketing Ocean. Get potential customers to tear your envisioned product offering apart. What's good? What needs improvment? How does this solve the problem better than current solutions? What competitors have you overlooked? Use mockups or wireframes to share early visions of the solution with customers without investing in building solutions as you transition to early design.

Next, it's time to identify the *must-have features* for an MVP. Develop the MVP to secure early paying customers. Now focus expands from Validation to Design and early Development. Startups can develop early visualizations of the MVP and then test them with potential customers. Envisioning and mapping the full-scale product with all of its bells and whistles is a good step. Then tear that product down to its core and identify the most important components of the MVP.

Map out a plan to get from MVP to the next couple of generations. Once you have an MVP, do some customer testing to try to break the product. Consider and observe all of the ways customers might actually use it. Update design specifications to try to minimize the downside of product misuse. This is the time to specify the design in more detail and make a development plan to work through those options.

At last, an actual product is in the hands of real paying customers. The launch design is done and in the market. Now, Development becomes the focus, with iterations back to Design. Customer product usage and customer service feedback are key. As customers are using the product, what works and what still needs more work? Run these new problems back through the design process. Update the backlog and keep new features prioritized with a team by following a solid process for capturing feedback and prioritizing development tasks.

Flesh out the development plan even more to bring on more resources to move through new product iterations faster and with higher quality. Consider whether you can outsource some aspects of development. Throughout, maintain quality-testing efforts. Good customer experience with early versions of the product will help a startup maximize its Early Growth stage.

As a startup reaches the Scalable Product and Business Model stage, the product needs to be scalable as well. The focus stays with Development, adding iterations back through Validation and Design. The first goal is to work through the backlog of features in a series of product updates. In addition, monitoring customer use and customer service issues can help identify even more product updates. The emphasis is now on continuous improvement. Monitor for signs of Poor Product Foundation as the startup grows rapidly.

A startup should continue to monitor competitors as well. If the customer is at the center of product development, a startup can start to move from simply meeting customer needs to anticipating them, heading off would-be competitors and copycats. At the same time, it should also look for early warning signs of product challenges customers might be experiencing. These kinds of product problems are easier to fix and less damaging when they are caught early. The following table highlights how the focus across the Seas in the Technical Ocean varies by startup stage:

Pre-Revenue: Developing Ideas	MVP: First Customers	Launch and Early Growth: Growing Customer Base	Scalable Product and Business Model: Exponential Growth
• Focus on validation. • Seek both positive and negative feedback. • Understand current solutions to the problem. • Test simple prototypes. • Identify the must-have features.	• Iterate between validation and design. • Assess whether now is the time. • Explore what the user experience needs to be. • Mock up a prototype/wireframe. • Develop the MVP. • Get customer feedback. • Use this input to finalize a launch design and scope a development plan.	• Iterate between design and development. • Build in testing and quality processes. • Begin developing features beyond the MVP. • Monitor the user experience and get feedback from customer service. • Maintain a prioritized backlog for continuous improvement. • Explore the build vs. buy decision.	• Continue iterating between validation, design, and development. • Engage in continuous product and feature improvement. • Use sprints to prevent burn-out and establish momentum. • Continue testing customer acceptance and technical quality of new features. • Validate the priority of new features in backlog. • Watch for warning signs of product-related problems.

Critical technical activities by startup stage

Most startups have a solution in mind when they start their journey. However, navigating the Technical Ocean is never a straightforward path. Startups can overcome many of the debtbergs that they come up against along the way by doing thorough validation early on. It's easy to let excitement carry you through this period, but decisions made now have the potential to grow into monumental debtbergs. A lack of navigation in the Technical Ocean can turn a startup into a castle in the sand, doomed to be washed away by the melted mélange of former icebergs. However, successful navigation can result in a robust product offering that delights customers and anticipates their needs and behaviors—and allows the startup to set sail and survive the journey.

CHAPTER 6:

CORE CONCEPTS of STRATEGY and UNCERTAINTY

"Plans are worthless, but planning is everything."
–Dwight D. Eisenhower

"Where are you going?"
–Dave Matthews Band

The company Webvan offers a great example of a lack of *strategy* and how the cumulative effects of icebergs in different Oceans can be disastrous. Webvan is one of the "poster children" of the dot-com bubble and the irrational exuberance of the late 1990s.[84] Louis Borders founded Webvan in 1996. You might recognize Borders as the co-founder of Borders Bookstore, which went bankrupt in 2011 after a long downward spiral. The concept behind Webvan was an online grocery store with home delivery, which was not a bad idea. Even better, Webvan was a first-mover—or at least an early-mover—in this space. Unfortunately, "leading edge" can also be "bleeding edge" if a company finds itself at the point at which leading the market becomes unsustainable.

At its peak, Webvan served ten cities across the United States and reached almost $200 million in sales. However, these accomplishments came with significant losses and unrealized expectations. The interaction of several icebergs across Oceans led to this titanic disaster.

On the human debt side, not a single executive, advisor, or major investor in Webvan had experience in the grocery business. CEO George Shaheen came from Andersen Consulting. Founder Borders had excellent book-retail experience (much longer product shelf life!) but no grocery store background. Growing a bookstore con-

---

84   Peter Relan, "Where Webvan Failed And How Home Delivery 2.0 Could Succeed," *Techcrunch.com*, September 28, 2013, accessed November 22, 2017, https://techcrunch.com/2013/09/27/why-webvan-failed-and-how-home-delivery-2-0-is-addressing-the-problems.

cept, where people like to spend time with a non-perishable product, is a bit different from launching and growing a grocery delivery service.

Webvan never established a profitable or scalable business even in its launch city of San Francisco, and its "disruptive" business model was unproven. Despite this, Webvan's investors pushed for extensive, expensive growth and drove the company to go public. The company received an **IPO** valuation of almost $5 billion in November of 1999. This lofty valuation came despite *cumulative* sales of just under $400,000 and cumulative losses of almost $50 million at the time of going public.

Enter *technical debt*. While still a fledgling organization with an unproven model, Webvan spent over $1 billion on warehouses plus a fleet of delivery trucks. The whole logistics process was complicated and torturous. According to Peter Relan, founding head of technology for Webvan:

> *I was responsible for the hundreds of engineers who built the software algorithms to make five miles of conveyor belts in our Oakland Distribution Center (DC) transport 10,000 totes around the DC daily. After conveying the item to automated carousel pods, which would spin like jukeboxes to transfer the item in question into the tote, the entire process would rinse and repeat until the order was completed and integrated at the shipping dock. Additional real-time inventory management algorithms would make sure that if a customer ordered milk on the website, it was currently in stock; software algorithms would route delivery vans to multiple delivery stops while minimizing drive time; and software on Palm Pilots in drivers' hands would deal with real-time delivery confirmation or returns.* [85]

Rather than building on existing grocery systems and infrastructure, Webvan attempted to build from scratch. Doing so not only cost tons of dough, but alienated the remainder of the market and set Webvan up in direct competition with the incumbent grocery store players.

Things do not get better as we shift our attention to the company's marketing debt. Remember the importance of segmentation and *positioning* to get the right value proposition for the segment? Webvan attempted to do both segmentation and positioning. According to Relan, the value proposition was "the high quality and selection of Whole Foods, the low pricing of Safeway, and the convenience of home delivery." Meanwhile, the segment was quality-conscious families who valued convenience and could pay for it.

---

85   Ibid.

The positioning of low pricing akin to Safeway did not make sense because high quality and convenience rarely accompany low pricing. The target segment was willing to pay for high quality plus convenience, while low pricing usually signals the opposite. Therefore, the pricing part of the positioning did not match the segment's needs and concerns.

The value proposition of low cost is also incompatible with a hugely complex and expensive technical process. Webvan's history says the mis-integration of technical and marketing elements presented some large debtbergs to navigate and was a major contributor to Webvan's demise. With losses totaling over $800 million and billions in lost investor dollars, Webvan folded in 2001. The combination of human, technical, and marketing icebergs proved devastating to the one-time darling of Silicon Valley.

Instacart operates a similar business to Webvan with home grocery delivery but made different strategic decisions from the outset. Rather than building infrastructure, Instacart relied on the stores already in existence. When a customer places an Instacart order online, a "shopper" goes to an affiliated store and makes a purchase. Then, the shopper drives the items to the customer's house. In fact, the way Instacart partnered with existing stores allowed the stores to take on Amazon and other online-only stores as the competition.

Instacart's shoppers quickly became a critical part of its value proposition for customers. Instead of viewing its shoppers as just a low-cost delivery method, Instacart invested in them, providing them training, maps of grocery stores, and tools to communicate with customers. These shoppers became the "complex packing and delivery system," leveraging their own cars. This makes for much lower capital expenditure for Instacart and is a great example of *bootstrapping* to get to market. The value proposition of Instacart became arming the shoppers with technology to be efficient and effective for their customers. Instacart's journey is still in process, but it has used a better strategy to avoid some of the icebergs that proved devastating to Webvan.

The examples above highlight the importance of strategy. Before jumping into the Strategy Ocean, though, it might be helpful to set the stage with a discussion of some of the core concepts of strategy. Strategy is a term that is often misused and misunderstood, whether in a large company or a small or new firm. This chapter discusses overall concepts of strategy. It highlights how these concepts relate to the interaction between human, marketing, and technical debts. Then, it introduces some of the strategy tools for establishing a unified approach across dimensions of *uncertainty* and activity as the *startup* moves from concept to launch to growth.

Defining Strategy

Let's back up and start with a definition. We define *strategy* as the *process* of linking *today's choices and actions* to tomorrow's *destination*, under conditions of *uncertainty*. Let's unpack the key components of this definition:

- *Process.* Strategy-making is a process, not an outcome. It is not the 100-page business plan that sits on the shelf gathering dust—it is an iterative and adaptive approach to navigating *venture* uncertainty. As Eisenhower noted, it is not the plan but the planning that is essential.

- *Destination.* There has to be a vision for where the startup is heading to guide the startup and inspire internal and external stakeholders (employees, partners, investors, and others). Find more on vision in the callout box.

- *Choices and actions.* While your strategy does include an ultimate destination, you have to connect that destination back to individual actions. This is not just the founder(s) and leadership team—all employees must understand how their choices and actions affect the startup's trajectory.

- *Uncertainty.* Little is known or guaranteed about the direction and market for a startup. The hypotheses and relationships between cause and effect, impact of competition, customer acceptance, technological performance, and funding create an ever-changing landscape where both possible outcomes and probabilities of those outcomes are largely unknown.

The Role of Vision

A definition of "strategy focusing on process" calls for a different metaphor than the often-used "road map" that guides venture development. Using a road map is a largely rational and thoughtful exercise where both the starting and ending points are known. Highways, mountains, and the connecting roads between the two points are clearly visible for the navigator. The startup road map would lay out where the startup will stop for the founders to refuel, with perhaps a search function for pit stops and fast food on the go. This is the world of the business plan, where most planning occurs in a basement, dorm room, garage, or library, with little-to-no interaction with the marketplace.

A road map is comforting because it has starting point A, destination B, and a detailed plan for getting from one to the other. However, it's not an accurate representation of the startup journey. In reality, founders almost never have such information

What is a Vision?

A vision is not a vacant promise or an ill-defined abstraction. In their book *Built to Last*,[86] James Collins and Jerry Porras suggest that companies that are successful over time have a relatively fixed vision, while their business strategies and practices adapt to market conditions. In brief, a good vision consists of two key components: a Core Ideology and an Envisioned Future.

The Core Ideology includes the following:

- Core Values or underlying principles that founders will not violate even for a strategic objective
- Core Purpose, which is how the firm improves the world or ecosystem in which it operates

The Envisioned Future includes:

- a Big Hairy Audacious Goal (BHAG), which is a bold statement of the company's challenging goal
- a Vivid Description of what the company will become as it evolves

Think of these pieces as the yin and yang of a powerful vision, as shown in the image below.

The components of vision

regarding the highways and byways of their path. Instead, the path itself is uncertain The founders resolve the uncertainty through iterative interaction with customers,

---

86   Collins, James C. and Jerry I. Porras. *Built to Last: Successful Habits of Visionary Companies.* New York: HarperBusiness, 1997.

advisors, and others. The strategy constantly evolves as internal resources, competition, and market dynamics change.

For such a dynamic process, strategy is much more like a set of sailing instructions. Even though sailing instructions don't specify particular roads, they still move you toward a destination. In fact, the paradise island that awaits when the startup succeeds is what motivates captain and crew. However, rather than following a set map, the whole crew must look for things that affect the ability of the ship to get to that dreamed-of destination:

- changes in wind speed (market growth)
- currents (changes in customer preferences)
- storms (competitors, changes in technology)
- icebergs (*hidden debts*)

Strategy is a constantly changing and adaptive process, with all on the ship engaged in continuous adjustment to stay on goal.

The startups we have consistently followed through the book provide a very interesting range of patterns regarding staying true to vision while adapting the venture strategy to meet market needs.

On one end of the spectrum are Steve Huffman and Alexis Ohanian of Reddit. They had an interesting idea in My Mobile Menu. They moved to a seemingly entirely different concept when they joined Y Combinator and embraced the feedback from potential investors. However, the Core Purpose of using technology to provide connections was central to both startup ideas. After joining Y Combinator, the Vivid Description changed significantly from connecting people with food to connecting like-minded people with ideas.

Mei Xu of Chesapeake Bay Candle and Joe Gebbia and Brian Chesky of Airbnb are in the middle of the spectrum. Xu experimented with multiple product categories. The Core Purpose of bringing fashion to home products permeated all of them.

Airbnb's Core Purpose to connect people with spare beds to travelers stayed constant. However, the target market of conventions as the context changed, and Airbnb's Vivid Description evolved as the founders realized that it needed to provide services to help its clients renting their sleeping spaces.

Gary Erickson of Clif Bar had a few false starts combining his family's culinary talents with food startups. In fact, the Core Purpose shifted from simply family-inspired food products (calzones) to fueling athletes on long adventures. It also incorporated the Core Values of family and food with a new product and market in energy bars eaten while pursuing adventures.

Randy Hetrick of TRX is on the other end of the spectrum. The original inspiration of the jiu-jitsu belt and parachute-webbing product for athletic training remain the Core Purpose of the business to this day. Yet, the Vivid Description has evolved from being transactional around a strap to being a technology-based workout partner.

Vision can be hard to capture and articulate in a powerful way. Alex Blumberg of Gimlet Media was disappointed—perhaps even disheartened—when he shared his vision for what was originally the American Podcasting Corporation with trusted advisor and potential investor Matt Mazzeo. Mazzeo reacted by saying that Blumberg's vision needed to be more ambitious. "I'm describing the biggest thing I've ever done…and it's not big enough," Blumberg notes when reflecting on the conversation.[87] Blumberg's vision of creating great content was solid, but in Mazzeo's perspective, it would be hard to scale without the incorporation of technology. After bringing on partner Matthew Lieber, broadening the Vivid Description to a media platform, and becoming Gimlet Media, Blumberg did indeed secure funding from Mazzeo and partner Chris Sacca.

There are many ways to *pivot*, or adapt strategy to context, based on market and investor feedback. Founders must determine what components will remain their "North Star"[88] to guide the startup as it navigates through perilous seas. Getting the vision right is a challenge for most founders, but essential for navigating around and through icebergs.

Beyond Vision to Uncertainty

Our definition of strategy recognizes the central role of uncertainty. Entrepreneurship is largely an effort of navigating uncertainty. In fact, we suggest that the primary job of an entrepreneur is not inventing a product, finding customers, raising money, or building a team—though it certainly involves all of those things. Instead, **the fundamental task of the entrepreneur is systematically navigating uncertainty** across these different Oceans. Understanding the primary sources of uncertainty, and how the Oceans of hidden debt relate to each other, is critical to startup strategy and success.

An important element to understanding *uncertainty* is to recognize how it differs from *risk*. This is particularly important as many often label entrepreneurship as "risky business." Risk is probabilistic. In a risk-based scenario, the range of outcomes and probabilities of their distribution are largely known. Think games of dice or cards.

---

87   Alex Blumberg, "Gimlet 2: Is Podcasting the Future or the Past?" September 5, 2014.

88   Prasad Kaipa, "What Wise Leaders Always Follow," *HBR.org*, January 18, 2012, accessed November 22, 2017, https://hbr.org/2012/01/what-wise-leaders-always-follo.

There are only so many combinations of a roll of two dice, and most of us know that the odds of rolling a seven (a three and four, a two and a five, or a one and a six) are higher than rolling snake eyes (both ones). Risk-based scenarios, then, involve a calculation of risk versus reward under these probabilistic conditions. While the popular opinion is that entrepreneurs embrace risk, or are not risk-averse, a strong body of research suggests otherwise. Entrepreneurs are no more likely to head to Vegas and gamble than the average person is.

Uncertainty is a different story (see callout).[89] Under conditions of uncertainty, both the range of outcomes as well as the distribution of probabilities are largely unknown. If a startup fails, how much time and money will be lost? If this startup becomes a *gazelle* or *unicorn* (high growth and very successful startup), goes public, and is wildly successful, how much might it be worth? How much *equity* will the founders give up in achieving success? What are the odds of achieving each level of performance, from the worst- to the best-case scenario? These are questions founders can't answer until they get in the game and try.

The Brain and Uncertainty[90]

Research suggests that different parts of the brain process risk and uncertainty. Specifically, the prefrontal cortex (PFC), which contributes to abstract thought, higher cognition, and executive control, is more active under conditions of uncertainty. The PFC area of the brain helps with constructing the rules for behavior in the current context, while also determining what the appropriate next actions should be. Uncertainty stimulates both halves, right and left, of the brain. As such, decisions under uncertainty integrate both a cognitive and emotional response.

On the other hand, risky decisions involve the parietal cortex on the left side only. This area of the brain is associated with reward-seeking by tracking and evaluating current choices in a more rational way. Whether the person perceives the possible outcome of a risky choice in terms of possible loss versus possible gain complicates the decision-making. Most people are less likely to engage in risky behavior when they see the outcome in terms of loss (you could lose everything) versus gain (you could make twenty times your money). Ongoing research using functional magnetic resonance imaging (fMRI) is yielding interesting findings on brain activity under risky versus uncertain conditions.

---

89   Hsu M, Bhatt M, Adolphs R, Tranel D, and Camerer CF (2005), "Neural systems responding to degrees of uncertainty in human decision-making," *Science*. 310,1680-1683. Also Campbell-Meiklejohn, D. K., et al (2008), "Knowing when to stop: The Brain Mechanisms of Chasing Losses," *Biological Psychiatry*. 63, 293.

90   For more information, see Laureiro-Martínez et al., "Understanding the Exploration-Exploitation Dilemma: An fMRI Study of Attention Control and Decision-Making Performance," *Strategic Management Journal*, 36 (2015), 319. Also Laureiro-Martínez D, et al., "Frontopolar Cortex and Decision-Making Efficiency: Comparing Brain Activity of Experts with Different Professional Background During an Exploration-Exploitation Task," *Frontiers in Human Neuroscience*. 7:927 (2014), 1.

Jim Koch, founder of Boston Beer Company, suggests different terminology on a similar theme. In his interview with Guy Raz for *How I Built This*, he contrasts engaging in activities that are **scary** versus those that are **dangerous**.[91] Scary, he says, is something you feel provides you a significant challenge and gets your heart racing, like rappelling off a sheer cliff face. With ropes and appropriate support, this is quite scary—but actually not very dangerous. A spring hike over ice floes, on the other hand, seems quite peaceful and does not get the adrenaline going, but instability in melting ice can be quite dangerous.

Starting a company is, at times, both scary and dangerous. It involves making a conscious decision to give up the day job (eventually) and undertake something new that could very well fail. That is scary. Staying at your corporate desk job, biting your tongue, and biding your time for the monthly paycheck are not scary. They can be dangerous, though—and could trap you for life.

If you are going to do something scary like rock climbing or rappelling, you should be familiar with the tools at your disposal to make a safe ascent or descent and limit the danger. You should also be aware of the specific dangers and risks you might encounter at each stage of your journey. The section below works through the types of uncertainty a founder must navigate by the stage of venture we have used throughout the book: Pre-Revenue, MVP, Launch and Early Growth, and Scalable Product and Business Model.

Uncertainty and the Human Ocean

People are one of the greatest resources for an emerging startup. However, involving other people potentially creates different types of debt at different phases of development as the founder navigates uncertainty. Here is a typical progression of uncertainty in the Human Ocean:

Pre-Revenue Stage

- *I have an idea and am enthusiastic.* Successful startups typically start with one or two people with a passion for solving a problem. The first step is having the core idea of what the product or service might look like. Sometimes this is a "eureka moment." However, sometimes the idea results from an emergent and evolutionary process that can take months or years—what Steven Johnson calls a "slow hunch" in his great book *How We Got to Now*.

---

91   Guy Raz, interview of Samuel Adams: Jim Koch, *How I Built This from NPR*, October 31, 2016, https://one.npr.org/?sharedMediaId=499205761:499297694.

- *I have someone else who is going to help me start this thing.* This is where founder debt comes in, but to overcome the dearth of diversity and attract investors a founder needs to start building a team.

- *We have some informal advisors who are helping us.* The next phase is to start cultivating relationships with a few folks who are responsive and provide valuable feedback. It also helps if they have connections to investors and/or customers. Founders may have to meet with dozens of prospective advisors to find the right fit, but founders do better if they are selective and limit close advisor status to a few people. A small, diverse group of advisors mitigates resource imbalances with roles and expectations.

- *We know someone who can help us build the prototype and MVP.* Many founders may have the *PEP*—the passion, experience, and persistence to get something going—but not the specific knowledge to build an app, develop software, or make a physical product. Finding a partner, co-founder, or vendor to do this without incurring too much hidden debt or breaking the bank is important.

MVP Stage

- *We can identify the right people to do necessary tasks.* As the startup moves to MVP, closes its first customers, and cultivates investor relationships, the founders need to start specializing to make sure the team can manage the critical tasks necessary for progress.

Lookout: *A founder who is still referring to the startup as "I" in this stage has not embraced the team approach!*

- *We have or can get key expertise in critical areas.* As the startup starts to get traction, it will need people in more areas of expertise to build, sell, deliver, and service customers. Balancing early employees with outside resources is challenging but essential in this phase.

Launch and Early Growth Stage

- *We have a founding team.* By now, or possibly even earlier in the process, the core founding team should be solidifying. Remember the 3 H's—Hacker (technology), Hustler (sales), and Hipster (visionary). These roles might be fulfilled by two people, but rarely by only one. There should also be a balance between an externally facing visionary or "face of the startup," who thinks big and sells the concepts, versus an internally focused champion of getting the job done, understanding cash flows, and setting up processes to be able to scale.

- *We have advisors.* Now is the time to convert that informal group of acquaintances and confidants into an advisory board.

 Navigation Plan: *Be sure to ask permission of advisors before you put them on a formal advisory board, and set expectations about obligations, time demands, and next steps.*

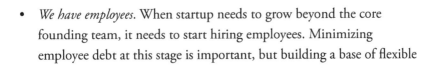

- *We have employees.* When startup needs to grow beyond the core founding team, it needs to start hiring employees. Minimizing employee debt at this stage is important, but building a base of flexible workers is necessary.

Scalable Product and Business Model Stage

- *We have investors.* Most high-potential startups entering this phase will need outside financial resources to continue to grow.
- *We have a board.* As outside money comes into the startup, it will be time to formalize a board of directors. Typically, a board consists of five people including one of the founders, two "outside" directors who are investors/advisors with deeper pockets for future growth, and a couple "insiders" who are confidantes of the startup and founders.

Uncertainty and the Marketing Ocean

Once the founder(s) has a solid core concept, talking to possible customers and users to get early feedback becomes critical. Here are some steps in navigating marketing uncertainty.

Pre-Revenue Stage

- *We talked to a possible user.* Before launching into even initial design and development and the associated costs and technical debt, a founder should talk to at least one user to validate the initial idea.
- *We talked to multiple users.* As the startup moves to develop a prototype, expanding the base of feedback to others is important. Ideally, this will include some acquaintances, not just friends and family! Seek input of devil's advocates and critics.

- *We shared mockups with users.* Before building the MVP, be sure to share designs, sketches, prototypes, or wireframes with potential customers.

MVP Stage

- *We have a customer who will try it (for free).* When the MVP is developed, get it in to the hands of potential users. See how they use it, break it, are confused by it, etc.

- *We have a paying customer.* MVPs and early feedback are nice, but until someone is paying for the product, the startup does not really have validation. Most people will download an app, try a sample, or test a new product when they do not have to pay for it, especially for a friend or family member. However, investors will look for paying customers, and a founder should as well. This separates the sleek sailboat with potential from the leaky rowboat bound for the ocean floor.

- *We understand how the customer actually uses the product/service.* As noted, Clay Christensen describes this as understanding the job that your product does for the user. It is not enough to have people using your product and paying for it—to continue progressing you need to develop a deep understanding of how they use it and why.

- *We understand and can communicate our value proposition.* From the observations in the previous step, the startup is in a much better position to articulate the value proposition for its target segment.

Launch and Early Growth Stage

- *We have several paying customers!* This is a significant hurdle, and critical to reach if the venture is going to be scalable. Having several customers lets you observe how different customers use the product in different ways and understand the different ways they perceive its value. These observations might result in different "use cases" or stylized stories of the value proposition for different users. However, if every customer has the product do a different job, it is almost impossible to market the startup effectively and scale the business.

- *We recognize and understand segments of customers.* These early use cases should lead to segments of customers. Are there groups of customers who have a high need for the product and who use the product in a similar way? If so, the startup can market to them in a similar way instead of having to market to each customer individually. Even better, are there several segments where customers within the segment have similar needs and each segment has different needs? This leads to focusing and targeting one segment at a time for maximum efficiency with an expansion plan over time.

- *We can sell, deliver, install, train, and maintain the product so it works for our customers.* To scale effectively, the startup then needs to be able to map the whole customer journey—from the opening interaction in the marketing funnel though installation and ongoing relationship. When and where does the sales-to-service handoff take place? How does the startup "upsell" or expand use within existing clients? What are renewal rates, and how does one increase customer lifetime value?

- *We have somebody who knows how to sell to customers.* At some point, the founder roles must begin to specialize. Scaling the startup and overcoming marketing debt requires someone who really knows how to close with customers. Initially many founders are able to get traction through connections and their networks and sell to customers in their own backyards. However, to scale and get growth funding, someone with sales experience must be able to sell to complete strangers.

- *We can use outbound marketing to bring in leads systematically.* As noted in the Marketing Ocean Chapter, getting leads—prospective customers—into the marketing and *sales funnel* is critical. Whether through emails, phone calls, conferences, or other outreach, figuring out how to target and appeal to new prospects are essential for scaling.

Scalable Product and Business Model Stage

- *We can use inbound marketing to scale sales.* In this stage, an inbound strategy must complement the already strong outbound efforts. Who is looking for the product the company offers or has the problem the company is addressing? What search terms do they use, and how does the startup get onto the first page of search results? Who are the key influencers in this market, and how does the startup turn them into advocates? Now, the startup can develop a comprehensive digital marketing strategy.

- *We understand the marketing funnel and how to get potential customers into and through it.* Systematizing inbound and outbound marketing efforts and coordinating marketing and sales to drive traffic into and through the funnel is the next step. Being able to quantify and replicate this process is critical for future growth and sustainability, including understanding customer acquisition cost and lifetime value.

- *We have multiple people who can sell to customers.* One good, or even great, salesperson is important and a huge benefit to a startup. However, someone—the same person or a different member of the leadership team—must be able to select, onboard, and train new salespeople to replicate this process. To scale effectively, this individual must develop the "playbook" for the sales process and implement it across multiple salespeople, likely serving different customer types or regions geographically in a repeatable and predictable way.

Uncertainty and the Technical Ocean

Similarly, the product/service evolves over time with uncertainty around a variety of issues. Here is a typical progression of uncertainty reduction on the technical front.

Pre-Revenue Stage

- *I have an idea.* Nearly all startups start with an idea—whether from a flash of inspiration like Hetrick with TRX, or a slow hunch from years of experience with a specific challenge, such as fueling your body on a long bike ride like Erickson with Clif Bars. Sometimes this idea stems from a problem—"I need tasty, healthy energy when biking." Other times it may originate as a solution in search of a problem—"maybe I can sell a night on my airbed to people coming to this design conference." However it starts, it starts with an idea.

- *We have a prototype.* The idea has to become something tangible—whether that something is a series of energy bar samples with no packaging, a simple and crude exercise strap that a user can hook over a door, or a few PowerPoint slides showing possible functionality. For software products, that something may be wireframes—a mockup to review with customers. Whatever way the founders choose, the idea has to move from a napkin to a simple model to show to customers and others.

MVP Stage

- *We have something tangible in the form of an MVP.* A startup achieves the MVP stage when it moves from prototype to the minimal set of functionality a customer can give feedback on—and, ideally, will pay for.

- *We have proof of concept.* The feedback starts coming in when the MVP is in users' hands. Now the founders start building a real sense of the job that the product or service does for the customer. In addition, the founders build some knowledge about the outcomes or benefits that customers get from the solution—as well as how they break it.

- *We know what parts of the value proposition we offer as a product versus as a service.* No matter what the product is, some aspect of early startup development involves helping users understand what they have and how to use it. The more unfamiliar, novel, or disruptive a product is, the more likely early customers will need handholding. See the Myth of SaaS callout box later in this chapter for more.

Launch and Early Growth Stage

- *We can reliably build the same product over and over.* Building the prototype and MVP is one thing. Being able to build hundreds or thousands of a product is quite a different challenge. Remember how Hetrick/TRX encountered manufacturing problems with breaking handles on their straps when they first outsourced production. Building a codebase for software that is durable and flexible enough to serve increasingly large numbers of customers is similarly problematic.

- *We know what parts we need to build and where to get everything else built for us.* At some point, the startup must also answer the classic "build or buy" decision. What pieces, components, or services are essential for the startup to "own" and provide in-house, versus buy from others? Koch/Boston Beer Company recognized that actually brewing its own beer was not a key part of the business. Instead, the recipe and quality control were. Gary Hirshberg, founder of Stonyfield Farm, on the other hand, attempted to have his company produce all its own product, and the resulting technical debtberg nearly sunk this startup.

Scalable Product and Business Model Stage

- *We can build the product and sell it for more than it costs us to make it!* Being able to reliably scale is only part of the equation. Understanding how much each unit costs and being able to sell it to customers for more than that is critical for sustainability. Ideally, the selling price also covers customer acquisition costs.

- *We need a plan for the next product/service extension to add revenue.* The team is not done! To continue to grow, the startup needs to think about the next thing. What additional products or services can be developed? How does the venture use knowledge and data to stay ahead of the competition?

The Myth of Software-as-a-Service (SaaS)

Investors and tech entrepreneurs love SaaS models. They are scalable, profitable, and the darlings of *angel investor* groups and VCs globally. However, the reality is that every technology startup is a combination of software AND service. At first, SaaS should really be "Software **and** a Service."

Second, while most startups think the S for "software" is the driver of the business—**S**aaS—in reality, the more novel or disruptive an offering is, the more customers or users will need help understanding the value. Airbnb, for example had to visit with a solid user base in person in New York to help them take pictures of and market their properties before Airbnb really started to see a substantial number of bookings. So early on, it is more likely to be a Saa**S** business until the startup and customers gain knowledge. This has important implications for startup strategy, staffing, and funding, as well as the oft-hoped-for scalability. Over time, the startup may become a **S**aa**S** or even a **S**aaS company—but this may take years.

📽 **Lookout:** *When looking at investing in SaaS businesses, dig into the service side—what it takes to install, maintain, and get meaningful adoption by users.*

Uncertainty and Venture Funding

The financial component of debt is not typically "hidden" and stays above the water in our iceberg metaphor. However, from a strategic standpoint, funding is the lifeblood of the startup that allows for progress along the above dimensions, and so founders and investors need to consider it as part of an integrated venture strategy. Here is the equivalent progression of uncertainty reduction on the financial front.

Pre-Revenue Stage

- *I have no expenses but have some cash saved up.* Even the leanest startup faces some costs. At a minimum, a domain name from GoDaddy may cost $19.99 for a year. Legal fees to incorporate and set up an operating agreement can run $2,000 to $5,000. In preparation for starting a startup, a founder would be well advised to put some money aside for incidental expenses, even if she does not quit her day job.

- *I/We can afford to build a prototype.* Most startups evolve from a solo founder and more than one bank account. Being able to build the prototype may take some of the founders' bank accounts or even credit cards. Costs here can vary significantly. Ideally, a startup gets the prototype built without outside funds from angel, institutional, or other sources. Remember, this can be as little as a wireframe or PowerPoint slide deck.

MVP Stage

- *We have invested as much as we are able and have an MVP (this can be an investment of up to $50,000 for stripped down but functional software).* Either at this stage or shortly after, the startup might need additional funds outside of the founder's personal savings. Building a solid MVP for an app takes some outside funding unless you have good programming skills in the founding team.

- *We have approached friends and family and raised another cash infusion.* By this point, one or more of the founders might have quit their day jobs, so a small salary is justifiable. Additional costs start to increase from sales and marketing expenses, additional product development, a good website, etc. Outside investors expect founders to have raised some money from *friends and family*. Individual angels or a small local angel group might also be part of the funding picture at this stage.

 Navigation Plan: *Yes, it is hard to ask friends and family for money, but it is even harder to tell an investor that your startup is too risky for you to ask friends and family for money! If you believe in your startup's potential, make friends and family aware of the opportunity, but also fully disclose the risk and let them know that they could lose it all. When you are wildly successful, they would be unhappy if they did not have a chance to get in on the ground floor.*

- *We have some (modest) revenue.* That first check from a customer is pretty awesome and great validation of the startup's promise. Finances start to become more complicated with both revenue and investor dollars coming in. Now might be the time to contract with an accounting firm or outsourced Chief Financial Officer to help manage the money. At this stage, founders should also make a strategic decision as to whether raising outside money is better or if spending that time selling customers and growing through funds from revenue is viable. Targeting big investor dollars and *venture capital* is the sexy thing to talk about, but it is not always necessary or desirable.

 Navigation Plan: *Raising external funding is not always appropriate. Consult mentors or advisors before taking outside funding, as it will drive many significant strategic decisions with their own associated hidden and visible debts.*

Launch and Early Growth Stage

- *We have raised our first outside dollars.* With multiple customers and revenue, proof of concept, and some real traction, a startup might be ready for a larger angel round and institutional investors. Keep in mind the investor debt challenges from the Human Ocean and seek strategic relationships, not just money (though dollars are necessary to build the team, marketing effort, and evolving product).
- *We can see a path to profitability.* Now is the time to be able to chart a believable path to being *cash-flow positive*, when more money is coming in from revenue on a monthly basis than is being spent. A growing startup might choose to invest more on marketing, growing its salesforce, and product development rather than show profitability—but this does not mean the startup could not plot a course to profitability if it chose not to raise another dime from investors.

Scalable Product and Business Model Stage

- *We have raised more serious money.* If appropriate, the *high-growth* startup might raise additional funds. At this stage, entrepreneurs and investors often call those funds the *A round.* The A round money could be $2 million to $5 million for additional growth.

- *We are cash flow positive.* At some point, a startup should show a profit—not just be able to chart a path to it. While there are examples of successful companies who have yet to show a path to profitability—and in some cases even a revenue model—their lives are often limited.

As you can see, uncertainty does not go away as the startup grows—but the nature of that uncertainty and the forms it takes changes over time in each Ocean of hidden debt. Think of it as a series of constraints that need to be resolved, as further described in the callout box.

Goldratt's Theory of Constraints[92]

One way to think about systematically managing uncertainty is that you are addressing constraints or bottlenecks. At each stage, a startup moves from one constraint to another. Identifying that constraint and overcoming it is the founder's main task. This brings to mind Goldratt's work in operations on bottlenecks, known as the "theory of constraints." The essence of this theory is that organizations are systems, not processes, and need to identify systematically the limiting factors that stand between the company and its goal.

Strategy and uncertainty are necessary companions with the founder on the entrepreneurial journey. Now that you have a deeper understanding of what these concepts mean at different stages in that journey, let's move on to the Seas and icebergs in the Strategy Ocean.

---

92   For more, see Goldratt, Eliyahu M. and Jeff Cox, *The Goal: A Process of Ongoing Improvement*. Great Barrington, MA: North River Press, 2004, and H. William Dettmer, *Goldratt's Theory of Constraints: A Systems Approach to Continuous Improvement*. Milwaukee, WI: ASQC Quality Press, 1997.

THE STRATEGY OCEAN

Anemic
Accountability

Meager
Measurement

Incomplete
Integration

CHAPTER 7:

THE STRATEGY OCEAN

"If you don't know where you want to go, then it doesn't matter which path you take."

–Lewis Carroll

"You can't always get what you want, but if you try sometimes, you just might find you get what you need."

–Rolling Stones

We have presented the key dimensions of hidden human, marketing, and technical debt as three Oceans to navigate. However, discussing these solely as three separate Oceans ignores the importance of the relationships among them. Navigating *uncertainty* in these Oceans needs to be part of a coordinated effort. The preceding chapter introduced some of the core concepts of *strategy*. This chapter details the Seas and debtbergs in the Strategy Ocean and offers some tools for navigating them. As in all of the core Ocean chapters, in this chapter we weave in the changes in White Star's and the *Titanic's* strategy over time.

The Strategy Ocean and the *Titanic*

Initially, White Star focused on clipper ship journeys to Australia. Over time, the model shifted to iron steamers and passage to the United States. Competitive factors drove a change from speed to size as the differentiator, with luxury and grandness an extension of size. Financial problems and investors contributed to strategic change by severing old partnerships and creating new ones. Funding, investor preferences, and competition are regular challenges in the Strategy Ocean.

These changes dictated seeking out and/or developing new technologies, which were not always effective. Remember that the iron hulls interfering with the compass contributed to the sinking of the RMS Tayleur. *Although the* Titanic *had a telegraph, the crew failed to process the telegraph warnings of icebergs appropriately on that fateful night. With new technical debt, the lack of human capital and skills needed to build and operate the* Titanic *clearly contributed to its demise. In addition, the operationalization of the strategic change from speed to size and luxury created considerable debts on the marketing side that strained the company's resources and ability to operate safely. In short, much of the human, technical, and marketing debt stemmed from strategic changes in direction, and the interaction of technology (Technical Ocean), people (Human Ocean), and customer targets (Marketing Ocean).*

Strategy Debt for Startups

Another company that demonstrates icebergs in the Strategy Ocean is Theranos. What Webvan represented in the tech bubble of 2000, Theranos exemplifies as a life-sciences *startup* collapse fifteen years later. Theranos was the brainchild of Elizabeth Holmes, a Stanford student who dropped out in 2003 at the age of 19 to pursue her entrepreneurial dream.[93] She eventually hit on the concept of disrupting medical testing through blood tests that require only a few drops of blood. Theoretically, this would encourage more people to get tests, be more cost-effective, and give faster results. At its peak, Theranos was worth more than $9 billion, including a $400 million raise from investors. However, due to the interaction of human, marketing, and technical debts, the sizzle definitely overshadowed the steak, and Theranos' lofty status was short-lived.

On the human side, Theranos had an enviable board and set of advisors, including former Secretary of State Henry Kissinger, software mogul Larry Ellison of Oracle, and former Senate Majority Leader Bill Frist. Unfortunately, none of the major investors or advisors had experience in life-science startups or with the regulatory requirements of the FDA. That experience is kind of important for a disruptive medical testing company! Holmes herself had some business training, but no meaningful medical training. Before long, former early employees, disillusioned with the lack of *proof of concept*, became whistle-blowers who alerted regulators to concerns about the technology. Founder, investor/advisor, and employee icebergs proliferated in the Human Ocean.

On the marketing side, Theranos was able to cultivate *channel partners* to distribute its "black box" technology. Anxious to expand health service offerings beyond the pharmacy and flu shots, established companies including Walgreens and Safeway

---

93   Andrew Pollack, "Elizabeth Holmes of Theranos is Barred from Running Lab for 2 Years," *The New York Times*, July 8, 2016, accessed September 22, 2017, https://www.nytimes.com/2016/07/09/business/theranos-elizabeth-holmes-ban.html.

signed partnership deals to bring the Theranos technology to the consumer. Safeway, for example, invested about $350 million in the relationship and built clinics in over 300 stores in 2013. By November 2015, Safeway terminated the relationship due to Theranos missing promised milestones.[94] In this case, partnerships formed before product development had a complete proof of concept. Promising the market cheap and effective testing as a value proposition far exceeded what Theranos could reliably deliver. Partners quickly retracted from the Theranos relationships as these deficiencies came to light.

At its core, the biggest failures of Theranos were rooted in the technical icebergs it encountered. Validation and development are iceberg drifts that startups cannot overlook or address superficially for long. While the idea of microtechnology for blood testing may have merit and promise in the long term, Theranos did not demonstrate validation of its technology through typical peer-reviewed processes. It did not have a scientifically valid, scalable proof of concept. When the startup's promises encountered scientific rigor, the technology did not hold up.

With a different trajectory, Theranos may have proved Holmes and investors right. It might have revolutionized medical testing. If the company had rigorously validated its technology before rushing to raise a big investment and securing significant distribution partners, we all might be going to Safeway or Walgreens for quick medical tests in the near future. However, the pinball effect of human debt hitting technical debt in close proximity to marketing debt caused irreparable damage. While Theranos still maintains modest testing and operations, its market value is well below 10% of its lofty peak. In addition, in 2016, regulators barred Holmes from working in medical testing facilities for at least two years, and subsequently pursued further legal action in 2018 for her role in misleading investors, partners, and customers.

The following sections further develop the Seas of the Strategy Ocean:

- **The Incomplete Integration Sea**—Coordinate all activities on the ship
- **The Meager Measurement Sea**—Know where you are and where you are heading
- **The Anemic Accountability Sea**—Make sure someone is in charge of key tasks

The cautionary tales of Webvan and Theranos set the stage for understanding and navigating these dangerous Seas.

---

94   John Carreyrou, "Safeway, Theranos Split After $350 Million Deal Fizzles," *The Wall Street Journal*, November 10, 2015, accessed September 22, 2017, http://www.wsj.com/articles/safeway-theranos-split-after-350-million-deal-fizzles-1447205796.

The Incomplete Integration Sea

The key to strategy is integrating across disciplines. Going back to our definition in Chapter 6, vision sets direction. However, vision must also link to everyday choices and actions by company representatives across all roles and disciplines. Founders typically encounter two drifts in the Integration Sea: Lack of Coordination across activities and Unbalanced Effort over time, when one Ocean gets more attention than another does.

Lack of Coordination

A Lack of Coordination across activities results in choices and actions that are inconsistent in different parts of the startup. In Webvan's case, for example, the extravagant growth goals and expense of building a huge storage and distribution center were logically inconsistent with "Safeway prices." Even within the Marketing Ocean, the inconsistency between "Whole Foods quality" and "Safeway prices" was hard for consumers to reconcile and sustainably support.

With the *Titanic*, marketing choices for luxury, like the two-story dining room, created technical debts in design and safety (bulkhead height) that human debts were unable to overcome (inexperienced crew). Startups need a plan that incorporates how marketing choices drive technology and staffing needs. Similarly, technology progression should dictate marketing strategies, hiring choices, and advisor input. Founders and employees must rise to the challenge of addressing technical and marketing uncertainty. Each of the Oceans affects the others. Startups cannot ignore the linkages and interchanges among them.

Coordination across Oceans can have important implications for funding and financial performance as well. For example, it is not unusual for a software startup to offer use of its nascent software product for free as an incentive to land new customers, get feedback, and possibly hook them on the product.

A free pilot program like this may run for a week, a month, or even several months. These free pilot programs help a startup avoid technical icebergs in development of ramping up an *MVP* into a sellable, scalable platform. However, they still require people to implement and service clients, and there is no revenue to offset these expenses. The fact that customers often do not pay for sixty-to-ninety days compounds the problem. The result of what may be a smart or necessary marketing tactic is significant cash burn. Moreover, it leads to much larger fundraising requirements, especially as the startup scales. Hiring personnel for sales, support, and product development often comes well in advance of revenue. A free pilot compounds this challenge. A sound integration strategy and coordination across Oceans can help navigate around this iceberg and set appropriate expectations for investors and others.

 Navigation Plan: *At the end of a free pilot, clients should have to "opt out" of an ongoing paid commitment, as opposed to "opting in," which would likely require a completely new approval process.*

Unbalanced Effort

Coordination across Oceans is one aspect of integration—the other is relative focus over time. Theranos serves as a good example of unbalanced effort. The marketing and fundraising function (Marketing and Human Oceans) were far ahead of the product development (Technical Ocean). It started selling a product it could not deliver. Webvan had the reverse challenge—it built a huge complex and made significant investments in technology and infrastructure (Technical Ocean) before proving the value proposition and target market (Marketing Ocean), in part due to human icebergs of a lack of depth of knowledge in the industry (Human Ocean).

One cause of Unbalanced Effort is the Dearth of Diversity iceberg drift. It is not unusual for entrepreneurs with a technology background to focus almost exclusively on the product and solving technical uncertainty, without commensurate effort on customer discovery, building a team, securing advisors, and establishing relationships for fundraising. Similarly, founders with sales or marketing backgrounds can have a tendency to sell a product well in advance of proving they can build it reliably and scale production.

 Navigation Plan: *Broadening the experience and functional reach of the founding team and/or advisors can help a startup navigate the icebergs of Unbalanced Effort.*

Visually, it is helpful to think about concentric circles of growth, reflecting the various steps in resolving uncertainty discussed in the preceding chapter. The types and sizes of strategy icebergs will likely differ at each stage of growth. At inception, the startup may be little more than a founder with an idea, no customers, and no funding. Visually, this might look like Figure 1:

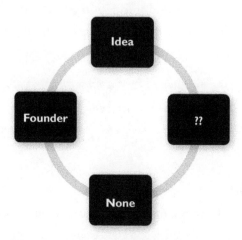

Figure 1: Pre-Revenue stage: first circle of startup growth factors

In the next stage, the startup has started to build a team, develop an MVP, and engage with customers for proof of concept, but may be largely self-funded or have used *friends and family* for support. Visually, this next stage looks like Figure 2.

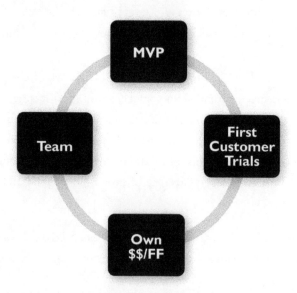

Figure 2: MVP stage: second circle of startup growth factors

As the startup further builds the product based on market feedback, develops a scalable base, acquires multiple paying customers, and starts to engage more formally with advisors—and maybe even hires first employees—it may be time for outside funding. Figure 3 represents this progression:

Figure 3: Launch and Early Growth stage: third circle of startup growth factors

It is after these three stages that a startup typically moves into the Scalable Product and Business Model stage. The Integration Sea threatens startups when there is little-to-no coordination across Oceans, or the parts of the company within those Oceans are at very different stages of development. The startup becomes unbalanced in its effort, and never achieves a Scalable Product and Business Model.

The Meager Measurement Sea

Many of us know some variation of the phrase "you can't manage what you don't measure," often (mis)attributed to management thought leader Peter Drucker or quality improvement guru Edward Deming. Once founders get beyond planning and move into launch mode, avoiding icebergs and systematically navigating uncertainty becomes an all-consuming task. Often, developing strategic metrics falls by the wayside. However, a ship that does not monitor wind, weather, tides, and location will not fare well in dangerous seas. Knowing where it stands today and how it is progressing toward tomorrow's destination is an essential activity for a startup. Putting these goals to paper and tracking performance metrics over time also becomes increasingly critical in earning the support of investors and advisors.

The Balanced Scorecard by Robert Kaplan and David Norton (1996) provides a foundational base for measurement of strategic firm-level metrics.[95] The thesis of *The Balanced Scorecard* is that, while financial metrics are important, they are the *lagging indicators* of firm performance. Financial metrics are a result of other important actions and activities that have already occurred, and the business should measure those important actions and activities (*leading indicators*) directly. These leading indicators drive firm performance for the future. In brief, the Balanced Scorecard tool identifies three perspectives that are leading indicators that drive firm performance, as shown in Figure 4 below:

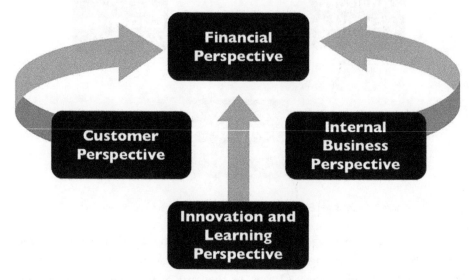

Figure 4: The Balanced Scorecard perspectives

1. *The Customer Perspective.* How do customers perceive the firm and its offerings?
2. *The Internal Perspective.* What must a firm excel at to establish and maintain competitive advantage?
3. *The Innovation and Learning Perspective.* How can the firm continue to improve and create value?

While startups and growing *ventures* may have different specific metrics for short- and long-term performance than Fortune 500 companies do, the Balanced Scorecard tool provides some good rationale and background for all firms. Identifying key leading versus lagging indicators and linking them to strategic objectives is a powerful and helpful way to navigate through the dangerous startup Oceans.

---

95   Kaplan, Robert S., and David P. Norton, "Linking the Balanced Scorecard to Strategy." *California Management Review.* 39: 1(1996), 53.

In the spirit of the Balanced Scorecard, each Ocean of *hidden debt* has some metrics that reflect future direction and outcomes. Some examples might include:

- *Human Ocean Metrics.* Early on, startups' human resources may be limited to one or two founders. As the startup hires its first employees, metrics like employee retention and satisfaction, support for corporate values and culture, onboarding success, and training results can be helpful. Even from inception, it's important to quantify goals for an advisory board (such as number and composition), target investors by stage, and assess partner performance.
- *Marketing Ocean Metrics.* Initially, undertaking customer discovery feedback should be systematic and involve multiple people. As the startup gets established, capturing and tracking hits on the website, customer acquisition costs, and *conversion rates* are critical. Eventually, the scaling startup should be able to quantify costs and yield of outbound lead-generation activities, conversion of inbound leads through the marketing funnel, renewal rates, an estimate of customer lifetime value, and other startup- and industry-specific metrics.

 Navigation Plan*: As noted in the Marketing Ocean Chapter, more than one person should be involved in getting customer feedback to be sure that personal bias is not driving which lessons are learned from these foundational interviews.*

- *Technical Ocean Metrics.* For product development and the Technical Ocean, someone in the role of Chief Technology Officer should be responsible for recall or failure rates, error statistics, server down time, and startup-specific product development and deployment goals.
- *Financial Metrics.* If the company has linked leading metrics to financial outcomes, then hitting financial performance metrics should flow naturally. However, metrics like cash (how much is in the bank), *burn rate* (how much it costs monthly to keep the lights on), and fume date (when the startup will run out of cash) should be top-of-mind for founders. Over time, the focus will shift from fundraising and the balance sheet—how much is in the bank—to incorporating cash flow and ongoing finances—how much comes in versus goes out each month. In the beginning, there is little cash flow to measure OR manage, but that has to change at some point!

> ⬛⬛ **Lookout:** *Track cash, burn rate, and fume date on at least a monthly or even a weekly basis once a startup has investments and expenses. When the fume date is less than six-to-nine months away, you need to start working on the next round of fundraising.*

Of course, measurement can also be overdone. The often-ignored rest of the Drucker/Deming "quote" regarding measurement is a caution about being so preoccupied with measurement that you do not get anything done. "You can't fatten a cow by weighing him all the time" is the alternative perspective. Indeed, many important elements of organizations of any size are impossible to measure.[96] Nevertheless, founders must craft a strategy and translate it into trackable metrics to successfully launch and scale their startups, while avoiding a metrics overload iceberg.

The Anemic Accountability Sea

While integrating Oceans and establishing metrics are important, the startup must still clearly delineate accountability. Who is responsible for hitting each milestone on time? Initially responsibility for just about everything falls to the founder(s). As the team grows, though, accountability and reporting for some functional metrics should move down to the next tier of the leadership team. The metrics noted above should fall on the shoulders of the lead marketing/salesperson, Chief Technology Officer, and lead human resources champion. Financial outcomes likely will remain with the founder(s). Eventually, a Chief Financial Officer or outsourced finance function may share these responsibilities.

Setting up the metrics is something that the founders and company leaders should undertake, perhaps in consultation with advisors or investors. The founders and startup leadership team must also still be accountable for specific overall venture metrics—hitting sales targets and cash burn rates, tracking overall customer acquisition, and mapping future products and services. However, over time more function-specific metrics must ladder down to the next tier of leadership. Theranos, for example, suffered from a lack of accountability for meeting performance targets, especially in the Technical Ocean. Only Holmes appeared to understand the performance of the core technology—or lack thereof.

Advisors and investors can help founders be accountable for venture-level performance. They can also provide insight into additional metrics that have been useful and predictive of performance for other startups. In addition to providing the fund-

---

96   Liz Ryan, "'If You Can't Measure It, You Can't Manage It': Not True," *Forbes.com*, February 10, 2014, Accessed September 22, 2017, https://www.forbes.com/sites/lizryan/2014/02/10/if-you-cant-measure-it-you-cant-manage-it-is-bs/#122a69107b8b

ing fuel to move the startup forward, an important value of advisors/investors is to help develop the metrics for performance and hold the leadership team accountable to these metrics.

Navigating Strategy Debt

Having identified some of the sources of icebergs in the Strategy Ocean and Integration, Measurement, and Accountability Seas, we now focus on some approaches to navigating these challenges.

At a mountain biking clinic in Utah, two of the authors of this work were introduced to the concept of Now and Next in mountain biking. When mountain biking, it is important to focus on where you are Now—the immediate surroundings, what is underfoot, where to bail if needed, and how to avoid rocks or roots that can take you down. Think what is under the bike and one-to-two seconds in front of you. The Next, however, is equally important. You must also be constantly scanning ten-to-twenty feet or three-to-six seconds ahead to see where the trail is going and what obstacles might come up immediately. This scanning tells you where the trail is heading so you can make the necessary adjustments to align yourself appropriately.

As professional mountain bike instructor and Trek Women's Advocate Kate Nolan notes: "One of the lessons I teach is terrain awareness—scanning and collecting information from the Now and the Next to learn how to ride more efficiently on technical terrain. We collect more information about the trail and better react and adapt to the ever-changing conditions through constant scanning. In order to be successful on the trail you can't only look at the Now **or** only focus on the Next. The best riders effectively use both the Now and the Next for a more controlled, efficient, and confident ride."

Founders must similarly pay attention to Now's choices and actions, as well as where the startup is heading Next. The Now for founders incorporates the immediate tasks that they need to do to move forward. Whether researching website domain availability, visiting with potential customers, exploring support from advisors, or experimenting with early versions of the product, there is always a plethora of tasks a founder must undertake. As one serial entrepreneur observes, "In the early stages, founders have to be willing to take out their own garbage."

Lookout: *Test founders who come from large corporations to be sure they are willing and able to "take out the garbage" and get their hands dirty. Big company experience can be helpful but can also blind founders to the Now.*

Persistence through these more tactical activities serves as the foundation for startup success. Consider lessons learned from our exemplar companies. Randy Hetrick/TRX spent over two years driving around the country visiting fitness centers to demonstrate the TRX product and train the trainers on how to use it safely and proficiently for athletes' benefit. Jim Koch/Boston Beer Company drove to bars and liquor stores around New England every day with seven cold samples in his briefcase to entice bartenders to carry his beer. Mei Xu/Chesapeake Bay Candle unloaded cases of candles by car headlight in the wee hours of the morning to meet orders for retailer Target. All of these founders indeed took out the garbage in their own way.

The Next for startups involves what happens in the coming days and weeks. Collecting and digesting patterns of feedback from customers, advisors, and others helps make sure the startup is on track. Filling orders and unloading pallets must be balanced with finding the next customer or investor, designing the next feature, and finding the next salesperson. To avoid many of the icebergs across Oceans, navigating uncertainty requires scanning for the Next series of icebergs. Then, founders must identify steps across technical, marketing, and human arenas to keep progress positive and effectively integrate these activities across disciplines. Fires will certainly come up that need immediate attention—but systematic review of the Next can minimize the fires and make sure the ship is on course.

We'll add a third concept: founders must allocate some time for Navigation to establish a vision and understand what happens after the Now and the Next. "If you don't know where you want to go, then it doesn't matter which path you take." Setting direction is a key part of leading the startup to the promised paradise island. This starts with developing and communicating the Core Purpose, BHAG, and Vivid Description. Then, determining the product development plan, identifying future hiring needs, monitoring implications for cash burn, managing key partnerships, and building customer relationships are all important long-term activities that require dedicated time and focus. At least one of the founders should spend half a day a week on these activities. In addition, regular sessions with advisors and investors can help the founder to engage in navigation activities because it forces the founder to articulate the broader vision to others.

Founders can err in both directions, building strategic debt. Some are a little too focused on vision and spend all their time gazing into the distance dreaming of the revolution their disruptive technology will spark. They might not even realize that the garbage can is overflowing. Others become so focused on the daily grind they lose sight of not only the future direction, but even the next stage of startup development. They take the trip to empty the garbage multiple times a day so that the trashcan always appears neat and clean. However, they just haven't gotten around to that advisor lunch to share the painfully slow progress with a supporter.

A founder needs to know her strengths and natural predispositions to avoid strategy debt. If she tends to be a "forest" person, most comfortable zooming out to focus on the big picture, she will benefit from an operationally focused co-founder. She needs to spend some time on the details and in the weeds. On the other hand, if a founder likes to be in the trees, maybe even on the branches looking at the leaves through a microscope, he might need to force himself to step back and look at the big picture. He will need to practice explaining the overall vision to others and work on the broader view of the startup, the market, and future trends—or bring on a co-founder who can do so.

A visual that helps strategically think about the different areas of focus for the budding entrepreneur captures three levels of analysis that all deserve attention, including the firm, the industry, and the macroenvironment—see Figure 5. At the core, what goes on inside the **firm** across marketing, technical, and human dimensions appropriately occupies the majority of the founder's time. However, how the firm interacts with customers, competitors, suppliers, and even new entrants is an additional level that needs strategic attention outside of the startup. It is virtually impossible to raise money from investors without being able to identify competitors and establish *points of differentiation*, for example. These elements are at the **industry** level. Finally, good strategy accounts for the **macroenvironment**—broad changes that affect not just one but many industries, including the following:

- new technologies, such as the Internet in the 1990s
- legal and regulatory changes, such as the Affordable Care Act
- social preferences, such as the importance of community
- economic trends, such as GNP (Gross National Product) growth and interest rates
- political changes, like major political party changes at the state and national level

Founders must not only understand the Now of these levels, but also what is coming down the road in the near future and what might happen in months or years to come. Now, Next, and Navigation for strategic vision incorporates all of these elements and levels.

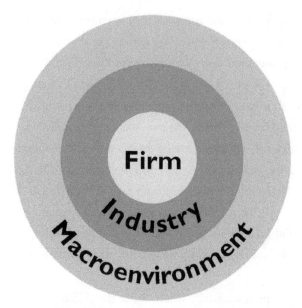

Figure 5: The macroenvironment in context

The Product/Market Matrix

Another helpful tool for thinking about the Now, Next, and Navigation comes back to core concepts introduced in the Marketing and Technical Ocean Chapters. *Product/Market fit*, or finding the right value proposition and functionality for the ideal market segment, can be elusive. At the genesis of the idea and in the pre-revenue stage, founders are rarely certain of the right product configuration, what to focus on for the MVP, or which customer segment to target. We call this the "We can also" phase—as a founder starts talking with friends, colleagues, advisors, and possible customers, more and more ideas of features and possible user segments seem appealing. "This tool is great for business education. We can also sell almost the same product to corporations for training!" Sounds like a great additional source of revenue, right? However, such an extension can create many additional icebergs of debt across Technical and Marketing Oceans.

Think of the strategic focus of the startup launch as finding the ideal intersection of product characteristics and functions, initially embodied in the MVP, and a target segment that is distinct, identifiable, and reachable. Finding this ideal intersection is the goal of early startup hypotheses and testing for validation. There may be several possible product configurations and a number of possible target segments. Figure 6 displays a simplified version of the possibilities, with three product configurations on the vertical axis and three potential target markets on the horizontal axis.

	Market 1	Market 2	Market 3
Product 1			
Product 2			
Product 3			

Figure 6: A simple product/market matrix

While it may be tempting to pursue all of the possible combinations of product/market targets ("we can also"), it is simply too expensive for startups to do so. First, it requires a bigger investment, and second, icebergs of hidden debt can accumulate across each Ocean and sink the startup. Some experienced entrepreneurs/investors refer to this as "boiling the ocean," trying to address too much and therefore not addressing anything at all. Instead, the savvy entrepreneur should run a series of experiments to establish the ideal beachhead or sweet spot for launch as part of the MVP and validation process. This takes the figure with nine possible points and focuses it to the most promising for launch and early traction, as Figure 7 shows.

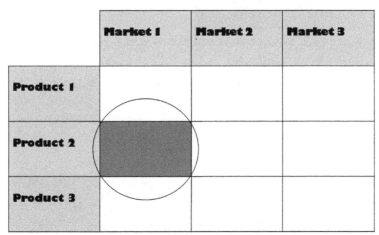

Figure 7: The beachhead for launch

The circled square, Product 2 for Market 1, represents that ideal product/market configuration for launch. That is the Now. What comes Next after getting traction in the sweet spot? Again, there is a temptation to expand on all fronts—to move from one square to all nine and maximize growth potential. Strategically, though, this risks overexpansion and fighting too many battles on too many fronts. Again, the startup will encounter significant icebergs of hidden debt. Instead, a startup should further experiment and determine which expansion path to take:

- Develop additional products and functionality for the existing market segment that it already knows
- Take the existing product to additional market segments—whether that is geographic, new demographics, or other segments as identified in the Marketing Ocean Chapter

The first option is *market specialization*, and the second is *product specialization*. Both appear in Figures 8 and 9 below.

	Market 1	Market 2	Market 3
Product 1			
Product 2			
Product 3			

Figure 8: Market specialization in the product/market matrix

	Market 1	Market 2	Market 3
Product 1			
Product 2			
Product 3			

Figure 9: Product specialization in the product/market matrix

Navigation Plan: *Hold a whiteboard session with three-to-five co-founders and most trusted advisors to plot the various opportunities in the matrix above for your startup. Build hypotheses to prioritize the top three product/market focal areas and develop experiments to test the viability of each one.*

An example of non-strategic growth resulting in a sunken venture comes from Jawbone. The company, originally named AliphCom, launched in 1998 as a supplier of headsets. The Jawbone product line grew rapidly for the next decade. The company had a clear market specialization strategy, improving upon its products with wireless technology and better clarity sound. Selling to a similar customer base, the company added speakers in 2010, fueling additional growth and raising significant capital. At one point, the company's valuation was over $3 billion, and it had raised nearly $1 billion.[97]

In 2012, the company, renamed Jawbone, expanded into a new arena with the UP band, a fitness-tracking device. This was both a product AND market expansion—think from circled square Product 2 and Market 1 above to Product 3 and Market 3. Strategic debtbergs emerged from the intersection of marketing, human, and technical challenges resulting from this stretch. Competitor Fitbit won the battles in this new arena, and by 2017 Jawbone shuttered. It is interesting that the name change from AliphCom to Jawbone in 2011 coincided with a change in strategy and core purpose that ended up sinking the company. The Strategy Ocean can be a harsh one, even for high flyers.

Industry Growth Models

Most of this discussion has focused on the firm and its intersection with customers. Founders must also pay attention to industry trends and growth of the overall market. Often entrepreneurs want to characterize a market in terms of straight-line growth that is linear over time. Unfortunately, market growth is more varied and hard to predict. Monitoring and understanding the industry growth trajectory can help startups better allocate resources and avoid debtbergs across Oceans.

Industry growth variants are many and complex, and each market follows its own trajectory. However, three models roughly characterize different growth patterns with important strategic implications:

- Bass Diffusion
- Crossing the Chasm
- Hype Curve

---

97   Emily Canal, "Jawbone, Once Valued at $3 Billion, Is Going Out of Business. Here's What Went Wrong." Inc., July 7, 2017, https://www.inc.com/emily-canal/jawbone-going-out-of-business.html.

The *Bass Diffusion model* is perhaps the most widely known and accepted, and captures markets with relatively slow early adoption, steady and significant growth in the middle time period, and slowing or maturing of the market in later years. Growth in unit sales and revenues in early years is minor as industry standards become established and customers learn how to incorporate the new product or technology.

The market then hits a significant growth period in sales- and unit-volume, with standards becoming established, new entrants coming in, and differentiation emerging for market segments. Competition increases during this period.

Following rapid growth, the market begins to cool off, and competitors often compete more on price. There is typically some consolidation in this phase, with some weaker competitors going out of business or consolidating with larger competitors. Unless there is a new innovation that sparks a subsequent new growth curve, these industries stabilize and face growth equivalent with GNP (Gross National Product) over the long term.

Markets for consumer goods from cars to computers to smart phones have followed this trajectory. Of course, the time for each phase of growth can vary substantially across product categories. See Figure 10.

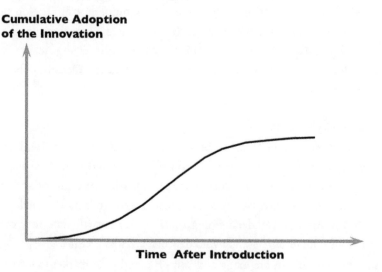

Cumulative Adoption of the Innovation

Time After Introduction

Figure 10: The Bass Diffusion model

A second growth trajectory originated in the book *Crossing the Chasm* by author Geoffrey Moore (1991).[98] In markets described by this model, the early growth and promise of a market stall until some intervention enters the picture. This intervention could be an outside force or technology, a competitor with a new busi-

---

98   Moore, Geoffrey A., *Crossing the Chasm: Marketing and Selling High-Tech Products to Mainstream Customers.* New York: HarperBusiness, 1991.

ness model or approach, or some combination of the two. Growth then increases significantly and in a big leap or step function. Often this means moving from a *niche* product, for a modest market segment of innovators and early adopters, to a mass-market product, for most segments or customer types in the early and late majority. See Figure 11 for a visualization.

Technology Adoption Life Cycle

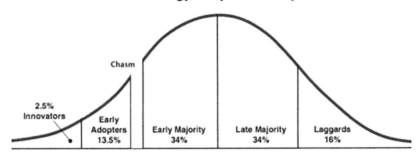

Figure 11: Crossing the Chasm model[99]

An example of this might be the explosion of digital music following the introduction of Apple's iPod. This was not the first such device in the market—the RCA/Thomson Consumer Electronics product Lyra, for example, predated the iPod by years. What Apple did to cross the chasm was introduce iTunes. iTunes was not just software. Apple also licensed access to individual songs as well as albums to overcome copyright issues that plagued Napster. Success came from layering this software on top of supporting macroenvironmental trends: home computers increasing, more widespread Internet access, and improvement in bandwidth/broadband access in the home. Following this combination, growth in digital downloads exploded.

A more recent model is the *Hype Curve* or Hype Cycle, coined by research firm Gartner. In this model, markets experience initial dramatic growth. However, after the initial excitement or hype wears off, sales of the product drop as only enthusiasts and hard-core users in a niche market continue to purchase it. If competitors survive, the market settles into a lower volume than at peak. It's smaller but still a respectable and sustainable level of sales.

The uptake of Pokémon GO is a recent example of this type of trajectory. Following its introduction in the summer of 2016, growth happened quickly to around twenty million daily users. We all might recall walking through parks, streets, and buildings regularly seeing people glued to their phones making jerky arm movements to capture the elusive characters. One year later, in the summer of 2017, daily users had fallen by nearly 75%. Pokémon GO still produces respectable revenue for Nintendo and Niantic: nearly $300 million in the first month and an estimated $1 billion

99   Source: http://www.theagileelephant.com/wp-content/uploads/2015/08/Moores-Chasm.jpg.

in the first year. However, the initial hype gave way to lower engagement over time with a sustainable base. See Figure 12.

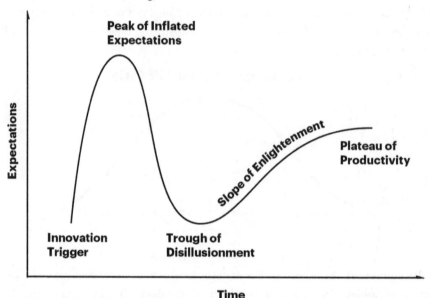

Figure 12: Gartner's Hype Curve model

At the product level, it is not just about the evolution of these markets, but the innovativeness of the offering itself. Innovative products hit the customers who are pioneers or innovators and early adopters, but imitator customers are necessary to penetrate the mass market.

Movies provide an interesting analogue on product uptake and innovation. Box office sales numbers for movies are easily available. Therefore, researchers have been able to model what makes movies innovative with sustained drawing power. The difference from normal product adoption and innovation curves is that movies typically start with peak demand and then have varying curves reflecting declining sales over time.

Probably you can readily think of blockbusters you've seen—an Avengers movie, perhaps? One of the Star Wars movies? Or surprise hits like *Get Out* or *A Quiet Place*? Most blockbusters are a prime example of the Hype Curve. They take off quickly and then have a dramatic decrease in sales. Still, some blockbusters stay in theaters for four, or even six, months because there is enough sustained interest to keep them.

Figure 13 shows what the sales trajectories for typical blockbusters might be. This figure includes Marvel's *The Avengers* (2012) and *Avatar* (2010). Notice that they both start in the $100s of millions. Within two months, revenues drop to around or below $10 million weekly. People generally regard *Avatar* as more innovative based on the 3D technology development it required. Notice how it generated a higher sales line for longer. In fact, *Avatar* achieved $760 million in US sales after thirty-four weeks in theaters. While Marvel's *The Avengers* came out stronger, its primary draw was the star-studded cast and writing from Joss Whedon. Its total US sales were an admirable $623 million, approximately 18% less than *Avatar*. It stayed in theaters for twenty-three weeks—impressive, but not as sustained as *Avatar*.

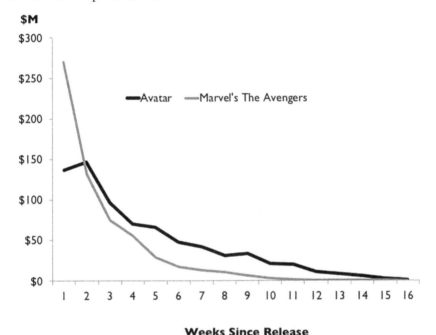

Weeks Since Release

Figure 13: Sales trajectories for blockbuster movies[100]

Next, we need to add the perspective of failed movies (also called "flops"). Note that movie busts not only don't get that early burst of sales, they also don't stay in theaters very long. *The Man from U.N.C.L.E.* (2015) generated a mere $44 million and was in theaters for only ten weeks. Likewise, Disney's *John Carter* (2012) lasted in theaters for only sixteen weeks with US sales of $73 million. Flops among movies and other products fade away quickly.

Movies can also provide an example of Crossing the Chasm from a niche audience to mass market appeal. These films start slowly and then build sales, typically due to Golden Globe and Academy Award nominations as well as positive word-of-mouth. Figure 14 shows the sales trajectories of *Crouching Tiger, Hidden Dragon* (2000) and *Slumdog Millionaire* (2008). Each started with weekly sales around or under $1 million. At their peaks, they crested $10 million in weekly sales. For both movies, total US sales topped $120 million, and they stayed in theaters for more than six months.

100   Source: http://boxofficemojo.com.

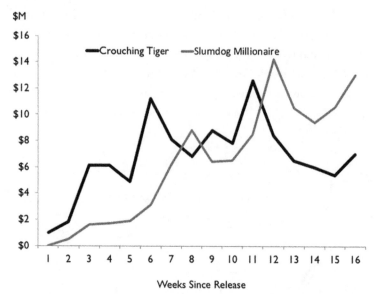

Figure 14: Sales trajectories for movies that Cross the Chasm

Translating Industry Growth to Strategy

How do these market and product trajectories affect strategy and create hidden debt? At the simplest level, these different patterns create very different implications for staffing and fundraising. If a startup hires too far in advance of market and firm growth, it will burn through its cash and sink. Investors have limited tolerance for funding growth that is always one or two years away.

However, shifts in demand also have implications for the startup's value proposition and target segments. It might have to change how to brand and message through the phases of market growth. Product development must similarly be mindful of industry uptake. If the market is still in the embryonic phase with limited growth, a startup should curtail too much investment in new products and product functionality. It needs to avoid being ahead of the market, on the bleeding rather than the leading edge. Bridging a market chasm is expensive and challenging. Most startups don't have the resources of Apple to create the next iPod/iTunes. Startups can rarely afford to educate mass markets to get them across the void. Here, time and competition can actually help bridge the market from early adopters to the majority. Let competitors help build the bridge over the chasm!

Of course, it would be great to have the crystal ball that allows a founder to predict exactly when a market will take off, when it will Cross the Chasm, or when it might hit a Hype Curve and crash. Even the most savvy and visionary founders and investors struggle to predict the market. However, as part of metrics, strategic founders should monitor not just their own growth and trends, but also those of competitors and the overall market. Tracking growth of and investment in competitors, attendance at annual conferences or conventions, and mentions of new technologies or startups in Crunchbase, PitchBook, or TechCrunch can all provide some signals of industry trajectory.

 Navigation Plan: *Develop three or four key indicators that reflect current and future market growth, such as online searches for terms related to your product, to detect trends in customer awareness and interest. Track these monthly.*

The Importance of Tradeoffs

This discussion of strategy has an embedded implicit idea that should be explicit and clearly understood. It is the notion of *tradeoffs*. Doing some things well or best means choosing to be average on others. It also means not doing some things at all. In our product/market matrix, by choosing one cell to focus on, a startup is choosing NOT to aggressively pursue eight other cells. Does this mean a startup turns down some business from new customers outside the focal target? It might.

As painful as it may be, each new customer represents a choice. If the costs of attracting, landing, or developing features for a new account outweigh benefits and are not a strategic fit, founders should just say no. Startups need to be clear and intentional on which customers and segments are worth pursuing and which they should abandon.

In terms of specific performance and functions, startups should also be intentional about where to differentiate from competitors and where parity is adequate. In fact, there are four levels to consider in terms of relative *positioning* on specific attributes:

- *Cede to competitors.* Particularly if the target market or functionality is not in the sweet spot, it is OK to let other players own the squares where a startup does not want to be.
- *Establish Parity.* "Just as good" can be good enough. On some elements, establishing parity with competitors is all you need.
- *Differentiate.* Being selective about exactly where and how you are better than your competition is critical. See more in Chapter 4.
- *Build Unfair Advantage.* Ideally, a startup has one thing that the market values where it has an unfair advantage—a person, technology, knowledge, head start, patent, or secret sauce that provides sustainable and inimitable competitive advantage.

Again, these choices reflect strategic tradeoffs that the startup makes willingly and intentionally in the Marketing and Strategy Oceans. Tradeoffs occur in other Oceans as well. Choosing outside investors, for example, seems to be the standard approach for a "successful" entrepreneur. However, this choice also comes with tradeoffs of giving up equity and control by reporting to a board with some outsiders. Tradeoffs abound in the Technical Ocean with how many platforms to build for (such as, iOS, Android, web app), internal versus outsourced development, and other choices that all help create opportunity but incur hidden and other debt as well.

Harvard strategy professor Michael Porter nicely develops the role of tradeoffs in his article on the topic of strategy.[101] This piece does a good job laying out some of the key strategic considerations both large and small firms should consider when crafting and implementing strategy.

Hetrick/TRX provides good examples of tradeoffs, competitive threats, and protecting the product. TRX invested about $50,000 early on to file patents internationally for its unique product design—a hefty sum for an early-stage company. After getting traction and growing significantly, TRX faced a wave of counterfeit companies making lower-grade products with what looked like the TRX logo. Companies also jumped in soon after with their own designs and logos that clearly were knockoffs of the TRX product. While it was a painful sum to invest with possibly no return, Hetrick was determined to protect his brand and market position. He spent an additional $2.5 million fighting the counterfeits and knockoffs in court. Though it took time and money, several years later he prevailed and received damages of more than $6 million. Without this illegal competition, TRX sales surged by more than 40% the next year. The tradeoff of the investment in protecting the design and brand ultimately paid off. It also helped limit future competitive rivalry.

Steve Huffman and Alexis Ohanian of Reddit, on the other hand, benefitted from icebergs that competitor Digg ran into. Circa 2010, Digg changed its technology platform in a way that created technical and marketing debt. Both partners and users rebelled, to the benefit of Reddit. Company leaders and users alike fled Digg due to a platform launch filled with icebergs of bugs and glitches. Digg was sold in three parts two years later. Part of monitoring competition is identifying moments of weakness where competitors are vulnerable to loss of customers—and key employees. Reddit continued to benefit from missteps of indirect competitors, as Facebook stumbled over data sharing of member information in 2018.

 Navigation Plan: *Track competitors and seize the moment to take advantage of windows of opportunity where customers and employees might be vulnerable. Note that this can be trickier if the competitor is local, as stakeholders such as investors may have overlapping interests.*

---

101   Porter, M. E., "What Is Strategy?" *Harvard Business Review.* 74:6 (1996), 61.

Surviving strategy debt and keeping the startup afloat requires a multitude of skills. To keep the crew and interested others (like investors) inspired, engaged, and on track, the startup needs a destination—the vision of what the startup can achieve, including a Core Purpose and a Vivid Description of how to get there. Passion and persistence for this vision can help the founders get through the tough early times (sometimes referred to as the "trough of despair"), when the startup appears to be foundering. Navigation and communication are critical elements for surviving this period. However, founders cannot lose sight of the Now and the Next, the everyday choices and activities they and their employees and supporters engage in to keep the ship afloat and moving forward.

Monitoring industry and macroenvironmental trends is an essential part of strategy. Anticipating and overcoming competitors and understanding customers must also be part of this journey. Tradeoffs as to what the startup should do (and what it should not) should be intentional—not accidental. Together, this approach helps startups overcome the icebergs of Incomplete Integration, Meager Measurement, and Anemic Accountability. You can't always get what you want—but with the right strategy, you might get what you need!

CHAPTER 8:

~~~~~~

THE ICEBERG INDEX

"Measure what is measurable, and make measurable what is not so."
–Galileo Galilei

"I want to be a billionaire so freakin' bad."
–Travie McCoy

Over the last chapters, we have introduced and discussed in detail some of the debtbergs across the Human, Marketing, Technical, and Strategy Oceans that can damage or sink a *startup*. Now, it's time to put all of these ideas together into a cohesive way to identify and assess the *hidden debt* that is lurking inside a startup. Allow us to introduce the Iceberg Index. The Iceberg Index is a tool to identify and measure hidden debt across Oceans.

First, we want to remind you that most startups and companies will take on many of the hidden debts that we've outlined in previous chapters. Just like people and companies take on financial debt in order to accomplish their goals, so too do startups take on hidden debts. Founders and investors should make *tradeoffs*—but intentionally and strategically. Our goal in creating this Iceberg Index is to make those hidden debts more visible. By knowing where debts have accumulated, startups will be better able to make plans to mitigate them.

Investors may want to complete Iceberg Index scores on current and potential portfolio investment companies. The Iceberg Index could be part of a *due diligence* process, and it can be a tool to help investors better guide founders as they navigate decisions while crossing these Oceans.

Let's start with a few important points in using this tool. We have tried to create a measurement system in the Iceberg Index that simplifies some very complex areas of *uncertainty* across areas of the firm. However, remember tradeoffs—simplicity can lack nuance and comprehensiveness. While our tables capture some of the more common debtbergs startups may encounter, we don't intend them to be complete and comprehensive. Revisit the core content chapters for more depth and nuance in each Ocean.

Each component in the Iceberg Index has a four-point scale. Decide which point best describes where the startup is on this continuum. Don't hedge your assessment—pick only one score for each component:

1. *Strong; smooth sailing.* This means the startup has fully addressed the debtberg.
2. *Some; rocky journey ahead.* The debtberg exists, but there is a plan to address it and minimize damage.
3. *Very little; need a navigation plan.* Without a plan to address it, this debtberg can damage or even sink the ship.
4. *Not at all; large debtbergs in sight.* Damage and failure are imminent, and immediate action is called for.

Second, the importance and threat of the debtbergs will shift over time. When a startup is in the first stage of uncertainty at all levels, while the founder still has the day job and has not raised any money, there is not much to sink. A low Iceberg Index rating is likely in the embryonic phase. The startup is still a rowboat that can turn quickly.

It is in the second and third stages—when the startup is hiring its first employees, moving from *MVP* to *Launch and Early Growth*, and growing a customer base—that strategy debt and other debtbergs accumulate powerful enough to sink the startup, immediately or in the next three years. The use of the Iceberg Index should evolve over time and be stage-appropriate for a startup, as you can see in Figure 1 below.

Pre-Revenue: Developing Ideas	MVP: First Customers	Launch and Early Growth: Growing Customer Base	Scalable Product and Business Model: Exponential Growth
• Be aware of taking on icebergs. • Use the Iceberg Index as a planning checklist.	• Move your Iceberg Index from a checklist to a more formalized set of metrics. • Track it across leadership teams and stakeholders.	• Completely implement your process for monitoring the Iceberg Index.	• Continue to use the Iceberg Index to monitor debtbergs. • Create a risk-reduction plan for large debtbergs on the horizon. • Track improvement on the Iceberg Index. • New product extensions and new hires create new icebergs.

Figure 1: How startups can use the Iceberg Index

Third, it might be helpful to have several people contribute to the process of completing the Iceberg Index. At first, of course, the founders may be the only ones available to complete the index, and they're completing it to get a sense of what's to come. During the *Pre-Revenue* phase, awareness of these concepts alone can be of value. Once the startup reaches the Launch and Early Growth stage, and as investors/advisors enter the picture, discussing the relevant Oceans with important voices in the organization makes sense. This also follows suggestions raised in the Anemic Accountability Sea—more people than just the founder should develop the metrics, and several individuals should be accountable for different measures.

 Navigation Plan: *A cool tool for alerting the growing startup would be a giant map that includes the Oceans, Seas, and drifts. Employees and stakeholders can put a red pin in areas of concern, where they perceive mounting iceberg activity. This can then be a good source of discussion for weekly team or company-wide meetings to make sure the whole group understands the nature of the hidden debt, and can work on a plan to address it. Think of it as your own "Ice Patrol."*

Now we dive further in to the Iceberg Index for each Ocean to explore some of the specific debtbergs that startups encounter.

The Human Iceberg Index

As a reminder, the three Seas where startups can encounter Human debtbergs are Founding Team, Investor/Advisor, and Employee.

The Founding Team Sea

Whether the initial idea is from a solo founder or a team of three, forming the founding team is an essential building block for the idea to become a startup. The first element to consider as a founding team is Misguided Motivation and Experience. When founders lack the appropriate passion, experience, and persistence (PEP), they bring considerable hidden debt to the startup from inception. On the other hand, founders must also balance that passion with being open to feedback. It is important that the team:

- care deeply about the problem the startup solves
- have experience to understand that problem
- be willing and able to persist through the stormy journey of venturing

Founders who are in it because they want to be a billionaire so freakin' bad should probably look elsewhere!

The next iceberg drift we discussed is Inequitable Equity. When a founding team allocates all of the equity at the start of the *venture* journey, it sets up uncomfortable discussions and decisions down the road. It can also negatively affect investor interest and ability to build the right leadership team over time. To address some of these debtbergs it is important to vest equity over time, commensurate with contribution,

Founding Team Sea		Strong – Smooth Sailing	Some – Rocky Journey Ahead	Very Little – Need A Navigation Plan	Not At All – Large Debtbergs In Sight
MISGUIDED MOTIVATION AND EXPERIENCE	The founding team includes people with the characteristics to succeed:				
	• has passion for solving this problem	o	o	o	o
	• brings prior experience with the problem	o	o	o	o
	• shows persistence to overcome hurdles	o	o	o	o
	• is willing to listen to feedback	o	o	o	o
INEQUITABLE EQUITY	The founders' vesting plan is strategic and encourages long-term participation:				
	• allocates equity over time	o	o	o	o
	• is based on contribution	o	o	o	o
	• has a pool of equity set aside for future allocation	o	o	o	o
DEARTH OF DIVERSITY	The founding team members have diverse perspectives:				
	• bring experience from various industries	o	o	o	o
	• offer technological competence	o	o	o	o
	• come from different functional backgrounds	o	o	o	o
	• come from different cultural backgrounds	o	o	o	o
LACK OF TIME AND SUPPORT	Members of the founding team are committed:				
	• have adequate time	o	o	o	o
	• can find financial and familial support	o	o	o	o

Figure 2: The Human Iceberg Index in the Founding Team Sea

and set aside some equity for future leadership-team members. Don't divide the whole pie before you bake it.

A startup team also needs to have access to diverse perspectives and avoid the Dearth of Diversity iceberg drift. Diversity breeds innovation and adaptability. Ideally, a startup team will have all of the following:

- some mix of experience launching and growing a venture
- education/training spanning various functional areas (technical/operations, financial, sales, marketing)
- a network (or the skills to build a network) with access to key resources, including customers, funding, and other connections

Obviously, very few startups possess all of these attributes from the start, but they are important goals to shoot for over time.

Finally, the iceberg drift of Lack of Time and Support can derail even the most promising idea. Having the time and energy to move the startup forward is critical for progress. This is a challenge if founders have a demanding day job, family obligations, and little spare time. It is also helpful to have family support and encouragement, or at a minimum, not have family resentment about the time and energy you put into the startup. This is where passion and persistence can help as well. Passion for a compelling problem can garner support from others.

The Investor/Advisor Sea

As the founders are navigating the uncertainty of launch, seeking feedback from advisors serves them well, and they may eventually want to seek funding from investors. These additional stakeholders can be an invaluable resource, but create their own sets of icebergs in this Sea.

The initial iceberg drift we discussed relates to a Resource Imbalance. This can come from having too many advisors—doing lunch with fifty people every month is tough! However, one single investor/advisor can be too influential and exert unwanted power, and is a sole voice. Being inclusive early and cultivating relationships with many prospective investors or advisors can be helpful, though demanding time-wise. Being selective and settling on a small, engaged group over time will help address some of the debtbergs these stakeholders can raise.

The next iceberg drift in this Sea is the Inappropriate Roles investors/advisors can play. As it is among founders, diversity of perspective and experience among investors and advisors is important. This set of stakeholders should add something new to the mix in terms of functional background, industry experience, and networks. These are not just cheerleaders—investors/advisors should provide a diverse set of voices that challenge and motivate the founders. Again, over time, founders should expect to settle on a small group that undertakes several roles and responsibilities as the startup grows. Advisors typically fill these roles early in the life of the startup, but investors enter the picture as the startup moves from Pre-Revenue to MVP and then Launch and Early Growth. Expect the board to grow when scaling.

Finally, Elusive Expectations of Behavior on both sides can create additional debts. The founders and the investors or advisors should agree on the nature of the relationship in terms of meeting regularity, expected contributions, and *quid pro quo* (or lack thereof). This is often clearer for investors—typically, a *term sheet* will spell out at least the investment terms, expectations, and possible board role. For advisors, though,

Investor/Advisor Sea			Strong – Smooth Sailing	Some – Rocky Journey Ahead	Very Little – Need A Navigation Plan	Not At All – Large Debtbergs In Sight
RESOURCE IMBALANCE		The startup has access to knowledgeable people:				
		• consults an appropriate number of advisors	o	o	o	o
		• chooses advisors who are engaged but not overbearing	o	o	o	o
INAPPROPRIATE INVESTOR/ADVISOR ROLES		Investors/advisors can help move the startup forward:				
		• know and understand the business and industry	o	o	o	o
		• have startup experience	o	o	o	o
		• include diverse perspectives	o	o	o	o
		• have more ability to invest	o	o	o	o
		• can network to customers and/or investors	o	o	o	o
ELUSIVE EXPECTATIONS OF BEHAVIOR		Investors/advisors understand the nature of startups:				
		• respond to requests for help	o	o	o	o
		• meet regularly but not too frequently	o	o	o	o
		• have reasonable expectations for returns	o	o	o	o
		• do not monitor too closely	o	o	o	o
		• can support future growth through funding or other means	o	o	o	o

Figure 3: The Human Iceberg Index in the Investor/Advisor Sea

this should be a topic of explicit discussion. Consider having a "two-coffee" rule: after the second informal meeting to share ideas, it is probably time to make sure elusive expectations don't create unwanted icebergs.

The Employee Sea

As a startup team moves from founders carrying the entire load to actually hiring employees and writing paychecks, the potential for employee iceberg drifts starts to surface. Startups have many needs, and very few can afford to hire all of the talent they would like. The first employees are critical.

Inappropriate Talent Versus Cost Tradeoffs are one source of hidden debtbergs. It would be great to hire a robust development team of engineers, a skilled salesforce, competent marketing help, and someone to do the accounting and finance. However, $100,000 monthly cash burn for labor is beyond the reach of most pre- and early revenue startups. Founders must balance the expense of an ideal hire (the experienced whale hunter) versus the lure of staffing up with cheap but inexperienced employees (such as interns). Specifically, avoid spending a big part of payroll on one superstar—especially if that superstar is a one-hit wonder.

A second iceberg drift in the Employee Sea can come in the form of Crazed Culture. Culture and core values can be a powerful source of alignment between the goals of the startup and the goals of the people who will move it forward. A powerful shared vision and strong positive culture help ease the challenge of late nights, missed meals, and tenuous paychecks. Startups should assess potential employees for cultural fit. The foosball tables, funky decorations, and gong-banging can create infectious energy. On the other hand, you want to avoid (or at least monitor) cultures that institutionalize unsustainable behaviors (like the expensive junket on investor dollars) or those that create painful moments in a downturn (like the lack of gonging). At a minimum, have a plan for how culture manifests and evolves in specific behaviors. For example, the founder lunch on employees' birthdays can shift to a monthly lunch with anyone who has a birthday in that month. Culture must evolve with the scaling venture.

Startups must also avoid Reactive Employee Resource Types that reflect a haphazard approach to building a talent pool. It is tempting to outsource everything and "run lean" until revenue justifies hires, but key hires are necessary to get passionate commitment and build skills over time. On the other end of the spectrum, hiring full-time employees to do everything is too costly: startup needs change too much to anticipate every skill that will serve current and future workforce challenges. Just reacting to product development and customer service demands creates additional human debtbergs. The staffing *strategy* should include a plan for which functions need full-time, dedicated talent, which can get by with part-timers, and which would do best with outsourced talent. A startup should have metrics in place that trigger converting a part-time to full-time employee—for example, when there are ten customers or $100,000 in monthly *recurring revenue*, employee X can convert from part- to full-time.

Employee Sea		Strong – Smooth Sailing	Some – Rocky Journey Ahead	Very Little – Need A Navigation Plan	Not At All – Large Debtbergs In Sight
INAPPROPRIATE TALENT VS. COST TRADEOFFS	The startup balances talent against cost:				
	• hires staff with enough experience	o	o	o	o
	• does not overpay for talent	o	o	o	o
	• inspires commitment in employees	o	o	o	o
	• chooses employees who can flex between roles or "wear multiple hats"	o	o	o	o
	• keeps productive employees	o	o	o	o
CRAZED CULTURE	The startup has a plan to manage culture:				
	• helps employees understand and buy in to vision and values	o	o	o	o
	• hires based on cultural needs and fit	o	o	o	o
	• relies on mission and values to guide decision-making	o	o	o	o
	• works to establish cultural norms	o	o	o	o
	• has plans to evolve how culture manifests	o	o	o	o
REACTIVE EMPLOYEE RESOURCE TYPE	The startup uses different kinds of employee types that are stage-appropriate:				
	• leverages outsourcing	o	o	o	o
	• brings required skills in-house	o	o	o	o
	• plans whom and when to hire	o	o	o	o

Figure 4: The Human Iceberg Index in the Employee Sea

The Marketing Iceberg Index

The hidden debts that challenge startups in the Marketing Ocean reside in three Seas: Segmentation, Positioning, and Tactical.

The Segmentation Sea

The first challenge that startups encounter in the Segmentation Sea is that their approach to segmentation is of Low Quality. The navigation plan to steer around this challenge starts by using a robust approach to finding segments. That approach should include a combination of the alternative bases for segmentation. At a minimum, it should use behavioral or customer needs indicators. Even better, add some psychographics. The best is if you can also add demographics. In addition, startups need a robust and in-depth understanding of these customer segments. Profiles that highlight each segment's needs, pain points, and desired gains express this understanding. Finally, these customer needs should include social and emotional needs, beyond simply functional needs.

Once a startup has a high-quality segmentation scheme, it still needs to avoid Poor Prioritization. Specifically, it needs to pick a primary market segment to target at the beginning and have a plan to expand that targeting over time. The goal is to target one segment that has a high interest in the product so that the startup can effectively pen-

Segmentation Sea	Strong – Smooth Sailing	Some – Rocky Journey Ahead	Very Little – Need A Navigation Plan	Not At All – Large Debtbergs In Sight
LOW-QUALITY SEGMENTATION — The startup has a robust segmentation scheme:				
• uses multiple bases	o	o	o	o
• includes functional needs	o	o	o	o
POOR PRIORITIZATION — The startup has a segment prioritization plan:				
• only one segment to start	o	o	o	o
• a list of subsequent segments to target	o	o	o	o
POOR IMPLEMENTATION — The startup has a deep understanding of customers by segment:				
• personas	o	o	o	o
• product needs	o	o	o	o
• pricing	o	o	o	o
• messages	o	o	o	o

Figure 5: The Marketing Iceberg Index in the Segmentation Sea

etrate the majority of the segment. Recognizing that startups have limited resources, the startup should focus on only one segment at the beginning. Success comes from a focused approach. Then, there also has to be a plan to expand across segments over time to maximize revenue potential.

Finally, a startup needs to avoid Poor Implementation in the Segmentation Sea. Trying to get by without the right information hampers implementation. Specifically, startups need to make sure that they have robust *personas* for each segment. These personas can help everyone in the startup understand how each segment thinks and feels. In addition, startups may need to be able to offer different product configurations for each segment and know how each segment will respond to pricing. Finally, startups must be able to reach each segment with the right messages in the right media.

The Positioning Sea

As startups move into the Positioning Sea, they have to explore how customers will evaluate them.

The first step customers go through is trying to categorize the product offering—what other products that the market already knows is this product like? When startups attempt to disrupt a market or offer something never seen before, they can bump into the challenge that their Market Category is Not Established. Initially, this situation may seem attractive because there are no competitors. More realistically, it means the startup has a lot of work to do, and will bear significant expense to create the category. Customers need a *frame of reference* to evaluate the offering. Startups want to be able to say what category its offering belongs to and have customers agree. That way, customers can identify the *points of parity* for the category, making it easier for startups to focus only on promoting how they are better than competitors are.

Once they've identified a well-established market category, the next challenge startups encounter is Weak Differentiation. People tend to behave tomorrow the way they behaved today. That means that they need a compelling reason to change before they will adopt a new product. If a startup wants to attract customers, it has to be able to tell customers clearly and unambiguously why it is better than competitors are. It has to have a compelling *point of differentiation* (POD). That differentiation has to be detectable by the customers, and offer something that is important to them. If they can't experience the difference for themselves or if the difference is something they don't care about, then the difference simply won't be a compelling reason to buy.

Once the startup has identified a compelling POD, the last challenge is Inconsistent Use. This area is risky for more than just the marketing function. The whole company has to be aware what the product's POD is and recognize it in their decision-making. All messaging should use the POD consistently across different media like the website, emails, blog posts, and social media. However, messaging the POD is not enough. This POD should also be apparent through product design, pricing, and other product-offering decisions. Finally, the startup needs to make a tradeoff between a POD that turns out not to be compelling, and *pivoting* direction. A startup should change when its product offering and messaging are not working, but every change means moving away from customers who have already signed on. It's best to get the POD right from the start and stick to it over time. Unfortunately, that doesn't always happen.

Positioning Sea		Strong – Smooth Sailing	Some – Rocky Journey Ahead	Very Little – Need A Navigation Plan	Not At All – Large Debtbergs In Sight
MARKET CATEGORY NOT ESTABLISHED	The startup has established a frame of reference to launch into:				
	• only one category	o	o	o	o
	• points of parity are known by customers	o	o	o	o
WEAK DIFFERENTIATION	The startup has strong differentiation:				
	• can say how the product is better than competitors' products	o	o	o	o
	• the advantage over competitors is meaningfully better	o	o	o	o
	• this advantage is easy to communicate	o	o	o	o
	• this advantage is important to customers	o	o	o	o
INCONSISTENT USE	The startup communicates its POD consistently:				
	• across media	o	o	o	o
	• over time	o	o	o	o
	• through all tactical implementation	o	o	o	o

Figure 6: The Marketing Iceberg Index in the Positioning Sea

The Tactical Sea

Once startups know to which audience they are talking and what makes their offering different and better, they still have a number of tactical challenges to work through.

The first of these is to make sure they are not offering a Customer Value Void. Sometimes, entrepreneurs see a problem and try to fix it, but the problem isn't important enough for customers to be willing to do something to fix. Alternatively, the solution isn't good enough to make adopting it worth the effort. To start, this problem should be something that customers already know is a pain point they feel—their needs are unmet. Then, the solution has to be both different from and significantly better than existing solutions.

If there is customer value in the solution, the startup now has to avoid a Price/Value Mismatch. Just solving a problem a better way is not enough. Customers also have to be willing to pay the cost to deliver that new solution. The price of the product offering should reflect the value it delivers rather than costs or what competitors are charging. One indicator is that customers are willing to pay to try it, rather than opting for a *freemium model*. Another positive indicator of a price/value match is that the revenue model depends on recurring purchase, rather than a single purchase opportunity. When customers come back for more transactions, the startup probably has a good price/value match.

Once there is a value customers are willing to pay for, startups then need to overcome the challenge that their Sales Process is Not Scalable. Very few products—especially new ones—sell themselves, whether B2B or B2C companies offer them. Startups need to plan for how they are going to close sales. Even if customers can go directly to the startup's website and buy, that buying process has to be well established and easy to finish. Startups need to know what the buying process is and have plans to minimize leakage from the *sales funnel*. More often, startups need *channel partners* to help them find and close customers. Selling to each individual consumer one-by-one is slow and difficult. Then too, startups need to plan for how to manage the sales force required to effectively close customers, including being able to afford the right salespeople, find them, and onboard them.

Startups cannot be successful with just a salesforce in the promotional mix. They also need to overcome the challenge of an Incomplete Promotional Plan. Unfortunately, *promotions* are expensive. As a result, startups often wait to plan for promotions until they have a budget. They start with a Facebook page and/or a very basic website. However, a successful promotional mix requires a number of critical investments. First, startups need to know where their target customers look for information. Then, they need a series of messages to communicate their PODs. These messages need to be apparent in search engine optimization and published through both inbound and *outbound advertising*. Finally, the startup needs to recognize the customer buying process so it plans for lead generation activities, lead nurturing activities, and an effective handoff from these marketing activities to sales closing actions.

Tactical Sea		Strong – Smooth Sailing	Some – Rocky Journey Ahead	Very Little – Need A Navigation Plan	Not At All – Large Debtbergs In Sight
CUSTOMER VALUE VOID	The product offers value to customers:				
	• addresses an unmet need	o	o	o	o
	• is a good solution to the problem	o	o	o	o
	• is a solution worth paying for	o	o	o	o
PRICE/VALUE MISMATCH	The startup can secure the value it offers through pricing:				
	• can price appropriately relative to competitors' products	o	o	o	o
	• can use value-based rather than cost-based pricing	o	o	o	o
	• can secure recurring revenue from each customer	o	o	o	o
SALES PROCESS NOT SCALABLE	The startup can create efficiency in sales:				
	• knows the buying process	o	o	o	o
	• has created a buying process that is repeatable	o	o	o	o
	• knows how to close sales	o	o	o	o
	• has a channel partner plan	o	o	o	o
INCOMPLETE PROMOTIONAL PLAN	The startup can create efficiencies in promotion:				
	• has a strong website with SEO	o	o	o	o
	• developed a well-formed inbound advertising plan	o	o	o	o
	• developed a well-formed outbound advertising plan	o	o	o	o
	• has budget for outbound ads	o	o	o	o
	• aligns its marketing process through sales and marketing	o	o	o	o

Figure 7: The Marketing Iceberg Index in the Tactical Sea

The Technical Iceberg Index

The hidden debts that challenge startups in the Technical Ocean drift into three Seas: Validation, Design, and Development.

The Validation Sea

The debtbergs in the Validation Sea revolve around making sure the startup is building the right boat. When founders begin the path of building a startup, they have their own assumptions about both the problem and the solution. Typically, they start asking friends, co-workers, and anyone they think might have the same problem to validate that problem. They want feedback on how good their solution is. It's human nature to try to encourage these budding entrepreneurs.

As a result, they end up running into the debtberg of False Hope. These early feedback providers tend to assure the founder that this is a good idea. Part of the Tactical Sea in the Marketing Ocean is to make sure that any new product addresses customers' pain points. In addition, the product development team also bears responsibility for validating potential founders' assumptions.

The best ways to do this are to seek out negative feedback. Often, we can't help ourselves. We want people to tell us we have a great idea. However, a startup must seek out alternative views—get someone to identify all of the reasons why this is a bad idea, including avoiding Unnecessary Solutions. While digging into why the idea is flawed, digging more deeply into how people are solving the problem today also helps. Maybe their current solution and competitors aren't the best solution, but maybe they are workable. A startup should ask itself: why has no one ever done this before? There are product and startup graveyards online that review why an idea failed. A startup can comb through these to learn from others' mistakes before starting design. Finally, a startup needs to think broadly about competition. Look beyond the exact solutions to other kinds of substitutes.

Once a startup knows current solutions aren't working that well, the next step is to find out if people actually intend to buy the new solution. Instead of asking potential customers if they like the solution, a startup needs to get their non-binding buying intent. If no one is willing to commit to buying, that's a warning flag. The time to pull the plug is now, before incurring the costs of building a product. During validation, it is tempting to start building something—but even building a prototype or wireframe should be part of the plan, to avoid the Overdo and Overspend iceberg drift.

It's nearly impossible to get all product features right the first time. The goal is to figure out what's required to launch and plan later for improvements. Before investing in designing and building, a startup has to discuss possible solutions with customers or it could Overdo. At this stage of validating assumptions, startups have to be careful to avoid testing every possible feature against its alternative, and pivoting features based on every piece of feedback. Either approach can lead a startup to Overspend. There is a delicate balance between getting feedback from the market and staying true to the startup's original approach. Remember that there will be changes in the future—start with the original plan, listen, and incorporate the ideas that make the most sense for what the startup wants to accomplish.

Validation Sea	Strong – Smooth Sailing	Some – Rocky Journey Ahead	Very Little – Need A Navigation Plan	Not At All – Large Debtbergs In Sight
FALSE HOPE — Founders check their assumptions:				
• don't present solutions prematurely	o	o	o	o
• seek negative feedback	o	o	o	o
• secure non-binding agreements to buy from potential customers	o	o	o	o
UNNECESSARY SOLUTION — The founders know the solution is needed:				
• understand current alternative solutions to solve the problem	o	o	o	o
• understand why past solutions were unsuccessful	o	o	o	o
• monitor a broad set of competitors	o	o	o	o
OVERDO AND OVERSPEND — The startup does not waste resources in validation:				
• avoids rushing to design before validating the customer problem	o	o	o	o
• is willing to accept a less-than-perfect product	o	o	o	o
• resists A/B testing every feature	o	o	o	o

Figure 8: The Technical Iceberg Index in the Validation Sea

The Design Sea

As a startup moves to actual product conceptualization and Design, it is trying to plot the right course for product development. It is tempting to rush to the MVP at this stage. Before doing this, though, a startup should begin by converting theoretical concepts to a simple prototype or wireframe.

This helps avoid the Missing Mockup iceberg of rushing prematurely to a developed product. This could even include a manual element or a "low-fidelity" version that minimizes investment until customers provide feedback. Don't spend $200,000 up front on software that could be first tested with pen-and-paper exercises and a little sweat equity!

This is also a good time to get out of the building and really interact with potential customers. Give them early versions of the product and get their feedback. A best practice is for the founding team to be actively involved in this feedback approach. Don't be a captain in the cabin letting everyone else see what's happening firsthand. Avoid the trap of Ivory Tower "Insights." At the same time, it's easy to be discouraged with the first prototypes and their feedback. A startup has to recognize that this is just a start. Early versions never look as good as they will end up being. The goal here is to get started and learn how to improve the product stepwise.

Now that feedback on early versions is coming in, a startup needs to be aware of Shortsighted Scoping. It can be easy to try to incorporate every piece of feedback into new designs. A better approach is to take all of the feedback, design a fully articulated vision of the product, and then tear the product back to its core. What features make the MVP and how can the startup iterate on those features over time? What are the core features that are absolute must-haves? What additional features can wait until later?

At the same time, a startup has to consider all of the ways that people might use its product differently than it expected. Not all of these uses will be positive. People use products at many different times, in different locations, and in ways that a startup may have never initially envisioned. It is important to work through some of these unexpected scenarios. What are the most likely ways that the product might be broken? How can the design help minimize these or overcome this possibility—or allow for a quick recovery to the right track?

Design Sea		Strong – Smooth Sailing	Some – Rocky Journey Ahead	Very Little – Need A Navigation Plan	Not At All – Large Debtbergs In Sight
MISSING MOCKUPS	The startup seeks feedback:				
	• develops a prototypes/wireframe prior to the MVP	o	o	o	o
	• gets customer feedback on these mockups	o	o	o	o
	• uses low-fidelity, manual tests where viable, before investing in technology	o	o	o	o
IVORY TOWER "INSIGHTS"	The startup maintains realistic focus:				
	• gets real user feedback on early versions of the MVP	o	o	o	o
	• gets founders directly involved in market tests	o	o	o	o
	• stays the course through the design process and doesn't pivot too often	o	o	o	o
SHORTSIGHTED SCOPING	The product design has flexibility over time:				
	• the startup designs first and iterates after	o	o	o	o
	• the design considers user experience	o	o	o	o
	• the base design includes all core features but not features unnecessary for the MVP	o	o	o	o

Figure 9: The Technical Iceberg Index in the Design Sea

The Development Sea

In the Development Sea, the goal for a startup is to figure out how to stay on course. Generally, the processes of validating, designing, and developing are iterative and ongoing. Where a startup can accumulate large debtbergs is in product development, when you start building something. By now, the founders have received a lot of feedback and decided to make a number of changes.

The startup needs to make sure it avoids a Mushy Process in development. Study after study has demonstrated that groups make better decisions than individuals do— the proverbial two heads are better than one. The same is true in product development. A team of developers is better than a lone developer. However, bringing on developers can be risky, as development skills may be difficult to assess. Startups should make sure that someone with good technical training is part of the recruiting process.

As product development progresses, there is a tendency for developers to work on what interests them, which might not align with startup priorities. It's critical to make sure that the team is keeping track of what it has already accomplished and what still needs doing. These steps, features, and changes need to live in some kind of list—a *backlog*, punch list, or some other type of list, with clear priorities for mission-critical development. Then, a team, rather than a single person, needs to continuously review the backlog and prioritize the next steps. The goal now is to move ahead as quickly and smoothly as possible. It's worth investing time to get a well-orchestrated process with which to move forward.

Once early versions of the product are available, assessing how good they are from a technical standpoint and whether they provide a base for scaling is important. A startup wants to avoid starting with a Poor Product Foundation. For a software development product, this means testing, grading, and getting a peer review of the codebase. For other products, this means detailed quality testing and quality controls. A startup wants to avoid building more features on top of a faulty foundation. Inevitably, over the course of the development process, more people will join the project. A startup needs to consider how to incorporate these new people into a complex development project, especially in the earlier development stages. Otherwise, they will be the new source of error.

Finally, a startup needs to consider if they will build this entire product in-house or outsource some of it (build versus buy). A startup should know its key competencies and be willing to seek high-quality outsourcing for the parts that are not its strengths. Selective outsourcing can be a more efficient and cheaper way to proceed as long as quality does not deteriorate. Even outsourced parts need to be quality-tested to make sure they will stand up to customers' requirements and not suffer from "quality fade."

At some point in the development process, products will be in customers' hands. While this is an exciting step, the development work is not complete. Now, Foggy

Waters can set in. In the Design Sea, the plan was to design for launch and iterate later. Now, a startup has to stay focused on its development plan and keep evolving the product. Most likely, the launch product was an MVP. It still needs to be improved. Here's a great place to get a different kind of feedback—the kind that comes from customers directly. Most products have some kind of user metrics. The startup can review these metrics to assess where the product needs improvement. Don't lose sight of either customers or competitors in the Foggy Waters of post-launch uncertainty.

Customer service can be another good source of customer feedback. Instead of just letting them manage customer support, a smart startup will use its service team to find out what kinds of problems customers are having and prioritize minimizing these problems. The customers and their needs should continue to stay at the center of ongoing product development efforts.

Development Sea		Strong – Smooth Sailing	Some – Rocky Journey Ahead	Very Little – Need A Navigation Plan	Not At All – Large Debtbergs In Sight
MUSHY PROCESS	The startup has set up a strong development process:				
	• creates a development team rather than relying on just one person, even if part of the team is outsourced	o	o	o	o
	• uses recruiting experts who can assess developers' skills	o	o	o	o
	• maintains a development backlog	o	o	o	o
	• sets backlog priorities and develops more important features first	o	o	o	o
POOR PRODUCT FOUNDATION	The startup maintains a strong product foundation:				
	• performs regular quality checks	o	o	o	o
	• has a plan to manage adding people to the development process	o	o	o	o
	• develops a build versus buy plan	o	o	o	o
FOGGY WATERS	The company is planning for long-term development:				
	• plans for managing changes over time	o	o	o	o
	• plans for continuous improvement	o	o	o	o
	• monitors user metrics	o	o	o	o
	• incorporates feedback from customer service	o	o	o	o

Figure 10: The Technical Iceberg Index in the Development Sea

The Strategy Iceberg Index

Now let's bring it all together. The Strategy Ocean includes the Incomplete Integration, Meager Measurement, and Anemic Accountability Seas. While many icebergs are in functional areas—the Human, Marketing, and Technical Oceans—Strategy spans all of these.

The Incomplete Integration Sea

The first debtberg in the Strategy Ocean is the Lack of Coordination drift. Large icebergs in this Sea would be things like the following:

- There is no plan or communication across areas of activity.
- Marketing and customer communication have little direction from or contribution to technical development and vice versa.
- Business needs don't drive leadership focus, investor/adviser input, and staffing, nor does uncertainty in the other Oceans.
- There is no vision guiding the startup.

This rarely occurs to such a degree, but we have seen entrepreneurs "wing it" with virtually no coordination of activities across the startup. Sometimes when an entrepreneur wants to be a billionaire so freakin' bad, they never really focus on their own passion and experience, and therefore lack persistence to follow through.

A middle ground exists where two areas have some coordination, but one area is on its own—for example, marketing and human areas of uncertainty are in sync, but the crazy development person is out in left field experimenting with who-knows-what. Without correction, this could create a bergy bit that causes serious damage.

Finally, at different stages, a firm may address coordination explicitly only on a quarterly basis, or around board meetings. While likely not devastating, this can create small icebergs over time that limit startup upside.

To address this debtberg, founders should spend at least one half day a week on navigation, including how the different functions relate to each other. A coordinated plan can help with many of these issues.

The next drift is Unbalanced Effort across areas. When one area of the venture receives most or all of the attention, the startup may resolve some uncertainty in that area but face increasingly hazardous icebergs in the others. As noted, this often occurs when the founding team lacks diversity, advisors are not engaged, and the team becomes singularly focused on solving one problem, whether the technical problem or the customer/market problem. More rarely, a startup will get preoccupied with building a huge team or raising money before they have resolved some of the market or technical uncertainty, but this happens as well, creating a large iceberg of hidden debt.

In more moderate situations, all the areas get some attention, but one area of uncertainty is the focus of most resources, discussions, and effort. It is not bad to have one area of uncertainty that drives the startup—for example, a technology that drives marketing and human resource elements, or a market problem and need that drives product development. However, this does not mean the other dimensions are less important in terms of resolving uncertainty and identifying icebergs of hidden debt. In fact, a lack of a consistent driver, with no seeming awareness of what really drives success for the startup, can create growler-sized debt. Companies in this situation can face a pinball problem of always bouncing from a fire in one area to a fire in another. In addition to coordination across areas, the navigation time founders spend should include mapping progress and the status of uncertainty in different parts of the business to maintain balance over time.

The Meager Measurement Sea

Setting up metrics and tracking progress is essential for a sustainable venture. A complete lack of attention to developing and maintaining a scorecard or measurement system for hitting milestones and making progress is a large iceberg that can, and eventually will, sink a startup. Either vague or generic metrics that have little grounding in the specific context (for example, total revenue or money raised) can create a good-sized bergy bit, as can over-measuring and having too many numbers to track. Metrics are important, but can be overdone. A sound set of metrics will be context-specific (to the startup and industry), cross all areas of the venture, and evolve over time—but don't expect to get them right the first time. Tools like the Balanced Scorecard can provide a useful model. Many successful startups have growlers of meager measurement debt that they navigate around and resolve over time.

The Anemic Accountability Sea

The next Sea, Anemic Accountability, does not contain the largest icebergs a startup might encounter. However, a complete lack of accountability, perhaps due to a lack of founder time and support, combined with elusive expectation of advisors, can cause significant damage. Having all accountability on the shoulders of the founders as the startup scales adds smaller debts, as does having multiple individuals accountable for the same area and metric. Again, accountability will evolve over time as the startup scales, and transition from founders to area leaders within the growing firm. Investors can be very helpful in navigating the Anemic Accountability Sea, even if they seem intrusive and create challenges on occasion. To navigate this iceberg, each metric should have an individual ultimately responsible and accountable for tracking performance relative to each individual goal over time.

Strategy Ocean			Strong – Smooth Sailing	Some – Rocky Journey Ahead	Very Little – Need A Navigation Plan	Not At All – Large Debtbergs In Sight
INCOMPLETE INTEGRATION		The startup integrates activities across Oceans:				
		• coordinates activities across Oceans	o	o	o	o
		• balances activity across Oceans	o	o	o	o
MEAGER MEASUREMENT		The startup monitors performance:				
		• links metrics to performance	o	o	o	o
		• uses stage-appropriate metrics	o	o	o	o
ANEMIC ACCOUNTABILITY		The leadership team designates individuals accountable for key activities and metrics.	o	o	o	o

Figure 11: The Strategy Iceberg Index

Many founders might be feeling overwhelmed by seeing there is a good deal of hidden debt in their startup. Remember, the goal here isn't to beat up founders and startups for the debts they've accumulated. The goal is to be able to identify those debts and start planning for how to mitigate them. Measure what is measurable—and make measurable what is not so! Startups will have hidden debts. However, they also have time to minimize the effect of those debts *before* the startup is sunk.

A startup should start with a simple checklist and have a plan for how to limit icebergs over time. As the startup moves through launch to growth, more formal use of the Iceberg Index can help systematically track and address debtbergs. Check out our online resources as our own Iceberg Index evolves at www.titaniceffect.com.

CHAPTER 9:

SETTING SAIL

"All journeys have secret destinations of which the traveler is unaware."

–Martin Buber

"Don't stop believing."

–Journey

Although prevailing wisdom suggests that the *Titanic* did indeed sink when it encountered The Iceberg, many alternative theories have arisen over the years. Some fall into the "conspiracy theory" category. In *Titanic: The Ship That Never Sank?*[102] Robin Gardiner posits that White Star's sister ship the *Olympic* was the ship that actually sank. Gardiner suggests that White Star swapped and "rebranded" the ships shortly before launch. The *Olympic* had taken damage in an earlier incident, so White Star planned to let the *Olympic*, masquerading as the *Titanic*, slowly sink at sea, allowing passengers time to disembark safely to rescue ships. By swapping, Gardiner argues, White Star could recover the loss via insurance. However, White Star didn't anticipate The Iceberg. Of course, many factors (and facts) render this story improbable.

To our knowledge, no alternative stories of the *Titanic* involve aliens or the Bermuda Triangle, but other fantastic versions do exist. One is worthy of a movie plot, complete with high-finance intrigue and sinister, self-interested actors.[103] This version holds that investor J.P. Morgan, whom you might recall from the Human Ocean Chapter, arranged for the ship to sink to take out powerful people who opposed forming the Federal Reserve Board. Three members of this faction, John Jacob Astor, Benjamin Guggenheim, and Isidor Straus, perished in the disaster. Morgan's last-minute cancellation of his own passage on the *Titanic* added fuel to this supposition.

---

102   Gardiner, Robin, *Titanic: The Ship That Never Sank?* Sheperton, UK: Ian Allan Publishing, 1988.

103   Mike Bird, "There's a crazy conspiracy theory that the Rothschilds Sank the *Titanic* to set up the Federal Reserve," *Business Insider*, October 12, 2015, accessed September 22, 2017, http://www.businessinsider.com/conspiracy-theory-that-the-rothschilds-and-federal-reserve-proponents-sank-the-titanic-2015-10.

Other explanations are less exotic but more plausible, suggesting other factors that may have contributed to the sinking. As we described earlier, watertight doors between bulkheads, substandard rivets, and the bulkheads themselves have all been fingered as suspects or accomplices. One theory that has received more interest and credence recently is that a coal fire started before the ship even launched and burned near a bulkhead for as long as several weeks. The theory suggests that this fire weakened the hull near where The Iceberg hit. While many steamers experienced the challenge of coal fires, this fire may have been more severe and longer lasting, leading the captain to prioritize speed over safety in iceberg-infested waters.[104]

In hindsight, it can be easy to find reasons for failure. We raise these alternative theories for the *Titanic's* demise not because they are viable, but rather to provide founders motivation to inventory sources of debt along the journey. Monitoring debts along the way may help a *startup* avoid the *Titanic's* fate. It may also help a founding team learn from failure for their next *venture*. We hope our work documents how a series of small decisions, of *hidden debts* occurring over weeks, months, years, and even decades prior to the maiden launch, contributed to the premature and infamous sinking of the grandest ship on the seas. These decisions and resultant hidden debts serve as a base metaphor to learn from in the hopes of preventing a similar fate for scores of startups embarking on the Oceans of *uncertainty*.

Bringing Closure to White Star Line and the *Titanic*

The White Star Line, launched in the mid-1800s carrying ambitious, gold-seeking voyagers to the Land Down Under, was able to survive the catastrophic loss of the *Titanic*. However, the company struggled during the next couple of decades, in part due to World War I, and then the Great Depression in the 1930s. Financial troubles similar to those experienced in the 1860s and 1900s led to multiple ownership and structural changes. The company's competitor, Cunard Line, eventually absorbed White Star Line in 1934.

The memory of the *Titanic* and attention paid to the tragedy ebbed and flowed over time. A wave of books and activity followed the sinking in 1912, but faded within a decade. Interest rekindled in 1955 with the book *A Night to Remember* by Walter Lord, and again with the ship's discovery on the ocean floor in 1985. Clive Cussler used the *Titanic* as inspiration for a fictional work *Raise the Titanic!* in 1976, with a similar effort by Arthur C. Clarke in 1990 with *The Ghost from the Grand Banks*.

Of course, the James Cameron movie of 1997 set records and garnered awards, and is the only filmed rendition to have actual footage from the decks of the ship

---

104   Telegraph Reporters, "Huge fire ripped through *Titanic* before it struck iceberg, fresh evidence suggests," *The Telegraph*, December 31, 2016, accessed September 22, 2017, http://www.telegraph.co.uk/news/2016/12/31/huge-fire-ripped-titanic-struck-iceberg-fresh-evidence-suggests/.

herself. While Leonardo DiCaprio and Kate Winslet are well known for their portrayals of passengers, other notable actors who have made appearances in *Titanic* movies include Barbara Stanwyck and Clifton Webb (1953), David Warner (1979), and a young Sigourney Weaver in an off-Broadway farcical play (1974). Alfred Hitchcock, on the other hand, declined an opportunity to be involved in a film adaptation of the story in the late 1930s.

What can a founder or investor learn from this narrative? We believe the metaphor of the *Titanic* raises a number of important points that parallel the startup journey and series of decisions and *tradeoffs* founders face. Startup failure similarly emerges from decisions made across Oceans, over time, and, in many cases, without the awareness of founders and key players.

Origin Story Updates

Throughout the book, we have referenced some ventures that paid a similar price to the *Titanic* and became instructive tales of loss and failure. We've described prominent examples of failure like Theranos and Webvan. We've also combed startup graveyards for examples of other, less well-known failures both in the United States and around the world.

Certainly, the challenges of navigating uncertainty claim many a startup. However, there are many noteworthy examples of startups that encountered debtbergs and continued their journey. As examples, we have also woven in the stories of startups that didn't just survive but thrived. Here is a status update on the ventures core to our narrative that we introduced in the opening chapter.

Clif Bars/Gary Erickson

From conceptualization in 1990 on a long bike ride to the success of today, Erickson faced a number of icebergs that challenged Clif Bar, but did not sink the ship. Instead, Clif Bar hit admirable metrics for an established company of 20% annual revenue growth while doubling its employee base in 2016. Clif Bar is a market leader in health and lifestyle bars with about 33% market share. While the company does not disclose sales revenue, it appears to be above the $1 billion mark. Its value far exceeds the $125 million offer to buy it received more than a decade ago.

Instacart/Apoorva Mehta

Instacart, founded in 2012, did many things that notable, failed predecessors like Webvan did not. However, that does not mean the venture did not face its share of bergy bits and iceberg islands. Still, in early 2018 it raised an additional $200 million in capital on a valuation of $4.2 billion. Revenue reportedly grew by 160% in 2017.

Instacart has eased the burden of the grocery store shopping chore for many, while providing employment for others.

Airbnb/Joe Gebbia

From having a stranger crash on his airbed in Providence to the launch and success of Airbnb, Gebbia and his team have overcome quite a bit of opposition. In doing so, the company has amply demonstrated that there is money in a sharing economy. Airbnb earned an estimated *EBITDA* of $450 million on $2.8 billion in sales revenue in 2017. The founders' stated goal is to be the first online travel company with a market valuation of $100 billion. That's a lot of airbeds!

Chesapeake Bay Candle/Mei Xu

Arguably, Xu and Chesapeake Bay Candle contributed to creating a whole category of household products incorporating fashion and function in new ways. Not satisfied with just the success of Chesapeake Bay Candle, Xu's holding company Pacific Trade International, has branched out into other home décor products, including fragrances and linens. As of September 2017, Xu agreed to sell Chesapeake Bay Candle to Newell Brands, the owner of Yankee Candle, for $75 million. At the time, Chesapeake Bay Candle had an estimated $55 million in sales.

TRX/Randy Hetrick

From a military mission hunting pirates to the launch of TRX eight years later, Hetrick serves as a great example of combining continued passion for a product, experience over time, and persistence in chasing the dream. Hetrick has successfully battled adversaries, both domestic and foreign. As of 2015, sales revenue was approximately $54 million. Because of TRX's success and a booming fitness market, several knockoff competitors have again emerged. In March of 2017, TRX won a $6.8 million patent infringement lawsuit against one of these knockoffs, WOSS Enterprises LLC. In the meantime, the company has been quiet about its success. The IHRSA recognized TRX as the Associate Member of 2017.

These founders and venture stories are worthy of celebration as well as study. But of course, they are also still on their journey—and it would not be surprising if one or more of them succumbed to the icy graveyard of venture failure by the time you read this.

Avoiding the Titanic Effect

The Titanic Effect occurs when a series of decisions and tradeoffs early in a startup's life make it more vulnerable to failure. These decisions are a necessary part of navigating the uncertainty endemic to the startup journey. However, they create unintended consequences, including hidden debts that can sink or seriously disable the growing venture.

- When the team needs to add a co-founder, but her role and contribution are unclear…
- When a company must change its brand and value proposition to reflect more accurately the job its product does for customers…
- When the startup needs to make a design choice to get the *MVP* in the hands of a customer…

These are necessary choices a startup makes. Startups have to navigate uncertainty, but the consequences do not have to be unforeseen. Awareness of the resultant hidden debts can help the tradeoffs be measurable and manageable. The goal of a startup shouldn't be to avoid taking on these hidden debts or debtbergs but rather to recognize them, track them, and mitigate them over time.

The Iceberg Index we discussed in Chapter 8 is our tool for identifying, tracking, and managing debtbergs. We encourage our readers and followers to go to our website (www.titaniceffect.com) and begin to build and track your own Iceberg Index. We hope to continue to aggregate and share findings over time as to how the Index benefits the founders, investors/advisors, and supporters of startups who use it.

Closing

Research on entrepreneurship offers two contrasting facts:

1. *High-growth* startups account for 50% of job growth in the United States, and yet
2. These very same startups are having even more difficulty in scaling growth now than similar businesses did in the past.[105]

Apparently, these high-potential startups are finding the environment less accommodating for scaling today than their predecessors did in the past. This comes on top of low survival rates to begin with. In short, it is darn hard to turn an idea into a product, launch a company around it, survive the icebergs, and evolve a Scalable Product and Business Model. The journey is not getting any easier.

We do not offer this narrative to dissuade would-be founders. Rather, we hope to help them navigate the uncharted waters in front of them. Every decision for startups involves tradeoffs. We hope that *The Titanic Effect* helps founders and others to recognize the pros and cons of the tradeoffs they are making. The sailing may not be completely smooth, but we hope you are better able to avoid or survive your own iceberg collisions.

---

105 Ewing Marion Kauffman Foundation New Entrepreneurial Growth Agenda, "Section 3: Entrepreneurial Trends," accessed April 9, 2018, https://www.kauffman.org/neg/section-3.

It would be a bit presumptuous to conclude that all a founder or investor needed to do to improve their success rate is to read our book. Clearly, the journey is more difficult than that. Still we would suggest that monitoring and mitigating debtbergs will help startups improve the likelihood of their success. In closing, we offer three principles to guide the startup journey.

Experiment often and fail fast. Startups almost never "get it right" the first time. Experimentation and learning from the results is important, not only within the lifetime of a specific idea, but also for the lifetime of a successful entrepreneur and venture community participant. That said, the experimentation should be deliberate and systematic, driven by specific hypotheses about what will work both from a technical and a market standpoint. With this approach, you will not fail—but instead have the opportunity to learn from numerous ways that don't work, without encountering life-ending icebergs. As Thomas Edison said, "I have not failed. I've just found 10,000 ways that won't work."

Seek feedback and advice through networking. Whether from possible co-founders, advisors, customers, design teams, or mentors, there is a virtual army of support for every would-be founder. We have found abundant generosity from captains courageous who have sailed and successfully navigated the iceberg-laden Oceans we chart here. In many cases they are willing to share their own navigation charts, connect you with past crewmembers, and perhaps even help underwrite your own vessel—we just suggest you do not call it the *Titanic.*

While seeking advice, startups should also build their networks. Think of it as degrees of separation. Almost every founder is three or four degrees of separation from the five people they need to know to be successful. Part of successful navigation is shortening those degrees of separation to one or two, to meet the people who can make you successful—and show them you have the *PEP* to win.

Make stage-appropriate decisions. Whether allocating equity, seeking funding, contacting prospective customers for feedback, building wireframes, or growing your team, moving too early or too late can yield devastating consequences. We have created models in each chapter that reflect the key challenges in Human, Marketing, Technical, and Strategic Oceans for Pre-Revenue, MVP, Launch and Early Growth, and Scalable Product and Business Model stages. As you map your journey and navigate uncertainty, don't create additional hidden debts by overextending into future stages. Trying to raise too much money, over-hiring, making promises to customers that you cannot keep, and overbuilding technology can all sink the overly ambitious startup. Similarly, not investing in people, markets, and products can have a similar effect if delayed too long.

Startups are the lifeblood of our future economy—the engines of economic and job growth, and the inspiration for future generations of Ericksons, Mehtas, Gebbias, Xus, Hetricks, Ohanians, Lincolns, and others. We sincerely hope that, by engaging more knowledgably in navigating uncertainty, founders, investors, and their supporters can better recognize icebergs, navigate, and realize the many benefits of startup launch and success. Most importantly, embrace the secret and unexpected destinations of the startup journey—they are rewards in and of themselves.

The *Titanic* set sail on a wave of ambition and promise. May your efforts do so as well, but with better outcomes. Don't succumb to the Titanic Effect. It's a book, not a prophecy!

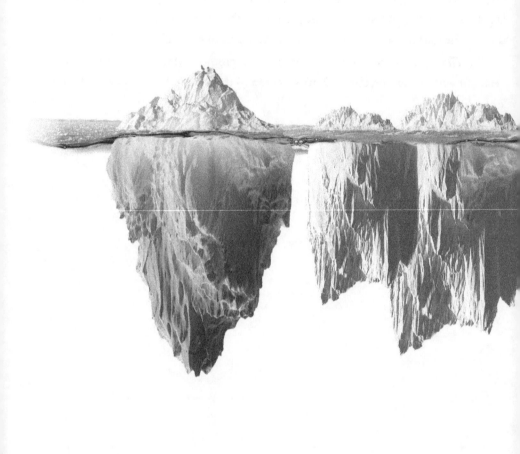

ABOUT THE AUTHORS

D r. Todd Saxton, Associate Professor and Indiana Venture Faculty Fellow at the IU Kelley School of Business, is an award-winning professor of strategy and entrepreneurship. Todd has advised, helped launch, and invested in hundreds of startups spanning life sciences, software, sports, consumer products, and services. Todd serves on the board of multiple entrepreneurial ventures, including VisionTech Angel Partners, the largest angel investing group in Indiana; Diagnotes, a venture-funded health IT firm he helped found; and Fight for Life Foundation, a not-for-profit providing social and emotional learning for the deserving but underserved. He co-founded the Indiana Chapter of The Society of Physician Entrepreneurs (SoPE) in 2018. He has published numerous book chapters and articles on corporate and startup strategies for success. Todd hails from New Jersey, and has lived in Virginia, the DC area, Pennsylvania, Wisconsin, and Bloomington IN, with stints in England and Australia. He currently lives in Indianapolis, IN where he enjoys training for endurance sports and water and snow activities of many types with his wife and partner Kim and their two daughters.

Dr. Kim Saxton has over thirty years of marketing and market-research experience, working with large corporations, startups, and medium-sized businesses. Currently, she is a Clinical Professor of Marketing at Indiana University's Kelley School of Business. Her teaching success has been recognized through numerous teaching awards, including an across-Indiana-University President's Award for Teaching Excellence. Kim's research on market segmentation, branding, promotional strategies, venture success, and venture ecosystems has been published in numerous international academic journals. She also serves as an Associate Editor for the *Journal of Advertising Research*. Kim is an active angel investor and advisor to high-potential startups. She is a member of the advisory board for The Startup Ladies, a community-based organization helping women launch their startups through training and access to investors. She has served as an executive mentor for a wide variety of women-founded startups. Kim grew up in Florida, went to school at MIT in Boston, MA, and has lived in the DC area, Pennsylvania, and Wisconsin. She currently resides in Indianapolis, IN.

Michael Cloran is a serial entrepreneur who has helped found startups in aviation education, bond-trading systems, Internet services, children's software, human-assisted customer-interaction systems, robotic beverages, and non-profit e-commerce solutions. His most recent startup, DeveloperTown, is a design and development firm with over fifty creative makers that has helped over 200 startups and larger companies build solid products and steer them to market. Michael grew up in Ohio and Yugoslavia and pursued ventures in Illinois, Texas, Florida, Germany, New York, California, and New Jersey before choosing Indianapolis, IN as the perfect iceberg-free place to raise his four boys with ship captain, Elyse.

GLOSSARY

A/B testing. An experiment between two variants to see which performs better. Also called split testing or bucket testing.

accredited investor. A person who meets the SEC's qualifications for participating in a securities transaction with a company that is not registered with the SEC, such as a *startup*. The SEC sets these requirements based on characteristics it deems make the investor able to withstand the economic *risk* of buying an unregistered security. It currently defines an accredited investor as one who has:

- an earned income that exceeds $200,000 (or $300,000 together with a spouse) in each of the prior two years and reasonably expects the same for the current year, OR;
- a net worth over $1 million, either alone or together with a spouse (excluding the value of the person's primary residence).

See the SEC rules at www.sec.gov/files/ib_accreditedinvestors.pdf

add-on service. An offering available for purchase only in addition to another, often base-level, offering.

Agile software development methodology. An approach to creating applications that is iterative and incremental. It includes adaptive planning, evolutionary development, early delivery, and continual improvement. It stresses being responsive and adaptable to change.

alpha testing. The first level of product testing. It is usually performed by internal users.

angel investor. An *accredited investor* who invests both time and money in early-stage *startups*.

API (application programming interface). Intermediary software that governs how one software application can talk to another. An API allows two different programs to integrate information from one to the other without compromising either program's integrity.

articles of incorporation. Formal legal documents, filed with the Secretary of State, that establish a company's existence. Typical information in the documents includes company name, address, basic purpose, incorporators, legal representatives, and the amount and types of stock that it may issue.

A-round funding. The money a *startup* receives for growth funding. This is typically the first round with venture capital investors. See also *first round or seed capital.*

backlog. A list of work to do, features to develop, or orders to fill.

bases of segmentation. Characteristics of customers that can divide the customers into meaningful groups. The bases include demographics, behavioral characteristics, and psychographics for consumer customer segments.

Bass Diffusion model. An algorithm developed by Frank Bass that describes how a market adopts new products. It includes parameters to describe the innovativeness of the new product and the degree of imitation, both of which affect the speed of adoption.

benchmarks. Standards against which to measure a *startup*'s progress. Some investors set benchmarks for their own investment. For example, a company must have a benchmark amount of *recurring revenue* after two years in the market. See the metrics section of the Strategy Ocean Chapter for how founding teams can also use benchmarks to monitor their progress.

beta testing. The second level of product testing. It is usually performed by customers and checks that the product not only works but also works the way that customers want. Beta testers are often allowed to use the product for free in exchange for their feedback.

bootstrapping. Accomplishing an activity using your own resources. In *startups*, bootstrapping refers to funding activities and growth from the startup's own revenue or the founders' personal funds instead of securing funds from outside investors. Generally, bootstrapping involves getting as far as possible with as few dollars as possible.

brand book. A set of rules that describe how a brand works, including the meaning behind the brand and how branding elements like a logo or messages should appear. Also called brand standards or brand guidelines.

break through. Stand out enough against competing ads to get target customers' attention.

bridge loan. A short-term bond or investment that provides cash to meet obligations between funding activities. It is short-term, carries a relatively high interest rate, and might be backed by some form of collateral, such as real estate or inventory.

B-round funding. The second round of *venture capital* funding. See *A-round funding* and *first round or seed capital.*

burn rate. The speed at which a *startup* consumes capital above revenue, usually expressed as a monthly amount. Total capital available divided by burn rate approximates the expected life of the startup (fume date) if it doesn't secure more capital.

Business Model Canvas. A tool related to the *Lean Startup movement* that maps out the key components of a *startup*, such as key partners, value proposition, and cost structure in a one-page format. It is conceptually on the opposite end of the continuum from a fully articulated business plan. See *Business Model Generation* (Osterwalder and Pigneur, 2010) or www.canvanizer.com for more information.

buying group. An organization where typically smaller businesses band together to coordinate their buying from vendors and negotiate better pricing and terms than they could get on their own.

buyout. The purchase of a controlling interest of a company, essentially "buying out" the existing owners. A leveraged buyout happens when the buyer borrows money for the purchase.

cap (capitalization) table. A list (via spreadsheet or table) of a company's securities and owners that includes equity shares, preferred shares and options, and the various prices paid by stakeholders for these securities. The table shows ownership stakes on a fully diluted basis, thereby showing the company's overall capital structure at a glance.

capped note. A type of convertible bond with a ceiling on the total valuation of the company before the note converts into equity. See also *convertible note.*

cash-flow positive. A term that describes a *startup* that generates more cash each month than it spends. Cash receipts include all paid customer purchases, interest, etc. Cash expenditures include operational expenses, investments in product development, and financing costs, among others. Theoretically, when a startup reaches cash-flow positive status, it does not need to raise additional investor dollars, though it might do so for growth.

channel partners. Organizations who sell, distribute, and service products created by another firm.

common stock. A security that represents ownership in a corporation. If the company has a *liquidity event* (see *exit*), common stockholders are repaid after bondholders, preferred stockholders, and other debtholders have been paid in full.

conversion rate. The percentage of people who took an action, typically describing the success of sales and marketing. For example, if 100 people visit a website and ten buy a product, then the conversion rate is 10%.

convertible note. A bond that a *venture* takes to secure capital when the value of the company is unknown. This note can be converted into a specified number of common shares in the future. Since it is a debt obligation, it has a specified interest rate and time horizon. The purpose is to allow a new venture to address some uncertainty before setting a valuation but still give investors an incentive to provide financing during the risky stage of the venture. Also called convertible debt.

CRM (customer relationship management). A *strategy* or approach that uses data about customer interactions to increase customer engagement and retention.

Crossing the Chasm model. Undertaking the required steps to help new products spread from "early adopters" to a larger market segment, including the "early majority." This term originates from the book, *Crossing the Chasm*, by Geoffrey Moore.

crowdfunding campaign. A fundraising event that asks many individuals to contribute small amounts, typically $10 to $100, usually either as a donation or as a pre-order of a future product. Most crowdfunding is accomplished through an online platform like Kickstarter or Indiegogo. Under the JOBS Act, crowdfunding can also include investing for equity by non-accredited investors.

debt financing. Borrowing money to use as working capital by promising to repay principal and interest on the debt. This is, in essence, taking a loan to fund operations.

down round. An event in private financing where investors purchase stock or convertible bonds from a company at a lower valuation than the company had in the preceding round. Down rounds are bad for founders and earlier investors whose previously purchased equity goes down in value.

due diligence. An analysis a potential investor makes of all the facts of an investment opportunity, the company's potential, and the founders' backgrounds before committing to investing. Can also include the analysis a founder does before considering an investor as well.

early-stage investor. People who support early-stage *ventures* with time or money.

EBITDA (earnings before interest, taxes, depreciation, and amortization). A measure of profitability. It provides an easy comparison between companies because it does not include effects from financing and accounting decisions.

equity. An ownership stake in a company.

exit. A way for early investors to secure a return on their investment. The exit brings new money into the ***venture*** and lets early investors "exit." Commons exit options are an ***IPO*** or ***buyout*** by another company.

first-round or seed capital. First official financing event for a ***startup*** from ***venture*** capitalists, usually to fund product development, early market research, growth, and/or building a management team. There can be several rounds of seed funding and they are usually labeled alphabetically as an ***A-round***, ***B-round***, and perhaps C-round.

four-bit hustler. Like a ***two-bit hustler***, but more expensive. Often costs twice as much, but not always worth it.

frame of reference. The category to which customers perceive a product offering belonging. A frame of reference for a new product offering gives customers a shortcut to understanding what the product is all about.

freemium model. A pricing approach where a basic product is given away free with the intention that most users will upgrade in order to access premium features, services, or virtual goods.

friends and family money. The most common form of ***startup*** funding, in which the founders' personal networks invest. It can take the form of a gift, loan, or equity investment. The SEC does not formally regulate this type of funding. This is a very risky stage of investment.

fully diluted shares. The total number of common shares of stock in a company that would be outstanding if all possible sources of conversion, such as convertible bonds and stock options, were exercised.

fund of funds. An investment device that invests in other types of funds. This investment portfolio contains different underlying assets instead of investing directly in bonds, stocks, and other types of securities, including startups. Also called multi-manager investment.

gazelle. An extremely fast-growing company that maintains consistent expansion of both total employees and revenue over an extended period, often five years or more. There is no single definition of what constitutes an "exceptional" growth rate, but 20% or more annually is a commonly used metric.

groupthink. A phenomenon where members begin to see a shared view of the world that may or may not resemble reality.

hidden debts. The unanticipated consequences of navigating ***uncertainty***.

high-growth. Quickly increasing in size, usually indicated by sales revenue. A specific description of a high-growth rate may vary over time and by industry, but is typically is several multiples over GDP growth.

Hype Curve model. A graphical representation of the stages of growth for technology products, branded by Gartner. A market described by a Hype Curve typically adjusts to a lower total level of value after a short period of irrational exuberance and high demand.

IPO (initial public offering). The first time shares of stock in a company are available on a securities exchange or to the general public. An **IPO** is a mechanism for raising capital. After an IPO, a private company becomes a public company listed on a stock exchange as regulated by the SEC. This provides an **exit** or **liquidity event** for early investors in a startup.

inbound marketing or advertising. Attracting customers who are already interested in your product category by providing "relevant and helpful" content aimed at the stages of the customers' buying process. It typically is predominantly online content via digital marketing and tied to online search by potential customers. This term originated from the company HubSpot.

lagging indicators. Metrics that focus on outputs and summarize what has already happened. Unemployment, for example, is a lagging indicator because it tells how many people were unemployment in the past time period.

land-and-expand strategy. The process of engaging in a small deal with a new customer intending to secure a bigger deal over time. B2B companies typically use land-and-expand strategies.

launch and early growth. The stage of a **startup** that comes after developing an MVP. A product or service is available in the market and revenue is being generated.

lead investor. A **venture capital** firm, **angel investor**, or individual investor that is the first to put up money and organize a specific round of funding for a company. The lead investor usually invests the most capital in that round and sets the terms, including valuation.

Lean Startup movement. An approach to creating new businesses, captured in works from Eric Ries, Steve Blank, and others, that advocates that new **ventures** should launch with rapid development and feedback from the market rather than extended planning periods. Through testing and **pivoting** based on market feedback, founders will better understand their market and potential. See *The Lean Startup* by Eric Ries (2011) and *The Startup Owner's Manual* by Blank and Dorf (2012). This movement is powerful in providing rapid feedback and experimentation, but also creates significant **hidden debt**.

liquidation. The voluntary process of terminating a company's operations and selling its assets.

liquidity event. A situation that allows early investors to cash out some or all of their ownership in a *startup*. This may also be an *exit*.

load testing. A quality check that simulates user demands on a software, application, or website to show its performance under different conditions, particularly as volume of users grows.

mass marketing. Targeting an entire market at once.

mezzanine debt. A hybrid form of financing that incorporates equity-based options with a lower-priority with borrowed money with an associated interest rate. The equity component is usually lower priority than earlier stage investors' equity, while the debt component is usually higher priority than existing owners' debt, in the event of bankruptcy.

minimum viable product (MVP). A new offering that has enough features to satisfy the first paying customers, but not enough to consider it a fully functional, scalable product.

must-have feature. A requirement that absolutely needs to be included in order for a product to be viable.

nice-to-have feature. A product requirement that is important but optional if resources are constrained.

niche. A subset of the market that has specific and focused needs. Usually it is a small segment, or even a part of a segment, in the market. Rhymes with "itch," unless you speak French, in which case you will probably say "neesh."

one-to-one marketing. When a company promises to deliver exactly what each individual customer wants. It is an extreme form of personalization that includes the product itself, its price, and how it is promoted.

outbound marketing or advertising. Promotion initiated by a company trying to interest potential customers in its products. Most traditional advertising (e.g. radio, TV, and print ads) are considered outbound marketing. It can also include direct mail, email (other than opt-in email), tradeshows, cold calling sales, etc.

PEP. The combination of passion, experience, and persistence, which are key characteristics of successful founders.

pitch or pitch deck. A tool *startups* use to talk to investors about their business opportunities. It is usually a presentation delivered face-to-face and includes information on market potential, the problem being solved, the solution being offered, the experience of the management team, and other details intended to show the startup is both scalable and investable.

pivot. Change direction in terms of product, business model, or target segment. A popular component of the *Lean Startup movement.*

points of differentiation. The attributes that make a product offering unique and are the product's competitive advantage.

points of parity. The attributes or characteristics common to all products in a specific frame of reference or category. They are mandatory for a product to be a legitimate member of a category. Because they are common to all category members, they typically do not differentiate a product. See also *frame of reference* and *points of differentiation.*

positioning. The value proposition a product offers to potential customers over its competitors.

post-money valuation. A company's agreed-upon worth after a capital infusion. For example, a *venture* raises $500,000 with a $2 million *pre-money valuation.* The post-money valuation is $2.5 million. As a result, new investors in this round own 20% of the company, or $500,000 of the $2.5 million post-money valuation.

preferred stock. An ownership share that carries a fixed dividend or return that is to be paid out before dividends carried by *common stock.*

pre-money valuation. The agreed-upon worth of a company before it receives an infusion of capital or before it goes public.

pre-revenue. The first stage of a *startup* where an idea is being validated and early product versions are in development. Because a product does not yet exist to sell, the startup has no revenue.

private equity. Securities of unlisted companies. The SEC does not regulate these equities to the same extent as stock offerings to the general public.

product/market fit. The quality of a new offering satisfying a strong need among the people who would buy it. It incorporates both the extent to which there strong demand for a new solution (market fit) and the ability of the new offering to be that solution (product fit).

promotions. Any marketing communication used to attract, inform, and persuade potential customers about a product's value proposition.

proof of concept. A demonstration that a new product idea can feasibly be developed and/or that there is a market for that product. It is the first test of a *startup* idea. It does not assess cost effectiveness, only the feasibility of the idea.

recurring revenue. The portion of a company's revenue that is expected to repeat in the next time frame, usually month or year. It comes from repeat buying, often occurring under contract.

reverse-vesting equity. A type of stock given to an employee that is subject to repurchase by the company for an at-cost purchase price, with the repurchase right lapsing over the *vesting* period. The idea behind reverse vesting is to give an incentive upfront but also protect the company with the option to repurchase these shares if the employee leaves the company.

risk. Possibility of a loss.

SaaS (software as a service) business. A company that delivers its product by allowing users to log in to the application, as opposed to users installing the application on their own computers or servers.

sales funnel. The process of converting potential customers into actual customers. The steps in the funnel can vary quite a bit depending on industry, brand, and target segment.

scalable venture. A company that has traction in its market and can grow rapidly and profitably. Scalability requires a replicable model that allows revenues to grow significantly without equally increasing costs. This is one of the more advanced stages of *startups* described in this book.

second-stage capital. Funds a company raises after it has already begun commercial manufacturing but before its initial public offering.

segment profile or persona. A description of the characteristics of a market segment and/or a semi-fictional representation of the ideal customer based on market research and real data about the segment. The profile often includes a picture as well as a description.

segmented marketing. The process of dividing a market into homogeneous groups and figuring out how to communicate with each group differently.

share of market. The portion of a market that one company or product holds, typically measured as a percentage of revenue or units sold.

sprint. A focused period of time in software development to complete specific work and make it available for review. It is one component of an *Agile software development methodology*.

startup. A new business at its earliest stage, maybe nothing more than an idea on paper. This term covers businesses from pre-revenue ideation to early growth and scaling.

strategy. A plan that links today's choices and actions to tomorrow's destination under conditions of *uncertainty*.

technical debt. Limits on a company's future scalability or growth potential caused by the early choices *startups* make about software and technology development.

technology stack. The suite of computer platforms combined to form a complete software solution. A technology stack usually minimally consists of a database to store records, a server-side programming language to write and read records and perform business logic, and client-side libraries and tools to build the front-ends that users interact with. Also called the stack.

term sheet. A nonbinding agreement that identifies the specific aspects and conditions of an investment. Once a term sheet is agreed to, a legal document will be drawn up. May also be called a memorandum of understanding.

tradeoff. A compromise that tries to balance between two desirable but incompatible choices.

two-bit hustler. A swindler or slick salesperson who asks for only two bits. Whether the price is fair depends on what the bits are.

uncapped note. A convertible bond that offers investors no guarantee of how much equity their money purchases or the valuation at which it converts. Contrast *capped note*.

uncertainty. A situation where the nature of the situation is unknown, the outcomes of the situation are unknown, and the probabilities of those outcomes are unknown.

unicorn. A company, usually a *startup*, with a stock market valuation or estimated valuation of more than $1 billion.

user experience (UX). All aspects of an end user's interactions with a product, including both functional and emotional aspects.

value-added reseller (VAR). A company that adds features and/or services to an existing product to customize it or make it turnkey.

value-based pricing. An approach to setting price based on customers' perceived economic value of the product rather than the cost to make the product.

venture. A risky *startup* that has the intent of being financially profitable.

venture capital. Money that investors provide to *startups* and small businesses that they believe have long-term growth potential. Startups often receive *venture* capital after funds from *friends and family*, *angel investors*, and as part of seed rounds. Startups receive venture capital during A rounds (typically $2 million to $5 million) or B rounds ($5 million to $10 million or more) of funding.

vesting. Accruing rights of ownership in a ***startup*** over time. Vesting also describes how retirement benefits accrue to an employee based on years of service to a company.

vesting schedule. A timetable detailing the when and the extent to which ownership rights accrue to a recipient. Once the ownership has accrued, the recipient may exercise these ownership rights or sell them, if there is a market for them.

vulture capitalist. An investor that buys distressed firms at a deep discount in the hopes of turning them around and selling them off again. Generally, vulture capitalists take advantage of early-stage companies during times of distress.

 Morgan James makes all of our titles available
through the Library for All Charity Organization.

www.LibraryForAll.org

Printed in the USA
CPSIA information can be obtained
at www.ICGtesting.com
JSHW082229140824
68134JS00017B/803